BIRTHMOTHERS

BIRTHMOTHERS

WOMEN WHO HAVE

RELINQUISHED BABIES

FOR ADOPTION

TELL THEIR STORIES

MERRY BLOCH JONES

AN AUTHORS GUILD BACKINPRINT.COM EDITION

AN AUTHORS GUILD BACKINPRINT.COM EDITION

Published by iUniverse.com, Inc.

For information address:
iUniverse.com, Inc.
620 North 48th Street, Suite 201
Lincoln, NE 68504-3467
www.iuniverse.com

Originally published by Chicago Review Press, Incorporated

ISBN: 0-595-00637-X

Printed in the United States of America

To my mother,
Elaine Judith Bloch

CONTENTS

ACKNOWLEDGMENTS

THIS BOOK COULD NOT HAVE BEEN WRITTEN WITHOUT THE PERSONAL commitments, candor, and honesty of the birthmothers who participated in surveys and interviews. I am deeply grateful for their contributions of time, emotion, private thoughts, and memories, as well as for their consistent support and encouragement.

I'd also like to thank:

my agent, Connie Clausen, for her enthusiasm, wisdom, and guidance, and her assistant, Amy Fastenberg, for her sincere dedication to this book;

Linda Matthews, Amy Teschner, and Erin Lydon of Chicago Review Press, for their care, sensitivity, and thoroughness;

Jan Thompson Dicks for the spirit of her art;

Sherrie Luce, members of the Adoption Forum; Barbara Gonyo, members of Truthseekers in Adoption; Janet Fenton, members of the Concerned United Birthparents, and members of the American Adoption Congress, all of whom supplied referrals, information, and support;

Nancy Hannon who shared her book of poetry;

Michael and Jan Molinaro who guided this book home;

Ann Rouse, Sandie Sher Sack, and Karen Greenfield, who contributed encouragement, advice, and assistance;

my sister, Janet Martin, who advised me to keep my eyes undistracted from my own path, and my brother, Aaron Bloch, who inspired with subtle wit and precise words;

my husband, Robin, who, even as he faced a surgeon's knife and an uncertain outcome, insisted that I leave the hospital and go work on this book; who proofread chapters before his staples came out; who has been patient, loving, and consistently positive, and who has shown me, by example, that it's OK to take risks;

Dr. Joseph Atkins, who was so careful;

Lanie Zera, who brought her exceptional mind and generous spirit to my family in the clutch;

my daughters, Baille and Neely, who have given me both quiet time to write and the unsurpassable honor of being their mother;

my mom, Judy Bloch, who has always known more than she's known she's known, who has demonstrated generosity, empathy, and the art of taking one step at a time, and who has helped me get through every crisis of my life, including the latest;

and my late dad, Herman S. Bloch, whose twinkle I hold in my heart and whose admiration I will always strive to merit.

INTRODUCTION

There is none
In all this cold and hollow world, no fount
Of deep strong, deathless love, save that within
A mother's heart.

Felicia Hemans, *Siege of Valencia*

We all know adopted kids and people who've adopted, but what about the women who bore the children? We never hear about them. What happened to them? Where are they?

Alexis, a birthmother

I REMEMBER WHEN A MAN I WAS DATING (WHO IS NOW MY HUSBAND) told me that he and his ex-wife had an adopted daughter. They'd adopted her when she was six months old. Born in Korea, she'd been abandoned at the age of four months on the steps of a police station. A letter attached to her blanket gave her birth date and name. It also indicated that she'd been breast-fed since birth.

I can still see my husband beaming, describing the day he met his daughter for the first time. And I can still feel the puzzling wave of sadness that passed over me while I listened to him describe his joy. For some reason, I was unable to follow his story; I was stuck on the steps of a police station, visualizing a woman wrenching herself away from the infant she'd nursed for months, knowing that she would never see her again. What could have forced her to do such a thing, I wondered. Was she ill? Poor? In trouble of some kind? Where is she now? Does she wonder about her daughter? Does she know that she's OK?

My husband-to-be was still telling me about the airport, about how a stewardess had called out his name and handed him a blanket stuffed with a chubby, cheeky baby, when I interrupted. I needed to know. "What about her mother?" I asked. "Do you know what happened to her? Do you know why she gave her up?"

In fact, he knew nothing about his daughter's biological mother. He remembered sending photographs to the agency for a few years. "They have a bulletin board on the street, where women can come to see pictures of the children that their 'girlfriends' had relinquished." But he had no idea who the woman was who had brought his child into the world. She would forever remain faceless, unseen and unheard.

My stepdaughter's birthmother has haunted me. Certainly, my husband's child was not the first adoptee I'd met. Like most people, I had several adopted childhood friends and many adult friends who'd adopted children. Still, the image of a woman, tenderly placing a precious bundle where strangers would find her, has remained with me for years. That image may be, in fact, what led me to write this book, which explores the effects of relinquishment on the lives of birthmothers. It searches for commonalities, consistencies, and patterns in their experiences.

The first hurdle in studying the experiences of birthmothers was finding them. Although there are an estimated six million birthmothers in the United States, this process was not easy. Since the late nineteenth century, adoption laws in most states have required "sealed" or "closed" records. Closed records were intended to "protect" all triad members: the adoptee from the stigma of illegitimate birth, the birthparents from the shame of bearing children out of wedlock, and the adoptive parents from gossip and invasion of privacy.

The secrecy enforced by closed records alone made birthmothers a difficult group to locate. Combined with social stigma, it made reliable statistical and demographic information virtually unattainable. I proceeded, therefore, informally, contacting national organizations concerned with adoption, seeking volunteers to interview. These organizations made my questionnaires available to their members, coast to coast. Responses came in from women in twenty states.

Not all participants were members of these groups, however. Dozens of birthmothers, not affiliated with any organization, found me via word of mouth that had been passed by an adoption agency, adoption attorneys, and networks of friends that spanned the country.

Initially, I'd hoped that for every ten questionnaires two or three would be returned. I was amazed that questionnaires came flying back to me by the handful, often with lengthy cover letters or notes written on the back. Birthmothers telephoned me to ask about the study, to find out where they could read the findings, to expand or update the events they'd described on paper. Many duplicated their questionnaire forms and passed them on to other birthmothers. Word spread; friends sent forms to friends and those friends passed them along to others. In a matter of a few months, I'd heard from over seventy birthmothers all across the country.

Some were suspicious. "Why are you asking these questions?" they demanded. They worried about how the information was going to be used, what "interest group" I represented, what "side" of the triangle I was on, what personal connection to adoption I had. As I explained, repeatedly, that I had no connection to adoption, no affiliation with any "side" or interest group, no ax to grind, I began to realize that, to birthmothers, relinquishment was more than merely a life-altering turning point. For most, it was an invisible barrier separating them from the bulk of humanity.

Even with their defensiveness, however, most birthmothers answered their questionnaires with candor. In fact, many spilled their hearts out, as if they'd been waiting for the opportunity to tell about what had happened. Although a stranger, I was greeted with disarming sincerity and openness. People I'd never even seen trusted me with truths they had hidden for decades, sometimes even from their spouses and closest friends.

Most questionnaires were followed up with in-depth interviews that lasted up to eight hours. Heart-wrenching and tear-filled, these interviews were often completed in stages, because the process of talking and remembering was too draining for one session. Some women admitted that they had never told *anyone* the details they were revealing for the book. Others, in the process of their interviews, recalled long-buried experiences for the first time.

For some, the interviews themselves became turning points, precipitating pivotal internal confrontations with their pasts. Speaking up about their relinquishments brought these women new perspectives and helped them define their losses, feelings, patterns, relationships, and goals. Releasing their deepest secrets was undoubtedly therapeutic for some. But I'm convinced that most of these women were motivated by a selfless, genuine desire to help others overcome or avoid the most disastrous aspects of relinquishment.

Even though many were willing to reveal their identities, the names and personal information of the women who participated in this book have all been disguised. Their stories, however, are real; the characters in the book are genuine in spirit and accurate in experience.

Nevertheless, with its relatively small, nonrandom sample, this book cannot hope to present a definitive portrait of the "birthmother experience." It does, however, portray the experiences of *some* birthmothers. In it, women who have come to terms with relinquishing, at least enough to be able to discuss it, share their insights for the sake of others. Although their wisdom and willingness to share undoubtedly set them apart from some others, the birthmothers in the book are generally "mainstream." They include accountants, nurses, psychologists, social workers, homemakers, lawyers, editors, and teachers. One is a diplomat, another is a wealthy socialite, a third is a waitress, a fourth is a retired WAC. They are active in country clubs, PTAs, politics, and charities. Socially, economically, and professionally, they cover a wide spectrum. Many are married, some for the second or third time; others are divorced or single. Most have other children or stepchildren; some do not. Some say they profoundly regret relinquishing; others say it was the best decision possible at the time.

Regardless of their differences, however, the women who participated have much in common. They all relinquished children at least seven years ago. They all believe that relinquishment profoundly affected their lives. They all hope that by sharing their experiences they will help others—in and out of the adoption triad—who are struggling with problems related to relinquishment. All generously volunteered their time, energy, and emotion to support that effort.

This book is certainly not about *all* birthmothers. It is not about women who intentionally conceived children with the idea of relinquishing them. It is not about drug addicted, chronically sick, or emotionally disturbed women who were too ill to keep their babies. It is not about women whose lives were habitually so dismal that relinquishment easily blended with other problems and passed almost unnoticed. And it is not, because I was unable to locate any, about women who relinquished happily.

Just as this book is not about all birthmothers, it is not about all adoptions. Neither is it about legislation, human rights, feminism, racism, sexism, politics, the evolution of the family, or postpartum depression due to temporary hormonal changes, except insofar as these topics are part of the chronicle of birthmothers' experiences. And, while it does not presume to offer easy solutions, it does present some ideas about the evolution of relinquishment practices and adoptive families.

Writing about experiences that have profoundly changed others has, in turn, profoundly affected me. In the course of interviews, I became startled by some of my own preconceived notions and prejudices regarding birthparents. I've also come to admire courage, strength, and self-sacrifice; to empathize with anger, anguish, longing, and love; to resent secrecy, shame, and victimization. I've accepted that, sometimes, there are no easy solutions for complicated problems, no convenient bad guys to soak up blame.

Most of all, though, writing this book has emphasized for me the inestimable value we place on our children, the persistence and strength of maternal desires, and the mysterious bonds that link us, mother to child, individual to individual. I have been awed by the power we human beings have to survive, overcome obstacles, and recover from loss. It is my hope that the contributions of the birthmothers who participated in this book will touch others and help anyone wounded directly or indirectly by relinquishment. I hope, too, that by honoring themselves and each other with openness, birthmothers will step out of the shadows and into the warm realm of the family, defining their own emerging roles. By doing so, they can hope to end the birthmother syndrome and ensure that their healing will be completed—or at least begun.

Discovery

1966: Escape

ZOE STARED, PANIC-STRICKEN, AT THE TATTOO. IT WAS JACK'S FIFTH, A serpent. It covered his whole forearm and coiled around a ribbon inscribed "Forever."

Zoe tried not to shudder as Jack cupped her chin in his hand, put his mouth to her ear and hissed, "Zoe, this one's for *you*. Forever."

Zoe Walsh was seventeen. Her parents were in the midst of a heated divorce in California and had sent her to stay with an aunt in the Midwest for her final months before college. Zoe spent her summer aimlessly hanging around with Jack, the mechanic at the local gas station.

"When I told Jack I was pregnant, he actually yahooed," she recalls. "He kept shaking his head and repeating, 'What do you know! I'm a daddy!' and kissing me. Then he jumped up and raced off on his motorcycle, yelling over his shoulder that I should 'call the preacher man.' He left me standing on the street in front of the gas station, with no idea what to do.

"See, I had no intention of spending forever with Jack. I was about to go to college and get back to my 'real' life. For me, being with Jack had been a 'kick,' a way to get through the summer, but certainly *not* a way to spend forever!"

Zoe's first problem was to tell that to Jack, a "greaser" with a gun collection and an erratic, uncontrollable temper. Jack's moods were unpredictable. She'd seen him beat guys up for offenses as slight as touching his motorcycle. Knowing how thrilled he was about the pregnancy, Zoe hesitated to tell him that she intended to get an abortion and had, in fact, already raised over half the necessary money.

Although abortions were not legal in 1966, Zoe knew of a doctor who would perform them. Finally, after days of false starts and fearful anticipation, she hinted to Jack that, if he were able to raise some money, they would be able to wait until they were older before starting a family.

"When he realized what I was getting at, Jack sat perfectly still for a few minutes without saying a word. I didn't know whether he hadn't heard me or if he was just going to ignore what I'd said. I was about to repeat myself, when he lurched at me and grabbed me by the back of my hair. He looked me in the eye and, real soft and slow, told me that if I killed his kid, he'd kill me. I had no doubt. I believed him.

"After that, I was too frightened to get an abortion. I believed that if Jack found out I'd had one, he'd kill me. I still think he would have.

"Jack had a dark side. I was sure that he would never let me go because I was carrying his child. In order to get away from him, I'd have to 'lose' the baby, but without an abortion. I prayed for a miscarriage. I hoped I'd fall down the stairs or get hit by a car. Anything to make me lose the baby. But, finally, one night, I just blurted out that I'd been mistaken, that I wasn't pregnant, after all. I said that I'd just been 'late.' I hadn't *planned* on telling Jack that. If I'd planned it, he'd probably have known I was lying. I just said it, spontaneously. He assumed I was sad about it, so he was nice to me, babied me, even left me alone sexually. Six weeks later, when I was about three months pregnant, I left for college. Nobody knew. Nobody."

1968: Accident

"We'd been using condoms for over a year. One night, as he sat up, Bob said, 'Oh, no, the rubber broke."

Sue was sixteen, a cheerleader, dating the captain of the football team. They planned to marry after high school.

"We didn't go crazy about the condom because we both thought girls could only get pregnant during their periods. We thought we were OK; we were so uninformed. But we'd also heard that if you douched after sex, you could stop the sperm, so we ran around trying to buy a douche bag, but we didn't know what they looked like and were embarrassed to ask. Finally, we went to Bob's sister and asked her if she had one. She did, but I didn't want to use it, you know, to use someone else's douche bag, so I just took a bath and tried to swish the water around and wash myself out.

"That month I missed my period. Bob cut school and took a urine sample to a hospital. The rabbit died, so he got me some kind of hormone pills that were supposed to help you abort if it was early enough. Again, we had no idea what the pills were or how they worked, but I took them. They didn't work. I woke up vomiting every morning, going to school and acting like everything was normal, and crying with Bob secretly every night. Our relationship deepened, and we talked about getting married as soon as we could."

By the time another month passed, Bob and Sue realized they would have to share their secret with their parents. "Bob came over and asked my dad if they could talk privately. I felt like I wasn't there. It was like I'd left my body and was watching from a cloud. I saw them walk into the den. When the door closed, everything seemed to stop and hang in suspended animation. Even my heart didn't dare to beat. I stared at the door, unable to move. There was a long, unnatural silence. Then I heard my father, my gentle soft-spoken father, scream, 'NO! Not my baby daughter!'

"There was some shuffle of furniture and my father, who'd never lifted a hand to anyone, shouted, 'If I had a gun, I'd shoot you! Get out of this house, while you still can!' He didn't sound like himself; he sounded like some cowboy hired gun. My mother must have heard and rushed in from the laundry room, asking what was the matter. I can still see her, as if it were today. She's got an armful of folded sheets and pillow cases. Dad bursts out of the den, storming towards me. I'm trying to talk, to tell Mom what's happening, but Dad's yelling, 'Bob has some news for you, Dear. Go on, Bob, tell her!' His face is twisted and furious. My mom's completely bewildered. Bob clears his throat and tries to sound calm. He says, 'Mrs. D., Sue's pregnant and we need your help.'

"My mom instantly crumples and dissolves into tears. She's sobbing and runs out of the room, dropping the linens. My dad chases Bob out of the house, tripping over the sheets, hollering for him to get out and stay out. I am frozen, unmoving. Out on my cloud.

"The most bizarre thing about that night was that we were expected to go to a family party, and we went. There was a complete break in the hysteria, rage, and crying while we sat at my aunt's house, eating pie and playing cards as if nothing had happened. That seemed strange to me, and unreal. But, actually, it was only the beginning of the secrecy. It was merely a hint of the way things were going to be from that day on."

1985: Betrayal

Sonia was twenty-three, in graduate school, studying foreign policy. She'd been seeing a high-powered attorney for almost two years. Although they had never discussed it, she hoped that one day, careers permitting, they would marry.

"I told him at dinner, in our favorite little restaurant. In our private, candle-lit booth. I knew he'd be upset, because he liked to be in control, and the pregnancy was certainly not part of *his* agenda. But, truthfully, I thought he'd marry me. I never could have anticipated what actually happened, or how stupid I had been. After I told him I was pregnant, Michael let go of my hand, looked away, and said three things. Only three.

"First, he said, 'How do I know it's mine?' Next, while I gaped at him, stung by the question, he said, 'Well, it's basically *your* problem, Sonia, not mine.' I was stunned, speechless. But, finally, I managed to argue that it was not merely my problem and to suggest the idea of marriage. He looked at his linguine and shook his head and said the third thing. 'That's impossible, Sonia,' he said. 'I'm already married.'

"After that evening, I never saw Michael again. He never even called to find out what I did about the pregnancy. And I never called to tell him."

Unwanted Pregnancies

Every year in our country, millions of women like Zoe, Sue, and Sonia face unplanned and unwanted pregnancies. Each year for decades, at least a million of these pregnancies have ended in abortion, whether legal or not. Even with the consistently high rate of abortion, however, many women carry their babies to term and deliver children they have not necessarily chosen to bear.

The situations of these women vary from poverty to wealth, from high school dropout to Ph.D. Some are married; others are single or divorced. In fact, more children are born to unmarried women in the United States than in any other country; over 20 percent of our births are out of wedlock.

Unplanned pregnancies occur to women of all educational levels, all professions, and, although about a million each year are teenagers, all child-bearing ages. Those who do not have abortions are usually faced with a single choice: keeping and raising their children or relinquishing them for adoption. This book tells the stories of seventy-two who chose to relinquish: why they relinquished, what happened to them afterward, and how they are managing their lives today.

The Adoption Option

Unmarried women with unplanned pregnancies today face less social pressure and have more options than those of a few decades ago. One source of change has been the consistently high divorce rate, which has diminished the stigma formerly associated with single parents. Unmarried mothers blend into society with divorced ones. The label of "bastard," considered so terrible in past generations, no longer exists; it has, in fact, been abolished by statute in many states.

As social attitudes have evolved, so has adoption. Although most states still adhere to "closed" or "sealed" procedures, many now question the wisdom of closed records and are considering legislation to "open" them, giving triad members legal access to adoption files, medical records, and birth information. Further, through the work of the National Conference of Commissioners on Uniform State Laws, the rights of adoptees and birthparents to get to know each other may someday be protected nationwide.

In the meantime, while laws are being reexamined and redefined, many new adoptions are being arranged privately, with "open" terms that vary widely and are usually unprotected by state law. Some private agreements guarantee not only that birthmothers be informed where and with whom their children are placed, but even that they can personally approve the prospective adoptive parents. Many birthmothers are guaranteed regular communication with adoptive families or even with adoptees. Occasionally, birthmothers become accepted as part of the "extended" adoptive family, attending birthday parties and holiday celebrations, just like aunts, close friends, or stepparents.

Although the specific terms of these private, more open adoptions vary, they usually relieve some of the agonies that plague birthmothers in closed adoptions. Through openness, birthmothers can *know* that their relinquished children are healthy, loved, and well cared for. They can be available to provide information as needed about the child's genetic, ethnic, or medical history. And they can help adoptees see themselves as "whole" people, loved by both adoptive parents and birthparents, not as having been "cut out" of one family portrait and "pasted onto" another.

Despite trends toward openness, however, many new adoptions are still arranged with traditional, completely "closed" terms.

Many birthmothers remain unaware of their options and their legal rights prior to, during, and after relinquishment. And, regardless of whether adoptions are open or closed, most birthmothers discover that the road after relinquishment is rocky, at best.

Birthmothers

Currently, there are an estimated six million American birthmothers. At least two million have relinquished in the last eighteen years. Not all birthmothers are unmarried or teenagers when they relinquish, but the vast majority fall into one or both categories. Of the half million teenagers who deliver babies each year, about one in five relinquish.

Although birthmothers in open adoptions are less limited than those in closed, many still struggle with the emotional aftermath of relinquishing their children. Regardless of the terms of their adoption agreements, most—even those who know that their children have been placed in loving homes and who would make the same decision if faced with the dilemma again—wrestle with inner conflicts.

One of the sources of these conflicts is clear. Although they come from all walks of life and all types of backgrounds, birthmothers share a common experience: they have each subordinated a most basic maternal drive for what they have been convinced is the good of their children. Regardless of what they believe or think about relinquishment, many continue to struggle with the emotional effects of suppressing these drives in the form of rage, frustration, sorrow, guilt, and self-doubt.

Granted, not every birthmother grapples with ambivalence or regret about her decision. Ellen, a birthmother who relinquished in 1987, had no job and two other toddlers still in diapers at home. The birthfather of her newborn was no longer in her life. She insists that she was not merely relieved but actually jubilant that a young married couple took the new baby off her hands to give him a loving home. "I was sad to lose him, but the last thing I needed was another baby to care for," Ellen remarks. "I just could not have managed another child on my own."

Lynne, also relatively untroubled, was a nursing student who became pregnant in an affair with "the wrong man" in 1986. Believing both the relationship and the subsequent pregnancy to be simply and completely "mistakes," she is philosophical about her decision. "I was glad to be able to help an infertile couple by presenting them with the child they had longed for. Their joy balanced all my negative feelings about the pregnancy. For myself, I just wanted the pregnancy to be over, so I could put the affair behind me and begin the rest of my life."

Neither of these birthmothers, to date, admits to any second thoughts about relinquishment. Perhaps they never will. Such carefree reactions, however, are far from ordinary. A Harvard University study recently estimated that 96 percent of all birthmothers in closed adoptions contemplate search and that more than 60 percent actually undertake them. While some birthmothers have, no doubt, found perfect peace and content- ment after relinquishment, many are troubled or curious enough to spend the considerable amount of time, emotional energy, and money required to search.

The birthmothers represented in this book are among those who have *not* found peace after relinquishing. They reveal their stories, hoping to help others who face similar struggles. Although they are not intended to define or portray the "typical" birthmother, they do present a wide range of experience and insight acquired, often with difficulty, in the years following sur- render. These women have relinquished as recently as seven or as long ago as thirty-one years ago. They describe experiences in both closed and open adoptions. Many have grieved; others have felt relief; a number have entirely repressed their emotions. Some have been open about their experiences; others have concealed them, even from their closest friends and family. Many have searched and some have experienced reunion, with varying de- grees of satisfaction. Currently married or unmarried, mothers or stepmothers or simply birthmothers, they share their stories and advice, hoping to help other birthmothers, women considering becoming birthmothers, and anyone, in or outside the adoption triangle, attempting to understand birthmothers.

To comprehend fully the experiences of these women, it is necessary to start at the beginning, with the circumstances that greeted their unplanned pregnancies. How these pregnancies were handled often set the stage not only for the futures of the unborn children but also for the directions of their birthmothers' lives.

2

Options
and Decisions

CINDY TRIED TO LOCK HER BEDROOM DOOR WHILE HER MOTHER threw herself against it, screaming, "Whore! Tramp! Let me in, slut!"

The door came flying open and knocked Cindy onto the floor. Something hard—a perfume bottle?—hit her on the forehead. She put her arms up and rolled over, trying to protect herself, but a vase crashed into the back of her head, sending pieces of dried flowers all over the carpet. Before she could move, her mother was on her, screaming, slapping her head and chest, and jabbing her knees into her stomach. Cindy rolled herself into a ball, hoping her mother would stop before she killed her or her unborn baby. Whatever it took, she'd have to get away.

Final Choices

"What 'decision?'" one birthmother demands. "There was no decision. The word *decision* doesn't apply to relinquishing a child. In fact, the word reflects the prejudice of society toward birthmothers. We are supposed to be unfeeling, inhuman trash, who *decide* to give up our children because life would be more fun, less expensive, and easier without them. That's hogwash. No mother in the world, human or animal, would *decide* to give up her baby. It isn't normal or natural. It wouldn't happen if mothers had the power to decide. It only happens when they don't."

When they discuss the events leading them to relinquish their children, some birthmothers insist that the term *decision* is misleading because it implies that they actively participated in the process or that they had other options to consider. For many, this was not the case. The "decision" to relinquish was often made by others, and, most of the time, it appeared to be the only choice.

The discovery of unplanned pregnancies can set off shock waves that reverberate not only through relationships and families but also across generations. How such pregnancies are handled and the related decisions made permanently affect the lives of everyone involved. It is important, therefore, to examine the dynamics involved in making the decision to relinquish, especially regarding the roles played by birthmothers.

Sex, Age, Money, and Power

Edie is a birthmother who relinquished in 1978 and earned a Ph.D. in anthropology ten years later. "Every society," she asserts, "no matter how democratic or egalitarian, is divided into groups that represent varying degrees of power. The divisions are usually determined by factors like age, sex, race, birthlines, education, and wealth. Traditionally, our society has counted wealthy, educated adult Caucasian men among its most powerful. Among the least powerful, despite efforts to equalize their rights, are women, particularly those without wealth or education, at either extreme of the age spectrum. Without the 'protection' of a strong male figure or the social status acquired through marriage to an empowered male, women of all races have been excluded from the inner circles of societal power and high status."

Although she admits that women today have many more options than in the past, Edie points out that there are still "rules" that define their roles in society and the means by which they enter them. "Modern women can achieve high social status without marrying powerful men, but to do so they must independently acquire wealth or higher education to ensure their own power. Without these assets, most young, single women with modest incomes and average educations are destined to remain among the least powerful people in our society. It is no coincidence that this is the group which most frequently relinquishes children for adoption."

The survival of any society, no matter how modern, depends on its women becoming mothers. Accordingly, every society defines patterns, rituals, rules, and routines to guide women through the critical process of mating and reproduction. In our society, adulthood, marriage, and independent financial resources are some of the prerequisites for motherhood. When unplanned pregnancies occur, women who lack some or all of these requirements find themselves outside the norms and, therefore, outside the margins of "acceptable" society. Lacking the power and status to defy the rules, many young and single women have found that their only hope of reentering "normal" society is to conceal and relinquish their unplanned children. In fact, most of the birthmothers interviewed relinquished not because they wanted to, but because their pregnancies broke the rules, opposed social standards, and threatened to leave them forever isolated from respectable society.

When Babies Have Babies

While many factors influenced the roles birthmothers played in deciding the outcome of their pregnancies, age had the most profound effect. In fact, age alone often defined their roles. Many birthmothers who were minors simply lacked the authority to make their own decisions. Their parents or guardians made their choices for them, and babies were taken from underage mothers without discussion, much less approval.

In 1964, Cathy was fifteen and pregnant. "My parents shipped me off to a home for unmarried mothers. I never saw the father of the child until it was all over. Nobody was allowed to visit me except my mom and dad. No one even knew where I was, except my parents and one aunt. I was just put in the home and told that I was going to give up my child. I didn't want to give up my baby, though. I tried to keep her—I ran away from the home twice but was found and taken back both times."

In recent years, because of cases like Cathy's, the parents and guardians of many pregnant minors have been prevented from taking complete control of the decision to relinquish. In many states, in fact, *both* birthparents must be involved, and minors are considered "emancipated" for the sole and express purpose of relinquishing their children. Unfortunately, even these regulations cannot prevent underage mothers from making näive mistakes. The act of signing papers does not guarantee either that the young birthmother has made a mature, informed decision or that she has made it willingly.

Within a year after giving birth at fifteen, Carla bitterly resented the fact that the state allowed her to surrender her child without her parents' permission. Today, she wishes she had allowed her mother to keep her baby until she could raise her herself. "How is it that I was an 'adult' for the sake of giving up my baby, but not for voting, getting married, or drinking? How can my judgment be considered sound for relinquishing and not for anything else?"

The sole responsibility for making decisions regarding relinquishment is, in fact, overwhelming to many teenage mothers. Candy says that her parents gave her, at age sixteen, complete authority to make her decision, before she was mature enough to understand the consequences of her actions. "They thought they were being fair by letting me figure out what to do. But I had no idea what I was doing and looked to them for an answer. They were impossible to read, so I asked another adult, my doctor, what to do. It was actually the doctor who made the decision, because he was the only one who had any opinion about what would be best. If I gave up the baby, he said, all the pieces of our lives would fall back into place. I could finish school and go to college. The baby would be better off with a good, two-parent home. Nobody thought beyond that."

The parents of many other young birthmothers took definite stands and insisted that they relinquish, convincing their daughters that it was the best solution, the only one that would enable them to become "normal" teenagers again, without the responsibilities of parenthood. Some birthmothers agree that they were better off relinquishing, in that they were able to complete their educations and mature before committing to family or parenting. Mindy, who was almost seventeen when she relinquished in 1966, says, "I felt I did the best I could for the baby and was able to straighten out my own life. I couldn't have done that if I had kept my baby without a husband, a diploma, or some means of child care."

Whether or not the decisions were "for the best," however, was often irrelevant to the effects the decision-making process had on birthmothers. Those whose opinions were ignored or overruled were often deeply and permanently traumatized by their powerlessness to influence these decisions that were so critical to their lives.

Powerless

"My mother said, 'There's no way you can keep it,'" Connie remembers. "I was thirteen years old. It didn't sink in. It didn't seem real. I was so young, even the baby kicking didn't seem real. I couldn't grasp that it was a life I was bringing into the world. I was too young to know my real feelings, let alone what my rights were. I was a child. I didn't know if I *had* any rights. I sank into a state where nothing hurt. I was numb."

Numbness like Connie's was common among minor birthmothers who felt powerless about what happened to their babies. Some experienced a sense of distance from reality or "unrealness"; others invented protective fantasies.

"Nobody ever asked me if I wanted to keep my baby or marry the father," Liz recalls. "It was like a bad dream. My mother and a woman from the county talked, and *they* decided it would be best for me to give up my baby for adoption. No one said anything to me, and I didn't say anything to them."

Buffering herself from her emotions required that Liz deny the truth of what was happening and invent a "pretend" solution to her problems. "On the outside, I went along with my parents. But I also went along with Joe, the birthfather, telling him I'd marry him and we'd keep our baby. I said whatever anybody wanted to hear, but inside I pretended that everything would magically be OK, that my parents would accept Joe and let us marry, even though I was only fourteen."

Castle in the Air

Fantasy was also a useful tool to young birthmothers whose pregnancies had crossed forbidden social lines. In the process of forming their own opinions and establishing their own identities, some broke through the boundaries of social prejudice, only to become trapped both between childhood and adulthood and between the mutually exclusive worlds of their parents and their lovers.

"I was fifteen years old, in love with a seventeen-year-old Mexican boy named Luis," Amber says. "My parents said he was 'trash.' If they'd allowed me to see him, the affair would probably have been over in six months. But because they forbade me to see him, it's gone on forever."

When she became pregnant, Amber and Luis hoped that her parents would let them marry for the sake of their baby. Instead, her parents threatened to disown her if she saw Luis again and warned her that she'd ruin her life if she married him.

"They said that Luis was no good, that he'd drop me after a year or two and that no one else would have me after I'd married a Mexican. They said they'd have nothing to do with me, so I'd be stuck with a mixed-race baby, all alone, with no education and too young to support myself. They told me I couldn't stay under their roof if I continued to see Luis. But I couldn't give him up. So I lied, hid our relationship from them, and pretended everything was fine."

Without the power to demand that their choices be respected, some young birthmothers adopted internal defense mechanisms that helped them survive the conflicts and confrontations that their pregnancies inspired. For Amber, the process of "deciding" what to do with her child involved fabrication, fantasy, and denial. If these defenses delayed her feelings of powerlessness and frustration, they were of little help in changing the final outcome.

"Luis saw what was happening," Amber says. "He tried desperately to adopt our baby himself or to have his parents adopt her. But, back then, in the early seventies, he couldn't get the baby. He was still a minor and a single male. And his parents already had four kids in a five-room house, so they didn't 'qualify' as adoptive parents. I wanted to sign the baby over to them, but my parents told me I couldn't, that I had no right to say where the baby went after I relinquished. I'm sure, now, that they knew I'd never give Luis up if he had our baby, so they made sure he didn't get her. I floated along, promised them one thing and Luis another. But, inside, I hid in my dreams, in a perfect fantasy world where I, my baby, and her father lived happily ever after, visiting Grandma and Grandpa on Sundays. When that dream world shattered, so did I."

The "Right" Thing

Some birthmothers who relinquished as minors *were* included in the decision-making process. Their involvement ranged from actively choosing surrender to merely being one voice of a "committee," which often included delegations from more than one family.

"The two sets of parents, Bob, and I all met in our kitchen," Sue remembers. "We were free to join in, but we didn't feel we could talk until our parents had finished. They already knew we wanted to get married, so we didn't have to remind them. They also knew we had another year of high school to complete, so the pregnancy was at least a year too soon. Still, I asked if we could go off to California and raise the baby there. My mother asked me how we would get along, raising a baby and finishing school, and I realized that that was only a dream.

"I remember the rest of the discussion like bees buzzing around my head. Sometimes I'd hear words. Mostly, it was just buzzing. Bob's mother offered to keep the baby until we could raise him. My mother vetoed that. Bob's father didn't want us to get married until after high school. My father didn't speak at all. He just sat there stony and silent—the same way I did."

Although birthmothers like Sue did not speak up much during the decision-making process, they were well aware that they had the opportunity to do so. No part of the process was hidden; they were invited to participate and informed of the reasoning, opinions, and motivations of everyone involved. Even if they were not pleased with the outcomes, they remained grounded in reality and in touch with their emotional reactions. This awareness often helped them understand and accept the decision to relinquish, but it rarely helped them sort out their feelings.

"I felt terrible grief as soon as the decision was made," Sue says. "But I knew there was no other choice, given our ages. And because I knew there was no other choice, I began to hide my feelings about it. I didn't want to hurt my parents further, by resisting the only decision that made sense. So I pretended to agree with adoption. I said what they wanted me to say, that I wanted to finish school, that I was OK, that I would wait to get married. I got good at telling untruths, doing what was expected, and keeping my true feelings to myself."

Many young birthmothers experienced a similar sense that their desires to keep their babies and their feelings of grief were "wrong" or "unacceptable." Guilty and ashamed, young women like Sue denied their true feelings and tried to live up to the perceived expectations of others.

"I felt it was wrong to be pregnant and even worse to be sad about it," a birthmother named Amy says. "I tried to close out my feelings and act 'normal' to please my parents. But I couldn't help crying late at night. I didn't know who I was anymore. My feelings had become so complicated. I loved the birthfather and wanted our child. But I was ashamed both that I was pregnant and that I *wanted* to be. I'd always been a 'good girl' and I needed to feel that

I deserved that title again. But, to be a 'good girl' again, my parents said I'd have to do the 'right' thing and give up my baby. But, if that was so 'right' and so 'good,' why did I feel so broken-hearted about it?"

Masking their feelings when they accepted the decision to relinquish, some pregnant young women divided themselves into "public" and "private" sides. By going along passively, they began a pattern of disguise in order to appear "normal" or "good" and please others. Like Sue and Amy, they became actors, playing parts, speaking lines, and behaving as they thought they should. Gradually, they began to feel absent or nonexistent, as if their relationships and even their lives were being conducted by strangers.

Survival and Lies

Some birthmothers had been powerless and passive long before they were ever pregnant, and not simply because of factors like age, gender, or economic status. These young women, often the children of emotionally disturbed, alcoholic, or drug-abusing parents, learned early in life to conceal their feelings in order to minimize the violence that dominated their families. Accustomed to neglect, beatings, or other mistreatments, they experienced the decision to relinquish as merely the latest of many uncontrollable losses.

Finding little or no affection in her family, one future birthmother named Cindy went searching for "love" outside the home before she was even a teenager. At fourteen, she was already promiscuous. Cindy was aware that her mother, Hilda, was schizophrenic. Hilda had what Cindy and her sisters called "fits," during which she'd rant about the evils of sex, taunt them about their bodies and sexual urges, and beat them with straps, blunt objects, or her fists. Cindy's father usually disappeared when Hilda's fits began and reappeared after she'd calmed down.

"Looking back," Cindy says, "I can see why I became sexually promiscuous. Sex was the closest I could get to love. My mother never told us about sex; she went into wild tantrums about it, using disgusting obscenities. I was scared, unloved, and alone. I reacted by becoming what you'd call a 'tramp.' I slept with everybody."

Without self-esteem, feeling unloved and unlovable, birthmothers like Cindy were unable to establish any meaningful relationships with peers of either gender and grasped sex as a substitute. When they became pregnant, some found new sources of comfort growing in their bodies.

"I was happy to be pregnant," Cindy recalls. "At fourteen, my little baby growing inside me finally gave me somebody to love. Maybe I'd *wanted* to get pregnant. Who knows? But I was scared to death of what my mother would do when she found out, so I hid my morning sickness and kept my baby to myself as long as I could."

Like Cindy, young birthmothers accustomed to violence often shielded themselves with secrecy and lies. However, the scenarios they invented, no matter how elaborate, usually failed either to insulate them from harm or to prevent the decisions that ultimately separated them from their babies.

"When she found out I was pregnant, my mother got very, very scary," Cindy recalls. "She demanded to know who the father was. I believed she'd kill me, or try, if she found out that I didn't have a clue, so I lied and said I'd been 'jumped.' It was a terrible lie, but I stuck to it. As it was, even when she thought I'd been raped, my mother beat me constantly for at least twenty-four hours. I was afraid for my baby—I was afraid for my life. She punched me, hit me with kitchen utensils, the broom, whatever she could get her hands on. I tried to get away from her, but she followed me, cursing and swinging."

Lying quickly and convincingly, Cindy dodged her mother to protect her pregnancy. When her lies failed to protect her from her mother, she tried them on her father.

"I pulled on his arm, showed him my bruises, and begged him to help me, whispering, 'She's going to kill me and my baby.' He knew she might, so he stepped in to help me. But if he'd known the truth, that I hadn't been raped, that I'd slept with so many guys that I had no idea who the father was, I'm sure he'd have killed me himself."

Although lying helped some pregnant minors temporarily, it also presented risks. Some lies became so transparent that they were eventually exposed; others grew beyond control, creating traps rather than escape hatches.

"My lies finally did me in," Cindy says. "I made up the story about the rape to save my baby. But, since my dad believed that story, he said I'd have to give her up. I asked him if I could keep her and he said, 'No, you don't want *that* baby,' because he believed she'd been conceived in rape."

Ironically, the web Cindy wove to protect herself and her baby ultimately separated them. Each lie led to another, until there were so many that Cindy became helplessly entangled. Even then, a captive in her own web, Cindy had to lie again.

"My dad told me to say that the decision to give up the baby was mine, so I had to lie once more and say it was all my idea and cosign the papers like he told me. I had no choice, really. But I knew, at fifteen, that signing those papers was wrong. It was a bigger lie than I'd ever told before. But I did as I was told. I figured I was being punished for all my other secrets and lies."

Exile of the Mind

Frequently, unplanned pregnancies among young, unmarried women were handled with extreme secrecy. These pregnancies were considered so threatening to the birthmothers' reputations and futures that secrecy appeared to offer the only chance of their return to "normal" roles in society. Maintaining their secrets, therefore, became the primary focus of these young women's lives. Ironically, the processes involved in secrecy often isolated and altered them so thoroughly that they found it impossible ever to enter society again.

Cammy remembers her first weeks of secrecy in 1965 as a blur of confusion and fear. "I was in college. It was my first semester. I couldn't tell anybody. Paul, the birthfather, was a guy from school who'd been sent to Vietnam, so I couldn't have married him, even if I'd wanted to. But I didn't want to. I didn't know what to do. So, instead of doing anything, I became obsessed with keeping the whole thing secret, as if that could make it go away. I ate only one egg and drank one glass of milk a day, so I could stay small. I took showers alone, late at night, when no one else was in the dorm bathroom. I made no friends. I wrote Paul a 'Dear John' letter and kept to myself. I wore loose, shapeless clothes to class and was completely terrified and alone."

Isolated by the pressures of secrecy, pregnant teenagers like Cammy were often unable to participate in their usual activities, much less to make sound judgments about their pregnancies. Fear of discovery, anxiety about breaking society's rules, and anticipation of social stigma plagued some so badly that they condemned themselves and even executed their own sentences.

"I thought I had done something horribly wrong," Cammy continues. "I spent my time waiting to be discovered and punished. Then, at semester break, when I was really showing, I went home and my mother found out just by looking at me. I was over five months pregnant by then. I never told Paul the truth. If I had, he might have told all our friends and ruined my life."

Young women like Cammy, previously unaccustomed to secrecy or deception, found that hiding their pregnancies changed them and their relationships. Trusting no one, they were unable to seek help. By the time Cammy revealed her pregnancy even to her mother, she had damaged both their mutual trust and their ability to work together to make the necessary decisions. Options had been limited not only by the advanced state of her pregnancy but also by the breakdown in communication she herself had created. Her obsessions with secrecy and social acceptability left her passive and powerless, too frightened to consider the deep and permanent issue of her pregnancy.

"My mom wanted me to get an abortion, but it was too late. So, to protect my reputation, she arranged for me to be an au pair in another state and to relinquish. There was nothing for me to say. I went obediently, trying to do whatever I could to make up for what I'd done. I never even considered what I wanted to do with the baby. I felt I'd better 'be good,' keep quiet, and do what I was told. I saw no friends, confided in no one, had no counseling. I was sent off alone, secretly. Even my father didn't know. The more time that passed, the bigger the secret became, and the more shame I felt. It was like a darkness that I wanted to get rid of, and I thought that if I did as I was told and gave the baby up, I could get rid of the haunting darkness and the shame, as well."

Old Too Soon

Childhood ended abruptly for birthmothers who relinquished as minors. No matter what role they played in the decision, none who relinquished continued their lives as carefree teens. Even those who insulated themselves with childlike fantasies were snapped to attention by the decision to surrender their babies. In the process of deciding, most lost their innocence. Some learned to deceive or to acquiesce. Their decisions drove many to immediate despair, others to cling to hopes for a fantastic miracle that would prevent surrender. Many waited their pregnancies out as if they were jail sentences that isolated them from "normal" life and set them forever apart from their peers.

Whatever roles underage birthmothers played in the process, reaching the decision to relinquish was traumatic. Those who were most powerless, who played no part in the decisions, who were passive, unacknowledged, or dishonest about their feelings, often experienced feelings of invisibility and developed patterns of reality distortion that shaped their adolescence and their lives. Those who were included in the process, even if their desires were ultimately overruled, were usually able to remain clearly in touch with reality and, therefore, to be better equipped to face the repercussions of those decisions later.

Between Mother Goose and Motherhood

Clearly, not all birthmothers were minors when they relinquished. For those of legal age, a blend of factors like financial independence, educational and career goals, marital status, relationships with birthfathers, social pressures, and self-esteem often influenced decisions to relinquish.

Some of the women considered "adults" by law were not yet prepared for the responsibilities of adulthood. Many remained financially dependent on their families pending completion of their college educations. Others were emotionally dependent, finding adolescence a difficult phase to complete. Although they were able to seek counseling and information about their options, many felt incapable of taking independent action and relied on others for all decision-related activities. Regardless of legal age, these women saw themselves as powerless to take charge of either their lives or their pregnancies.

"I never made a decision," Beth says. "There was only one horse in the stable, so I got on it and rode it in the direction it took me." Twenty-one when she got pregnant, Beth first turned to the birthfather for a solution. "He said we could get married, but that I'd have to convert to his religion. So I took instruction in his faith. We found an apartment, bought wedding rings, and got our blood tests for a marriage license. Then his family decided he couldn't marry outside his church. He was nineteen and his mother would have had to sign for him, since legal age was then twenty-one. She refused."

Left literally at the altar, Beth turned to her family. "They were embarrassed and ashamed. They sent me out of state to work for a family until I could relinquish. They never told me I had any options, never suggested counseling. I had no idea what to do. I was all alone and just did what my family thought best."

Legally adults, birthmothers like Beth nevertheless perceived themselves as weak and subject to the judgments of others. When they talk about their decisions, they emphasize their lack of power and their sense of victimization.

Broke, Broker, Broken

Some adult birthmothers reached their decisions to relinquish based primarily on finances. Bonnie, married at the time, remembers that she and her husband were on the brink of divorce owing to financial problems when she became pregnant in 1964. At that time, the couple could not afford the additional stresses and costs of a baby.

"Having a baby right then would have been the final straw," she sighs. "I was working full-time to help put my husband through medical school. If I'd kept the baby, we'd have lost my income and my husband wouldn't have been able to finish school. We already had thousands of dollars of loans to pay off, so we'd have been left with tons of debts and no medical career to pay them off with. It was awful. I had to choose between giving up my unplanned child or giving up my husband."

Other adult birthmothers, unmarried and struggling to make ends meet, fought to overcome their emotions and do what rationally seemed best for their babies. Money issues so overwhelmed them that even some who faced only short-term shortages abandoned hopes of raising their babies themselves.

Although today she is senior partner in a lucrative accounting firm, in 1973 Pam found that money was scarce. One of seven children, she knew what it was like to grow up with barely enough and was terrified of raising her own child without ample finances. She saw her university education as the key to a good profession, a lucrative salary, and eventually a financially secure family.

"A month into my pregnancy, I had to drop out of school," she says. "There was simply not enough money to pay for the medical bills and college, too. I took a job at a bank, but it was hard to live on what I earned. Jeff, the birthfather, came from a wealthy family, but I'd broken up with him and was too proud to ask him for money to help with the pregnancy, even though I was desperate."

Without the resources to complete their educations, birthmothers like Pam saw their prospects as bleak, at best. Many looked for supplementary sources of support before settling on adoption. And some believe that they were deliberately misled by adoption authorities who tried to convince them to relinquish.

"Before I finally agreed to give my daughter up," Pam recalls, "I asked the agency about loans or other financial help that would enable me to keep her. They told me there were none, even for my medical bills, and that my only choice was to relinquish. I *knew* there were social programs, like welfare, that could see us through the year until I'd graduated, but the counselor told me I wasn't eligible because I wasn't married. I believe she lied to me and deliberately distorted the facts to sway me toward relinquishing. At the same time, the agency brainwashed me, telling me I was incapable of raising a child and unworthy to try because I was unwed. They insisted on seeing me every week. I thought it was to help me, but now I think it was so they could control me and convince me that adoptive parents would be *much* better than I was, that they never err, never die, are always stable, and are generally eligible for sainthood."

Even adult birthmothers like Pam, who did research, selected adoption agencies, and reached their own decisions, often felt angry and discontented afterward. Several months pregnant, unmarried, emotionally vulnerable, and overwhelmed by financial problems, many agreed to solutions that later seem extraordinary.

"I could have made it," Pam insists. "I was an adult, close to graduating from college. If any single mother had a chance at making a home for her child, I was it. I just needed help for a year, but I listened to my fears and took bad advice. It seems incredible to me, now, how insurmountable those temporary problems seemed. But I couldn't see my way through them. I went to price cribs, intending to buy one, but they cost $100. I just sat down and cried, right in the store. I didn't have $100. And I was so alone and defeated that I couldn't imagine that I ever would."

Money and the Protection of Men

Finances were important, but money alone rarely led birthmothers to relinquish. More often, compounding factors such as marital status tilted the scale. In 1971, a college junior named Peg felt abandoned and vulnerable when Peter, her baby's father, refused to marry her. Rejected and alone, she determined to protect her child from growing up as she had, without a father. "My father died when I was ten, leaving my mother to raise five kids on her own. Without a father, I always felt different than the other kids and I wanted my child to feel normal and safe, under her daddy's roof. I kept hoping Peter would come through and marry me. But, as the pregnancy neared its end, I realized I was on my own. I knew that if I kept the baby, I'd never finish college and we'd have to live without much money. But, more important, I knew that my child would grow up without a dad, just like I did. It's hard to have no father. You *want* your dad. You want him on Father's Day, Christmas, graduation, and birthdays. You want him just at dinner. I know how it is to be without a dad. And my dad died; he didn't reject me the way Peter rejected our baby. I couldn't stand the idea of having my child grow up with that rejection. I thought it would be better for the baby to have two parents, even if it meant that I wouldn't be one of them."

Swayed by finances and her own childhood experiences, Peg's scale tipped toward relinquishment. Nevertheless, like many other birthmothers, she found this solution unbearable and remained reluctant to accept it.

"I seriously considered abortion. I thought, if I couldn't accept the responsibility for a baby, I shouldn't give birth to it. But I couldn't go through with the abortion. I actually made the appointment—I changed it twice, but I canceled at the last minute each time. It wasn't a religious decision. And it wasn't a moral one, either. I have friends who had abortions and I don't think they were wrong to do so. My decision was purely personal. To me, the baby was a person who was relying on me and I didn't want to let her down. The trouble was, I had no choice. It wasn't a question of whether I'd let her down, but of how."

Birthmothers like Peg who grew up feeling "different," saw surrender as their children's opportunities to enter the traditional structures of society and "normal" family life. For these unmarried, unwealthy, unestablished young women, relinquishment presented a chance to give their children acceptability, security, social status, and, possibly, power. Coming from backgrounds like Peg's, they could not imagine themselves providing as much with mere maternal love.

The Price of Independence

More recently, other single young adult birthmothers have relinquished because of a need to attain or retain their hard-won self-sufficiency. Although they still lacked sufficient resources to keep and raise their babies, many were beginning to acquire personal assets, strong identities, and personal power and felt confident enough to make their own decisions about how to handle their pregnancies.

Although many young women today are independent, ambitious, and outspoken, in 1982 when Laurie became pregnant during a casual affair, she was a groundbreaker.

Breaking rules was not new to Laurie. She was the first woman in her family to attend college. Her parents could not see why she thought education was important for women; they thought she was educating herself "right out of the marriage market." Her three brothers mocked her for being "uppity" and "too good" to get married after high school. Undaunted, Laurie pursued her own dreams and supported herself by working two jobs while she attended college. Her commitment to attaining her potential and her goals, even at great sacrifice, was unshakable.

"I knew I couldn't keep my baby," she admits. "I had friends who'd had babies and had to leave school. For me, to keep her would have to mean providing for her and affording quality day care without financial support from anyone else. I couldn't do that. So I searched for an alternative, combing libraries for books on adoption and interviewing agencies."

"Interviewing agencies" was a new concept when Laurie undertook the process. Agencies were unaccustomed to assertive birthmothers who required certain conditions, asked questions, and demanded answers. Birthmothers with a new profile, who were unashamed, open, and self-empowered, were emerging. Laurie was among the first.

"I wanted to see if I could trust an agency with the responsibility for my child, so I made a list of requests. Would they guarantee that I could communicate regularly with the adoptive parents? Would they let me know their educational, religious, medical, and fertility histories?

"Well, agencies were astounded that a birthmother would ask *them* questions. The prevailing attitude was that I should submissively hand over my baby with no questions asked. One agency asked me to 'please leave now, since it's obvious we can't service you.' They thought I should be grateful for whatever they'd give me. I left. I was determined not to give up my child until and unless I could find a way that would meet my requirements."

With the emergence of open adoption, more agencies have become willing to provide information about and contact with adoptive parents. When birthmothers took active roles in selecting the agency and the adoptive family, some found that their decisions to relinquish become easier.

"When I found an agency that would agree to my terms," Laurie says, "I felt profound relief. I knew I could go through with the adoption in good conscience and that I could finish school and continue to pursue my goals."

Because they exerted so much authority and imposed such strict terms during the decision-making process, birthmothers like Laurie were often surprised at their dissatisfaction with the outcomes. Nevertheless, they clung steadfastly to their independence and refused to dwell on these feelings, believing that uncontrolled emotions, like the unplanned pregnancies they stemmed from, could only hold them back. Faced with the dilemma of sacrificing their dreams or their unplanned babies, they made the choices that they thought most practical, that would leave them with the most security, independence, and control. Most, however, remained painfully ambivalent, rationalizing or avoiding thoughts of their decisions.

"After my pregnancy, I kept busy working and studying," Laurie says. "I left myself no time to think about emotions. It's been ten years, and I wonder if I've ever dealt with my feelings about my decision. Probably not. I seem to push them away by keeping busy. I'd rather work until I drop than let them come out. Frankly, I don't know what good they'd do. There was no perfect solution. I selected the best available alternative. And I made a choice. Dwelling on it could only hurt."

Independence on Crutches

For a few young women, relinquishing reflected a struggle not just for independence but for actual survival. Pregnant within long-term abusive relationships, they were convinced that the fathers posed threats to both their own and their children's lives. In 1983, Donna was a self-supporting college graduate, twenty-one years old. She lived alone but had been seeing Nick "on and off" for several years. Donna loved Nick. The only problem with their relationship was that Nick beat her from time to time, sometimes severely.

"I got my period the first month," Donna recalls, "so I didn't know I was pregnant. Shortly after that, Nick beat me up so bad I ended up in the hospital. My left eye was swollen shut and I had stitches under my chin. He'd broken my thumb and punched me in the abdomen, the ribs, the face and head. For the next two months, I missed my period, but the doctors said that was probably due to internal bruises and emotional trauma. I took a pregnancy test right away, but it was negative and the doctor told me not to expect regular periods for up to three months. Meantime, I was depressed, eating a lot and gaining weight, so I didn't pay much attention to my expanding waistline. It wasn't until a few months later, when I felt life, when I felt the baby *move*, that I knew for sure that I was pregnant. And, by then, there weren't many options left: I was five months along."

Women who became pregnant in abusive relationships were often more concerned for their babies than for themselves. For the first time, some began to assert themselves, to separate from long-term abusive partners and to assert independence in ways that they would not otherwise have dared. For Donna, pregnancy presented the final incentive to break away from Nick. The safety of her baby was all that mattered.

"I took off, moved, got an unlisted phone. It was the pregnancy, definitely, that gave me the nerve to break away. And the odd part is that I thought I was going to have an abortion. It didn't make sense, really, to hide and protect a baby I was going to abort. But, still, I protected her. I told no one that I was pregnant. Not anybody. I just cleared out, laid low, and kept my child secret and safe."

Having escaped imminent danger, however, women like Donna confronted the frightening and complicated repercussions of their pregnancies. Marriage was out of the question; they were afraid even to inform the birthfathers of their pregnancies. Further, as newly independent adults, most were unwilling to ask their parents for help; parental rescue would mean the return to dependency and the loss of their still unstable adult identities. Finally, abortion was out—sometimes because it was illegal, sometimes because it went against their beliefs, sometimes because it was simply too late. For Donna, abortion was her clear preference, and she still wonders what led her to choose relinquishment instead.

"What I needed to do for myself, back then, was to stand on my own two feet, without Nick, without my parents and, certainly, without a baby. I would have freed myself easily if I'd gotten an early abortion. But because I denied my pregnancy for over five months, I couldn't. Somewhere, I must have known that I was pregnant. Ignoring the pregnancy, pretending that it was just 'internal injuries,' must have been my way of protecting my baby, so that I couldn't decide on abortion, no matter what else I chose to do. Looking back, I see denial as my first maternal act. I hid and protected her not only from her birthfather but from myself."

Till Secrets Do Us Part

"My husband never knew about the baby," Joyce confides. "He was in the war, and I didn't see him for over a year. It was a mistake, over and finished by the time he came home. I went crazy, covering my tracks, hiding the truth from anybody who might eventually leak my secret to him, but I didn't want him to find out because it would have broken his heart. Luckily, I had no stretch marks, or it would have been all over."

A few birthmothers, like Joyce, were married women who relinquished because their husbands were not the babies' fathers. Joyce had a fleeting affair in 1968, while her husband was away in Vietnam. "I never even saw the baby," she says. "I just made my mind up to get her a good home and tried to put the whole mistake behind me. I was so busy trying to keep my secret that I had no time to think about the baby. I didn't let myself do that for years."

Julia became pregnant in 1979 while she and her husband were legally separated. "When we got back together, we didn't realize I was pregnant. When we found out, we both knew that Larry couldn't have been the daddy, since we'd each been seeing other people, not each other. Part of putting our marriage back in shape meant getting rid of our other relationships, and I couldn't ask my husband to raise another man's child. It was enough that he stayed with me through the whole pregnancy and that he understood. I was very depressed about the baby. It was a tough time, a hard decision. But it had to be."

Ashamed

Regardless of age, money, and social status, one of the major factors influencing birthmothers to relinquish has always been the judgments of others. Even today, society subtly frowns on women who have children out of wedlock. The stigma is certainly less severe than in past years, but it still intimidates some women so thoroughly that they surrender, even if with great sorrow.

Sonia, who became pregnant while in graduate school, relinquished in 1985. When she learned that the father of her child was married, she turned to her family. Instead of support, however, her father reacted with shame and panic. Dean of students at a small college, he feared that his career and the reputation of the entire family would be ruined by Sonia's "scandalous indiscretion."

He insisted that Sonia stay away from the family for the duration of her pregnancy and forbade her to keep her child at the risk of being disinherited. These threats of rejection, abandonment, and shame overpowered Sonia; she felt she had no choice but to relinquish.

If social stigma posed a threat to women in 1985, it overwhelmed them two decades before. Jean relinquished in 1966. Newly divorced, twenty-seven years old, she had been told during her marriage that she could not have children. After years of tests, hormonal therapies, and fertility experiments, she and her husband adopted a baby boy and, a year later, divorced. Her first romantic relationship after her divorce resulted in pregnancy.

"I couldn't believe I was pregnant," she says. "It seemed impossible. We didn't use birth control because I knew I couldn't get pregnant, but I'd been taking tranquilizers due to the stress of my divorce, and I guess the pills relaxed me enough to allow conception. At any rate, the guy refused to marry me, so there I was—divorced, with a baby and pregnant."

Embarrassed, Jean began to wear her old wedding ring. She told nobody that she was divorced and pretended, even at her new job, to be married. Her mother, who lived with her, was ashamed to see her in her "condition," so Jean hid in the bedroom of her own house, internalizing the shame. She felt that, by conceiving, she had done something terribly wrong. The counseling she received only confirmed those feelings.

"I developed such bad feelings about myself that I thought my baby would be better off without me. The counselor I saw advised adoption. Still, I couldn't help thinking, after all those years of trying to get pregnant, 'What a lovely thing to happen to me! I *can* have children, after all!' I wanted her. I kept searching for alternatives that make it acceptable for me to keep her, but there weren't any in 1966. I was a marked woman, hiding my head in shame."

Like many others, Jean could not withstand the pressures of social stigma. She fought the decision to relinquish, however, until the stigma threatened to affect her children. "My mother visited me in the hospital the day after I gave birth. She said that, if I kept my baby out of wedlock, I might lose custody of my adopted son. She told me I'd be considered immoral and unfit, and that my ex-husband could take him from me, or that the courts might. At the time, I believed her. But whether or not it was true, my mother and the rest of our community would have made life impossible for me and my little girl. I saw that there was no way I could keep her. I'd been worn down.

"So I walked to the nursery. Somebody was rocking her. She opened her eyes, and I remember that they were brown. I hadn't known that babies could be born with brown eyes. They didn't give her to me, but I whispered, 'I love you.' I had every negative, painful feeling a person can have, but I decided to surrender her. It seemed to be not the best but the only choice."

Despite their maturity and apparent authority, many adult birthmothers felt, as Sonia and Jean did, that surrender was their only option. Often, the powerlessness they experienced in reaching these decisions irreversibly lowered their self-esteem. Many blamed themselves for not finding ways to keep their babies and sank into depression. Some pretended to be "fine" while secretly despising themselves. A few, however, did not turn their frustrations inward; they saw their lack of options as the fault of others and aimed their anger, accordingly, at them.

Amputation of the Heart

Some women who felt that society forced them to surrender were infused with a permanent fury. The anguish they felt at surrender both strengthened and alienated them. Even if they were self-sufficient, mature professionals with more than adequate financial resources, they felt powerless in the face of tradition, judgment, and social pressure. Indignation and rage usually offered neither solution nor relief, but motivated and empowered these birthmothers to express their permanent discontent and actively work for social change.

Sylvia, a professional diplomat, was thirty-seven when she relinquished in 1962. "Reaching my decision," she recalls, "was rather like hanging off a cliff by my fingers. As each of my options disappeared, it was as if I'd had another finger hacked off at the knuckle, until there was only one finger left to hang by: adoption."

Sylvia's first choice would have been to conform to the dictates of society and marry Girard, the birthfather. Because he wasn't free to marry her, she considered her second choice, that of raising her son herself. In 1962, she felt that society made that choice impossible.

"I was angry. I felt that my baby, if I'd kept him, would be held hostage by values I didn't share, that he'd be persecuted for being illegitimate. I would have stood up to anyone, gladly, if it meant keeping him. But I didn't think it was fair to ask a newborn infant to enter the world fighting a moral war. It's hard for people today to understand what it was like then. My child would have been a bastard. In those days, prior to the 'revolutions' of the sixties, he'd have had a lot to contend with. It would have been like putting blood on a chicken; the others in the coop would peck him to death. I didn't want other kids to do that to *my* son."

Sylvia's third idea was to take her child abroad to live in a more tolerant country. "I thought of going back to work abroad and taking him with me. But I was afraid that, as we'd move to another country, we'd become too dependent on each other and that my child's whole life would revolve around mother. I saw that as horribly damaging."

Birthmothers like Sylvia saw themselves as the victims of their times. Although attitudes were evolving and becoming more tolerant of single parents, many women who were pregnant during the transition period were unwilling to gamble that society's changes would take place fast enough for their children. They abandoned the idea of openly taking on the role of unmarried mothers. The only way they could consider keeping their children was by cloaking themselves in acceptable fictional roles.

Accordingly, Sylvia's final choice, other than to relinquish, was to move to another city and claim to be divorced or widowed.

"I was afraid of living lies, of raising a child under the shadow of false origins. That was also why I didn't ask my brother's family to raise my baby. I wouldn't have wanted to come by, after a decade or more of being his aunt, and tell him I was actually his mother. And even if we'd told him the truth, he'd become rooted there. I knew I could never really reclaim him once I'd put him there. I thought he'd be better off rooting outside, where shame, judgments, and lies couldn't reach him.

"So, having abandoned the options of marriage, of running off with him here or abroad, and of placing him with my family, the only finger I hadn't yet chopped off was adoption. But I was angry, furious, that relinquishment was all that was viable for us."

Some birthmothers who reluctantly accepted that they and their babies were being separated because of values they did not share were paralyzed by frustration and defeat. Others, however, like Sylvia, became energized and driven, thirsting for an unattainable revenge against the society they blamed. Despite their systematic, seemingly rational, assertive roles in their decisions, these birthmothers remained outraged and devastated by the choices they felt powerless to avoid.

"I was willing to do *anything* in order to keep my child and live by my own standards," Sylvia declares. "I was not ashamed of myself or of being pregnant. But I needed to think about the child. I had to give him his best opportunity, and that meant protecting him from the judgmental hordes. But I've never gotten over it, never forgiven society for forcing me to make that choice. I've alienated myself. I've become forever an outsider. And I've done whatever I can to stir things up and make changes in society or just to get even however and whenever I can."

Indecisive

As painful as the decision to relinquish was, it was at least a decision. Despite the pain, some birthmothers found that reaching a decision, even an unsatisfactory one, brought them a degree of relief. Many were convinced that only by reaching a decision could they begin to heal or "move on."

Some, however, were not able to accept the idea that a definite decision was in their own or their babies' best interests and delayed taking permanent steps as long as possible, hoping that better solutions would emerge.

Annie was twenty-one when she had her baby in 1969. A political radical in the antiwar movement, she believed that the adoption system itself was an offshoot of a racist society and refused to agree to relinquish the child. "If I'd been black," she insists, "everybody would have assumed I would keep my baby. Because I'm white, everyone was pushing me to surrender, because there was a big demand to adopt white babies. It was like a supply and demand issue, and I could help supply the demand.

"Today, it's more acceptable for single white women to keep their babies. But, back then, the pressures were incredible. I refused to give in."

Accordingly, Annie determined to take a stand. She hung onto the hope that Dave, the birthfather, a political activist and draft resister, would miraculously conform to traditional values enough to marry her. They were both twenty-one and, she thought, old enough for marriage.

"Abortion was legal, then," Annie recalls. "When I told him I was pregnant, Dave just shrugged and told me to get one. Just, 'Oh, really? Well, get an abortion.' Marriage never even occurred to him. Problem was, though, it was too late for an 'easy' abortion. I was almost six months pregnant. When I pointed that out, Dave lit a cigarette and coolly informed me that he was seeing someone else. 'We're basically done, you and I,' he said. 'So do what you want to do.' I was crushed. Destroyed. In shock."

Annie, who had hoped that her pregnancy would secure her relationship with her boyfriend, found that it trapped *her* instead. Frantic and rejected, she lost control and her sense of perspective. "I ran out of the room. I didn't even get my coat, just my bag with my car keys. It was an icy night. I started the car, floored it, spun on the ice and skidded down the street. Finally, I smashed into a parked van. I demolished my car. I wasn't badly hurt and neither was the baby. But I wished I had been. I wanted to die. I really did."

But she didn't die. She panicked, instead. Forced to give up on Dave, she hoped that her liberal parents would step forward to help her raise her child outside the parameters defined by society. That hope, too, went unrealized. Finally, with no way to support her baby, Annie signed papers releasing him for foster care rather than adoption.

"It turns out, that was the worst thing I could have done," she says. "In order to get him back, I would have had to go to court and prove I was a fit mother. You can't just take your baby back from foster care, but I didn't know that, and nobody advised me. If, on the other hand, I'd changed my mind after giving him up for adoption, I'd have been able to reclaim him within the grace period designated by the state, without any court hearings or having to prove myself 'fit.'"

Desperate, unable to reach the decision to keep or relinquish, a number of birthmothers fell into traps like Annie's. By extending the decision-making process, they rarely found new alternatives and often cut off some of the old ones. Ironically, by trying to protect and hang onto their babies, some may actually have harmed them.

"I visited my son once a month for a year," Annie explains. "That was a whole year in which he could have bonded with me or with adoptive parents. Instead, he was stuck in a foster home, where any bonds he formed had to be broken."

Like Annie, many birthmothers received counseling biased toward adoption. "They saw me constantly until I decided to relinquish, then they dropped me. They had no interest in how I was or what I felt. They only wanted my baby. But I was muddled, exhausted, convinced that I was no good, because I hadn't wanted to give up my baby. The baby's father had dumped me, so my self-esteem was not great. But the counseling I received about relinquishing finished me off. My ego was so low that if someone had told me to kill myself, I'd have said, 'OK. That sounds right.' But I wouldn't have taken the initiative to do it myself. I wouldn't have thought *any* idea I had was any good."

Overwhelmed with emotional and personal issues, many women who were ambivalent about surrender did not fully understand their legal options or the ramifications of the decisions they made. Some, even in open adoptions, learned too late the meaning of the terms to which they had agreed or about the existence of alternatives they would have preferred. The effects of their misunderstandings were both devastating and permanent.

"I was dead wrong about everything," Annie says. "Each mistake compounded another. I hesitated to act because I knew I'd just mess up again. But I had no idea what to do. I was a coward. I gave in and gave my son up, and my contempt for myself for doing that has never gone away."

After the Choice

Almost two-thirds of the women interviewed said that, facing the same circumstances, they would refuse to relinquish their babies, no matter what problems or issues would ensue. A quarter would relinquish again but qualified that with comments like "I was too young to do anything else" or "It was the only choice I had." The remainder do not know what they would do if given the chance to make the choice again.

Many birthmothers saw the "decision" to give up a child for adoption not as a matter of choice but as a trap set by circumstances such as social stigma, parental authority, financial hardship, or their own youth. Others found alternatives, like abortion, either unacceptable or unavailable. And many were simply uninformed about programs, such as public welfare or personal financial loans, that might have enabled them to keep their children.

Many of the women interviewed received no professional counseling or support whatever. Others felt that the counseling they received was biased toward relinquishment, that "professionals" were far more concerned about acquiring a baby for adoption than about the birthmothers' feelings, goals, or ultimate well-being.

Without neutral, in-depth counseling, many were unable to explore their feelings and, consequently, unprepared for the emotional reactions that followed their decisions to relinquish. Further, because of the betrayal or abandonment they felt when they sought help, they often faced issues of broken trust in addition to those of relinquishment. Some have blocked out their thoughts and feelings related to the painful process of decision making; others remember, but with varying levels of clarity, numbness, and grief.

Looking back, birthmothers often feel guilty, angry, or unsettled about the events leading to their "decisions" to relinquish. Many, even those who were powerless, dependent minors when they gave birth, do not forgive themselves for failing to question authority, defy social pressure, and seek impartial legal, financial, and emotional counseling. Some angrily insist that they were lied to by adoption professionals. A number, adults as well as minors, blame their parents, the birthfathers, or society, but, ultimately, most turn their anger inward at themselves.

Whomever they blamed, whatever led them to their "choices," most birthmothers were left alone with secret rage and pain. Some who felt powerless about the decision drifted into protective fantasies or recurring depression. Others, who actively took part in the process, were often left with intense guilt and feelings of being "bad," "shameful," and deserving of punishment. Some split themselves into a "public" side that reunited with society, conformed and did everything acceptably, and a "private" side that hid, grieved, and felt unworthy.

A few became so enraged by their helplessness about their decisions that they declared outright war against those who influenced them, alienating themselves from families, social rules, and society at large.

Some birthmothers were convinced that relinquishment had been the best available option for all concerned. Even so, many of these women did not feel good about it and went along with it because they felt unable to do anything else. Some admitted to conflicted and lingering feelings of loss, emptiness, or anger. Others said that they generally avoided the topic of adoption, burying the associated memories and trying to hide their secret pain, even from themselves.

3

Waiting Days and Birthdays

SOMEBODY WAS SCREAMING.

It was a woman's voice, but Zoe couldn't tell where it was coming from. It just screamed on and on, in rhythm with a white-knuckled fist that pounded on green cement walls.

And then it was quiet. The fist relaxed, revealing chipped red nails. Zoe panted, smeared sweat across her forehead with wet arms. Propping herself up onto her elbows, she searched the long hallway for help. Her eyes darted down green linoleum floors and matching green walls to stark white curtains, not quite wide enough to cover the cubicles behind them. Muffled voices mumbled, veiled and unseen. Stripes of white neon buzzed above her. Empty stretchers stood in line behind. In another minute, it would begin again.

Down the hall, one of the curtains opened. Someone . . . a woman in white . . . a nurse . . . a nun came out. She wore glasses. She was coming toward Zoe. She would help. It was going to start again.

"Help me!" Zoe reached for the nun. "Can you help me? Can somebody get me something? . . ."

"You'll have to be quiet. You're disturbing the other patients." The nun walked on.

The screaming began again, suddenly. White pain that screamed lifted Zoe and hung onto her, squeezing, owning her. From nowhere, lots of large hands appeared in long white sleeves. They grabbed her fists, pulled them away from the pounding wall and tied them down, one on each side. One big hand came down and crushed Zoe's mouth. The screaming stopped, even though the blinding pain roared on. A big head appeared over her face. It had droopy skin and glasses, marble eyes and no lips. Instead of hair, it had gray paper held on with elastic, and when it spoke, a line opened in its chin. The face spoke to her. It spoke alien sounds.

"Getayholduvyorself. Iymgoeentooshayvyew. Iymiytkutyew, ifyewdontkuntrollyorself. . . ." Zoe fought to free her arms. She wanted to bite the hand, but it squashed her jaws together too tightly. She heard, she thought, the word *enema*, maybe the word *doctor*. Eventually, the hand released Zoe's mouth and the face stopped talking, disappeared below her belly. The screaming wanted to start again, but, stifled and afraid, it hunkered into a low, bellowing moan, escaped from her throat and rolled heavily down the corridor.

Delivery

When she gave birth to a baby girl in 1966, Zoe was seventeen years old. She had received no information to prepare her for childbirth, no education about what to expect during labor or delivery. She was alone in the hospital through it all. During contractions, she believed that she was dying.

Zoe's experience with childbirth is not unlike that of many other birthmothers, particularly those who delivered a decade or more ago, as teenagers. For months, Zoe looked forward to having her baby, so that she could end her pregnancy-imposed isolation and return to life as a "normal" teenager. She hoped that her dark moods and depression would end with childbirth.

Birthmothers like Zoe, however, who expected that they would be "delivered" along with their babies, were often disappointed and shocked that normal life continued to elude them postpartum. Many found that the experiences of pregnancy had changed them so completely that giving birth became just one of a continuing series of isolating and anguished secrets. Unlike women whose pregnancies were planned or desired, women waiting to surrender their babies experienced reproduction as a series of losses rather than gains. Many of these losses were unanticipated; most were unarticulated and unacknowledged.

Obviously, women about to relinquish expected the loss of their babies. In addition to their babies, however, they were also about to lose, at least temporarily, the role of mother, which, under traditional circumstances, would have improved their social status, marked their passages from girlhood to womanhood, and brought them recognition as honored individuals, important to the basic framework and survival of society.

Further, with pregnancy and birth, most birthmothers lost their innocence, self-esteem, and prospects. Along with their babies, many relinquished their trust in others and their sense of identity within society. As if these losses weren't enough, many felt that their most important relationships, including those with birthfathers, parents, or peers, were damaged beyond repair. Instead of the traditional joy, fulfillment, and hope associated with pregnancy, most birthmothers experienced the antitheses. As their pregnancies advanced, so did their despair and their distances from "normal" life.

Incubating

For almost three-quarters of the birthmothers interviewed, pregnancy literally meant banishment from society. Sent away for the duration of their pregnancies, they lost their homes, friends, and families. Almost half of those interviewed spent several months of their pregnancies in homes for unmarried pregnant women. Although most of these institutions are defunct today, they were standard residences for birthmothers through the fifties, sixties, and most of the seventies.

A fifth did not go away to homes but were sent instead to work as au pairs or nannies for families in other cities. About one in six moved with their families or a family member to another city for the duration of the pregnancy.

The remainder, many of whom delivered in the 1980s, remained at home, living either with their families or on their own. Even if they stayed home, however, many lost any sense of "normal" life. Dropping out of school, changing jobs, and isolating themselves, most invented elaborate cover stories to avoid stigma, minimize embarrassment, and protect themselves, their families, and their newborns under intricate cloaks of secrecy.

The "Home"

Women who went to institutions for unmarried mothers were separated from familiar people and environments for months. Many found that being displaced and resettled with a bunch of other pregnant women was almost as traumatic as their unwanted pregnancies.

"My first thought," says Toby, "was that it was a luxurious, splendid mansion. You walked into a magnificent foyer with marble floors, a domed ceiling, and a winding staircase. A very pretty girl, about eight months pregnant, was playing a sonata on a grand piano in a formal sitting room to the left of the entranceway. I was nervous, so I walked over and asked her if she knew how to play Claire de Lune, my favorite song. I thought it might calm me down. She motioned for me to sit next to her on the bench, and I did. She played it beautifully. I thought what a wonderful place this must be, how elegant and gentle. As I listened, I closed my eyes and began to relax. When the song ended, I turned to thank the girl. Looking at her, I became startled and uneasy. There was something wrong with her face, although I couldn't identify what it was. From far away, she'd seemed perfect and serene, but up close, something was wrong. Not wanting to stare at her, I dismissed it and forgot about it in the confusion of moving in. Later, I saw her tugging on her eyelids and learned that she pulled all her lashes out. I suppose it was nervousness. Everybody had some outlet. That was hers."

At the home, many young women found, as Toby did, that things were not as they appeared to be. First, despite its epithet, the place was *not* home. Rather, it was where unmarried pregnant women went when they were sent *away* from home.

Second, the relationships made there were often deliberately temporary and artificial. In the interests of anonymity, no one revealed her real identity. In some homes, false last names were given; in others, no last names were used at all. Some allowed only last initials.

"At the end of our pregnancies," says Barbara, "we were supposed to give up everything. Our babies, our past 'sins,' *and* the few supportive friends we'd made there. We were supposed to go on as if nothing had ever happened there, or as if we'd never been there at all."

Another false aspect of homes was the cover stories created to explain the absence of pregnant women from their homes and families. Rheumatic fever or kidney problems were popular excuses. Others were "sent to study abroad" or to "help a sick aunt" or other relative in another state. The stories varied but lent a consistent air of deceit and secrecy to their lives. Often, these cover stories required other falsehoods to support them, such as false addresses and means of forwarding mail or consistently fabricated answers to concerned acquaintances who asked after the missing young women.

Finally, homes prevented any involvement by birthfathers in the pregnancy and birth of their babies. Because unmarried women and birthfathers were separated, marriage and legitimization of their unborn children became impossible. Birthfathers, in fact, were often encouraged by authorities and family to date others, so that cover stories would seem more believable. While many young birthfathers obediently played the field, their pregnant girlfriends sat in the homes, often idealizing their relationships and dreaming unrealistic dreams. "I fantasized about Rick day and night," says Jill, who relinquished in 1970. "I imagined that we'd get married and have other babies, and I decided to save the names I liked best for the babies we'd have later and be able to keep. Meantime, Rick was keeping the eyes of the community off our problems by dating other girls, including my best friend Trish. He'd moved on while I was stuck with my fantasies of him and our seven-pound, eight-ounce case of 'rheumatic fever.'"

Many birthmothers felt that the homes were not merely false; they were actually punitive. Because their emotional needs were so often overlooked there, some angrily referred to homes as "baby factories" for adoptive parents. In many homes, residents were allowed visits only by their parents or female friends or relatives. Some homes, however, forbade visits not only by birthfathers but by *any* men, including the residents' own fathers. In many homes contact with the outside world was tightly controlled and used as a means of manipulation; in others, it was lost altogether.

"If I did something wrong," Cindy says, "I wasn't allowed to have visitors. The staff had the power to isolate us completely. There was one nun who was especially mean. She didn't like me and made me dust all her religious statues over and over again. We were like Cinderella. If we did something a nun didn't like, we'd be punished. We were prisoners, waiting out our sentences."

Nine Months to Life

Although few of these homes exist today, many birthmothers still feel the effects of having lived there decades ago. At least a few had valid reasons for feeling like prisoners during their stays. Pregnant before they were of legal age, they had obviously participated in illegal sexual activities.

"My boyfriend and I had planned to marry," Cathy says. "But we were only fifteen and his parents opposed it. They agreed to pay for an illegal abortion, but my parents vetoed that because they were afraid that, if it got botched, I'd be damaged for life.

"My boyfriend's parents became so worried about having to pay medical expenses or child support that they reported me to the juvenile authorities for having sex as a minor. They wanted to make me seem promiscuous, so they wouldn't be held financially responsible. After all, I couldn't prove that their son was the only boy I'd ever slept with. The officer asked me, 'How many times have you had sex, young lady?' I lied and said, 'Only once,' because I was afraid they'd send me to Sing Sing.

"As it was, they put me on probation until I was eighteen. I was on parole for having had sex. I had a police record. I had to drop out of school and was sent away to a home. My boyfriend snuck in once to see me, but they found him and pulled him out, literally, by his ear. My father was so ashamed that he wouldn't visit me. He wouldn't even *talk* to me. My mother visited but kept asking how I could have done this to her. To *her*! I'd confided in a few girls from my school and they came to see me once, but it was out of curiosity, not concern. They wanted to see 'the pregnant girl,' the same way they'd want to see 'the fat lady' at a circus. Once they saw me they never came back. I was on my own, without friends, boyfriend, or family. I was bad, sent away, being punished for having had sex."

Sue likens her stay at the home not merely to prison, but to a death sentence. "I knew, at sixteen, that my life was over," she says. "There was no way I could ever return to it. I'd never again be a child or even a normal teenager. Instead, I was like an old Eskimo, left on the ice to die alone. There was no hope of rescue. My boyfriend, Bob, felt so guilty and powerless about the pregnancy that he ran off to another state. He was missing for most of the time I was in the home. Without Bob, I had nobody to turn to. The only companions I had were the other girls like myself. Other abandoned Eskimos without last names, drifting on the ice."

Like many birthmothers, Sue remembers the staff of the home as judgmental and sometimes cruel, deliberately "punishing" pregnant young women for their "sins," as if exacting punishment were part of their job description. While living at these homes, many pregnant women felt powerless to communicate with the staff, much less to disobey them or defy their authority. Under such harsh conditions, some lost their sense of perspective, others their sense of self.

"They made us scrub the toilets and wash the bathroom floors on our hands and knees, even on the hottest days of summer," Sue recalls. "I felt faint from the smell of the disinfectant and from the heat, but I had no choice. They constantly reminded us that we had to atone for what we'd done, start a fresh life by hard work and prayer. They told us that, unless we hated our babies, we'd give them up. They said we shouldn't dwell on the past, that we should move on and not look back. I listened to them. I trusted them. I prayed and felt close to God. But I couldn't do what they said. I couldn't just move on. I pretended to, but secretly I cried myself to sleep every night. I thought I was wrong, that I was bad because I couldn't discard my feelings or forget my past. I didn't know how. I wanted to die."

The Loneliest Number

For some pregnant women, the home was not so much a prison as a refuge. A number of birthmothers relied on the home as an escape from abusive relationships. Many of these women, long accustomed to hiding their fearful secrets, remember the home as just another site of unending loneliness, one in which their problems separated them not only from the other pregnant women but also from any staff who tried to help them. For some, pregnancy itself provided the only comfort.

Cindy's father pulled her out of high school as a sophomore and sent her away where she could be safe from her mentally ill, violent mother. "The other girls were nice enough," she recalls, "but they talked about their boyfriends, schools, their families, and friends. They talked about the lives they'd go back to after their babies were born. I had nothing to say. I had no boyfriend, no friends to go back to. No family that I could talk about, anyway. Sometimes they talked about giving up their babies, and I couldn't stand to hear it. It scared me to death. So I kept to myself. I didn't talk to anyone. But I didn't feel lonely, really, since I had my baby with me."

Birthmothers whose extreme family problems led them to the home often felt isolated by their secrets. Although help was sometimes available, attaining it, for young women like Cindy, seemed to require too great a risk.

"Most of the people at the home didn't care about us," she says. "But there was one counselor who wanted to talk about my feelings about sex. She was concerned that I'd been raped and thought I needed help about that. But I hadn't really been raped. That had been a lie, something I'd made up so my mother wouldn't find out I'd been sleeping around. So I had to lie again, to satisfy the counselor, and make up a whole story about the rape and how I was really OK about it now. If not for the rape story, even she wouldn't have cared about my feelings, though. I would have been just another pregnant girl with another baby for adoption."

For young women in situations like Cindy's, the home provided temporary safe housing, board, and prenatal care. Ultimately, however, it left them to their own resources in dealing with their problems. Counseling, where it existed at all, was minimal and slanted toward relinquishing. Most women felt that they were left to handle their emotional conflicts and relationships on their own.

"It was a place to eat and sleep," Cindy says. "It was a place where I'd do my chores and hide in my room so I didn't have to lie to anyone or realize how much of a freak I was compared to the other girls. I'd curl up on my bed, on my side, and poke my belly just enough to make my baby move. Feeling him move was my only joy, the only time I had any peace or, at least, relief from pain."

Two Hearts, a Pass, and One Dummy

Not all women at the home were passively sent there. Some were there by choice, paying their own way. One divorced birthmother in her late thirties checked into a home because she didn't want her college-age children to know she'd become pregnant during an affair. She told them, as a cover, that she was traveling for a few months. Another, temporarily separated from her husband, was there because her husband was not the father of the child. These women, older and more mature than most residents, were better equipped to control their activities and experiences during their stays.

For Sylvia, the home provided a place to roost comfortably while waiting out her pregnancy. "I played bridge all day long," she remembers. "I had plenty of money, so I paid my own way. I saw a psychiatrist privately. And I learned a lot about my childhood, about growing up with an alcoholic father, about how his problems had made me the 'adult' in our family when I was just five or six years old. My time in the home gave me time to concentrate on who I was, on why I always felt the need to entertain people and be the life of the party. Essentially, I learned that I had a need to control everyone, keep them calm, keep the lid on. Even as I came to understand all this, however, I continued the behavior by making the people at the home have a rather merry time. We played cards constantly. It was an ongoing party. My best friend and I snuck into the kitchen at night and ate ice cream by the carton. We were so very jolly that when we got caught by one of the night staff, we just invited her to join us and the three of us sat up joking and gossiping until dawn. The gaiety, I suppose, was a ruse. But I was unwilling to sit and mope for four or five months. And so, for myself, I kept the peace by playing and chattering all day until I'd drop."

Women like Sylvia, mature and accustomed to independence, often viewed their time in the home as respite from the pressures of career, romance, or the responsibilities of "real" life. Some used their time for introspection, others for relaxation. Because they paid higher fees, they were generally exempt from the tedious chores assigned to other residents. And unlike the others, they had life perspectives that kept them relatively unintimidated by the rules and staff of the homes.

"I thought the enforced anonymity was positively ridiculous," Sylvia says. "I made lifelong friends there. We were not about to lose each other because some narrow-minded prigs ordered us not to reveal our last names! Confidentiality, after all, was not promised us; it was forced upon us. It furthered the aura of shame surrounding our pregnancies. My friends and I saw no reason to cooperate with that. I may have been the instigator, but my few friends and I were certainly all rebels. We shared our real names and addresses and determined not to let other people's attitudes dominate or defeat us."

Birthing at the Home

Even if some strong women were able to thrive in the environment of the home, most found their experiences both debilitating and disorienting. When the time came to deliver their babies, many were unprepared about what to expect. Information came as often through rumor as through formal channels.

"Girls from the home were given less pain medication than the other patients," Sheila claims. "The idea was that we should be taught a lesson and punished for our sins so that we'd refrain from having sex again, at least until we were married."

Whether or not this allegation is true, the belief was common among the birthmothers interviewed. Many feared childbirth, expecting danger and pain. For some—particularly the younger birthmothers—there were other fears, as well. Cindy says, "I thought I was dying when labor began. I had no idea how to react. I panicked completely. The panic wasn't just about dying, though. I'd heard about girls getting false labor and having to return to the home, sometimes three or four times. I remember, when they put me in a taxi to go to the hospital, I was terrified that my pains would stop and I'd have to go back, because they'd only given me enough taxi fare for one way. That seems silly today but, at the time, I was petrified."

Some birthmothers looked forward to delivery as a way to get out of the home and back to real life. It was not uncommon for birthmothers to idealize birthfathers and the romantic relationships they'd left behind or to fantasize unrealistically about their futures. Some, however, were without illusion about the events awaiting them, starting with the birth of their babies.

"I tried to hold the contractions back," Sue recalls, "because birthing my baby meant losing him. When labor started, I didn't tell anyone for about five hours. I just stayed in my room, rubbed my belly, and sang songs to my baby between contractions. Finally, I went to the hospital. I was alone because my parents didn't arrive until the next day. The nurses were distant and indifferent. They told me to dig my nails into my palms to ease the pain. After about fourteen hours and torn, bloody palms, the doctor finally gave me a spinal, but I was awake the whole time. Finally, at 2:47 a.m., October 13, 1967, I heard a smack and a cry. My baby had been born! I had to ask the nurse if the baby was a boy or a girl. She announced his sex and weight but wouldn't let me hold him. He was crying. I wanted to comfort him and pleaded with her to give him to me, if only for a minute. The nurse refused. Mechanically, she took my fingerprints and his footprints, ignored his wails and my tears, wrapped him in a blanket, and carried him away, leaving me there crying, begging, aching to see, hold, and kiss my son."

Even decades later, most birthmothers, like Sue, can cite the exact minute that their babies were born. Many who spent their final months of pregnancy at homes described the experience of having their newborns ripped away from them at birth, without even a brief opportunity to view or hold them. "I woke up after my C section," one birthmother says, "and saw that the doctor had written on my arm in magic marker the date and time of my baby's birth, as well as her sex and weight. That was the only communication I had about her, and when I asked to see her, they told me I had to wait until I was strong enough to walk to the nursery and view her through the window. When I did, I stood there leaning on the glass, crying. They wouldn't let me hold her. I could only stare at her and ache."

Unnaturally Natural

Even many birthmothers who were well informed about childbirth experienced difficulties from medical staff during and after their deliveries. Sylvia and her friends read extensively about natural childbirth and practiced breathing, timing contractions, and performing relaxing exercises together. When Sylvia's labor began, she and her best friend walked and timed and breathed together until contractions were regular and less than five minutes apart. Even with her preparation for childbirth, however, Sylvia was unprepared for the attitudes of the hospital staff. "The head nurse was very hostile. She whisked the baby away before I could even look at him. I demanded to see him, however, so she brought a baby to me. When she unwrapped the blanket, I knew that the baby she brought was not mine. It had very long legs, a small head, and a skinny frame. I told her that the baby wasn't mine; she flatly insisted that it was.

"Later, in the nursery, when I was shown my baby, he had a large round head, short chubby legs, a long torso, and looked very much like his birthfather. I confronted the labor room nurse and asked her why she'd shown me the wrong baby. She shrugged and walked away, saying, 'What difference does it make? You're giving him up anyway.'"

Although outraged at the treatment they received, birthmothers had little recourse in the days of the home. Many accepted the punitive and harsh attitudes surrounding them as normal, expecting the world to condemn them for having had illegitimate babies. Although they were repeatedly told that they were doing the "right thing" by relinquishing, many faced scorn precisely because they were relinquishing. Even the strongest among them, like Sylvia, were powerless to prevent condescending attitudes or to defend themselves against the judgments of others.

Au Pairs and Despairs

As an alternative to an unmarried mothers' home, many women with unwanted pregnancies were sent, through various charitable or church-related agencies, to work as nannies or au pairs for "respectable" families. In exchange for child care services, they received room, board, medical care, and a means of concealing their conditions from most of the people who knew them.

"My mother sent me to work for a rich family, taking care of their infant," Zoe says. "If she'd sent me to a home, I might have made friends. As an au pair, I had no one to talk to, just the baby I was watching. And the one I was carrying."

If birthmothers at homes experienced loneliness, many who worked as au pairs endured complete isolation. Although many themselves came from wealthy families and were sent to work in lavish settings, they spent the final months of their pregnancies basically as servants, not as part of the family. Some found the people who took them in to be kind and supportive; others, however, thought they had acted out of a sense of superiority or false charity. Few pregnant au pairs received any professional counseling, preparation for childbirth, or information about their legal options.

"At night," recalls a birthmother named Tammy, "I stayed in my room, read books, and chain-smoked. I read until dawn. I went through seven or eight books and a carton of cigarettes each week. On Sundays my mother and one of my girlfriends drove ninety miles to see me. They brought a new supply of books and cigarettes. I survived, Sunday to Sunday, waiting for a few hours of real human contact."

Other birthmothers were not as lucky as Tammy, lacking even those few hours of reassurance and comfort. "The only time I really had off," Sonia says, "was to go to church or the doctor. I received religious counseling, but I wouldn't confess. My only sin was naïve trust of a man who deceived me. I was sorry I'd brought pain to my family, but I did not believe I'd done anything wrong. However, my family, the people I worked for, and the church had other opinions. When I left town, my mother wouldn't kiss me good-bye. She announced sharply, 'Good girls don't have bastard babies.' After I left, no one from my family spoke to me for the duration of the pregnancy. It was as if I had died and gone to purgatory, pending the birth and relinquishment of my child. Knowing I'd have to give him up, I felt my baby kick and grow. It was torture, actually, to care for other people's children during my pregnancy. The daily routine of giving baths, reading stories, and patching knees made my upcoming sacrifice that much more real and, therefore, that much more cruel."

Although some au pair experiences were gentler than Sonia's, many were so painful that they left permanent scars. "I still can't go back to Chicago," Debbie says. "My life ended there, in a way. I was a glorified maid to wealthy people who felt very proud about their charitability in taking me in. But they really weren't aware of me or interested in how I felt. My body, my surroundings, and everyone around me seemed strange and unreal."

The feelings of "unrealness" Debbie describes are common among women who worked as au pairs while pregnant. Without choice or preparation, many were suddenly sent away from their homes and families. Merely being away from home made some feel lost and disoriented; moving away combined with the physical changes of pregnancy and the unfamiliar duties of an au pair overwhelmed others. Birthmothers who served as au pairs, like those from homes, commonly suffered feelings of anonymity, low self-esteem, isolation, and depression. Even those who worked for sympathetic or supportive families often longed for familiar surroundings and continuity with their "real" lives.

On Familiar Turf

Even in the heydays of the homes, not all birthmothers went there or off to jobs as au pairs. Many tried to keep their pregnancies secret by staying with relatives or friends in other cities. Even today, women facing unplanned pregnancies sometimes find it impossible to remain at home.

"I pushed my parents away and they allowed me to do it," says Amy, who gave birth at seventeen in 1986. "They were distraught and embarrassed, as if I'd done something to *them*, to deliberately disgrace them. They never saw this as something that had happened to *me*. My mother kept asking, 'What will the neighbors think?' My father called my boyfriend's father and demanded that my boyfriend marry me. His father refused and called me a whore, so my father slammed the phone down and that was the end of that. I couldn't stay with my parents. When they looked at me all I saw was shame, so I went to live with my aunt in Colorado. I'd suddenly developed very bad 'asthma.'"

If an unmarried woman's pregnancy brought embarrassment in 1986, it brought ostracism in 1968. Liz's family sent her across town to live with her grandmother, so that neighbors would not find out. "I changed high schools," she says. "They made my grandmother my legal guardian and sent me to school near her house, so none of our friends would find out. My grandmother's biggest concern was that I finish school. She wanted me to have a better life than she and my mother had had. So she helped me hide my pregnancy through the seventh month by dressing me in girdles and loose dresses. She wrote notes to get me excused from gym class. That worked for a few months. But, finally, the principal called me into his office and asked me if I were going to have a baby. I couldn't lie; I said yes. He said, 'Well, you can't stay in school. You're going to have to leave.' So I left. That broke my grandmother's heart. I was just fourteen, you see. And I never did go back to school. After the baby, I wasn't a kid anymore. I couldn't be with other kids. I wasn't like them, anymore."

Some birthmothers were welcome to stay at home but chose other options. Some wanted to keep their pregnancies secret; others sought to pursue personal goals away from home, even during their pregnancies. "I wanted to stay close to Dave, the baby's father," says Annie, who delivered in 1969. "I moved in with friends of his, a married couple. I hung onto the hope that, as the pregnancy progressed, he'd come around and ask me to marry him. I was sure he'd forget about me if I left town, so I stayed in his inner circle. But it was no good. He was barely civil to me, and, as time went on, I felt like the baby and I were nothing more than interferences in his plans. It was very difficult to be around him; he had moved far away from me emotionally. But there I was, tied to the past by the baby's umbilical cord. And I refused to let go. I hung on, no matter how humiliating or futile it was."

Whether or not they were successful in hiding their pregnancies, protecting their families from embarrassment, or attaining personal goals, women who lived with family or friends during their pregnancies were generally less isolated and lonely than those who worked as au pairs or who went to homes. The continuity of identity, roles, and familiar relationships allowed them to avoid much of the disorientation and sense of loss, abandonment, and punishment experienced by those who were sent away to live among strangers.

Home and Not Alone

About a quarter of the birthmothers interviewed remained at home during their pregnancies. Although some lived with their parents, many were independent, working and living on their own. Even though they did not change residences or lifestyles, most found that their lives changed profoundly.

"I woke up happy every day," Pam says. "I *liked* being pregnant. I couldn't help it. I was carrying a precious life inside me, and that gave me an inner peace, a glow, even though everything around me was falling apart. My boyfriend didn't want the baby, and I had very little money, but being pregnant gave me a mission, a purpose more important than anything I'd ever known before. I had a reason to get up, fight the hurt and depression, and take good care of myself. I believed that moods involved chemicals in the body and that any depression I felt could harm my baby, so I didn't let myself slip into it. I bonded with that baby as deeply as I bonded with those I had later, in marriage, and I did my very best each day to make sure he or she would have a good start."

Even when their families were understanding and helpful, birthmothers like Pam, who relinquished in 1973, could find little support elsewhere. When they stepped away from their families, they encountered the same loss of respect and harsh attitudes as other birthmothers. "My family gave me lots of hugs and offered to do whatever they could. But they were not in a financial position to help me keep my baby. I fooled myself for nine months, pretending that my boyfriend would magically change his mind and marry me, but as I went into labor, I realized the horrible truth—that I was going to have to give up my baby. My labor was short. I delivered only an hour and a half after arriving at the hospital. I was dazed, unable to adjust to the fact that the baby I'd been carrying and nurturing so closely all these months had actually been born. A part of me was suddenly apart *from* me. I was sort of in shock. But, even in my daze, I remember one of the nurses scolding that it was too bad I'd not had a more difficult time, to teach me not to do this again."

Secrets, Skeletons, and Lies

Sometimes birthmothers' pregnancies unlocked closets full of family secrets, causing them to lose their trust in or concepts of their relatives. Several remarked that their families had been particularly upset because of prior experiences with illegal abortions or illegitimate births. One women learned that her grandmother had died as a result of an illegal abortion. Another learned that her mother, too, had relinquished a baby before marriage. Occasionally, family reactions to relinquishment reflected even darker secrets.

In 1966, Jean was twenty-seven years old, divorced, and the working mother of an adopted one-year-old boy. Her mother moved into her home to babysit while Jean worked. "I started a new job, just about the time I found out I was pregnant. Nobody knew me there, so I pretended I was still married. I *had* to work; it wasn't a matter of choice. I had a son to support and a home to run. Every day at work I lived the fantasy that I was delighted to be pregnant and that the baby was legitimate. When I came home, I faced the reality of my mother's reproachful disgust and hid in my bedroom to avoid her humiliating comments."

Although her mother's condemnation was difficult for her to understand or endure, Jean believed that it merely represented the social mores and attitudes of her times. She had no idea that her mother's reaction was compounded by family secrets and bizarre twists of fate. "All during my pregnancy, despite my mother's attitudes, I planned to keep my baby," Jean says. "I couldn't understand why none of my family—neither my mother nor my wealthy brother—would support me in my desire to keep my biological child. My son, although adored, was *adopted*. This child was *blood*—theirs as well as mine—or so I thought.

"It wasn't until years later, at my brother's fiftieth birthday party, when he'd had much too much to drink, that I learned the truth. My brother blurted out that I wasn't his 'real' sister, that *I* had been adopted. I was forty-six when I learned this. My mother had died the previous year, so I couldn't even ask her why she'd kept it secret! And, nineteen years after I'd relinquished my only biological child, I found out why *my* bloodline had made no difference to my mother and brother: they had no blood in common with me or with my child!"

Another birthmother, named Claudia, was eighteen when she became pregnant in 1986. Her father, an adoptee himself, pressured her to have the baby and relinquish rather than to get an abortion. "I just assumed he felt so strongly because he was adopted. After all, where would *he* have been if his biological mother had aborted? It was only later, after the baby was born and the papers signed, that I found out the whole truth from my mother. My dad's girlfriend had gotten pregnant in high school and she died as the result of an illegal abortion. My pregnancy was like a bad recurring dream for him, and he was terrified that it might end the same horrible way."

Although revelations like Jean's and Claudia's gave them more realistic and true impressions of their families, they often left birthmothers shaken by a sense that they had been deliberately lied to or deceived in their closest relationships. Even if these women understood the reasons for the secrets, the truth, once revealed, left them wondering whether their pregnancies had been dealt with wisely or, rather, been fended off like dreaded ghosts of their relatives' pasts.

Held by the Arms of the Triangle

Not every birthmother has endured trauma, stigma, and shame during pregnancy and birth. As social tolerance has increased, many have discarded the traditions of imposed secrecy and anonymity. Some have become quite assertive while pregnant, devoting much time and energy to planning the terms of the upcoming adoptions.

Lynne, a nursing student, continued to work until she delivered her baby in 1986. Not only did she remain grounded in her own identity, home, and career during her pregnancy; she also initiated a close relationship with her baby's prospective adoptive parents. "I did a lot of reading about adoption and finally decided on an open one. That was the only option that made any sense to me," she says. "I answered an ad in the paper and got in touch with a private attorney who introduced me to a couple who wanted to adopt. I interviewed them in person, and we talked on the phone dozens of times. Once I decided that they were the right parents, they became involved in my pregnancy, like partners. They helped with my expenses, and I kept them informed of what happened at my checkups, how big the baby was, how much weight I'd gained, and so on. The pregnancy became easier for me, because I had the support, encouragement, and affection of a wonderful couple whom I grew to care about and who I knew would love my baby very much. When the time came for me to give birth, I called them and they came out to be at the hospital when the baby arrived. I had no fear or doubts about what would happen to my child, and I did not feel alone."

Like Lynne, a number of birthmothers involved in open adoptions insist that they have no second thoughts about relinquishing their babies. For these women, finding the best possible home and family for their children was of paramount importance. Lacking the ability to provide adequate care for their babies, some never thought of themselves as "real" parents; they saw themselves as carrying infants into the world for other mothers and fathers. Ellen, who already had two toddlers at home, no job, and no contact with the birthfather, said, "I knew that the pregnancy was not right for me. I did not love her father. And I was having enough trouble raising the kids I already had. But I knew, all during my pregnancy and even during my labor, that I was doing the right thing. My baby would have three parents, in a way, because of the openness of the adoption. I was not *losing* the child; I was giving her benefits I alone could not have given, and I was not going to disappear from her life."

A Mom but Not a Mom

Although openness in pregnancy and adoption procedures helps some women through pregnancy and birth, others find that open adoption is merely the most tolerable of several intolerable options. Donna gave birth in 1984. "I was severely depressed during my pregnancy. I worked all the time and went back to school. I rarely left the house, except to go to work or class. I wouldn't answer my phone. I couldn't sleep; I was always on nervous alert. I kept busy so I wouldn't have to think. People withdrew from me when I withdrew from them. I didn't tell anyone I was pregnant and, since nobody close to me *saw* me, nobody knew. My friends and family thought I was upset about how my boyfriend and I had broken up. But it wasn't my boyfriend that upset me; it was our baby. I was terrified about what I was about to do."

Donna was one of many birthmothers who felt that even open adoption was not desirable, even though she could see no viable alternative. She found the prospect of single parenting financially and logistically unrealistic. As a last, desperate resort, after months of searching for another way out, Donna reluctantly settled on a privately arranged, "partially open" adoption.

"I knew I could not afford to be a parent yet. I wasn't ready," Donna says. "I was working but having trouble making ends meet as it was. I played the lottery every day, praying for a miracle. I had wonderful fantasies about keeping her. I delayed selecting an agency until days before the baby arrived, which meant that I didn't have a chance to meet or interview the adoptive parents. I approved their profiles, in terms of education, professions and medical histories. We agreed to the specific terms of the adoption through the agency and by mail. I insisted, for example, that we'd write to each other at least once a year and that my daughter would be given the opportunity, when she was older, to meet me. But, even as I agreed to these terms, I secretly planned to continue to play the lottery so I could get my baby back. I knew I'd have several more months until the adoption was finally legal, and I was not going to give up my child and all that it means to be a 'mommy' if I could help it."

Ambivalent about relinquishing, some women chose open adoption as a way to "hang on" to their babies. Relinquishing the role of mother, like Donna, they saw open adoption as a way to retain a fragment of the title.

Waiting Days

Whether or not the outcomes satisfied them, birthmothers who remained on their own turf and active in their own lives were less devastated by loss than those who were sent away. Unlike women nesting at the home or working as au pairs, they were spared the disorientation and shame of temporary exile, were able to retain their identities, and could sustain as many of their relationships as they chose. Remaining grounded in their own lives, they were less likely to retreat into unrealistic fantasies or suffer from feelings of rejection, punishment, and low self-esteem than those who were sent away.

For some of those involved in open adoptions, the ability to set conditions, establish communication with the adoptive parents, and make some of the critical choices for their babies' futures eased the process of letting go. Very few of those interviewed, however, included their families, the birthfathers, or the birthfathers' families in arranging these adoptions. Most, in fact, had the unhappy sense that they alone were responsible for determining the direction of their babies' futures. For many, even openness did not help; pregnancy was a torturous nine-month countdown in which zero hour would bring a heartrending and possibly permanent good-bye.

Hush and Deliver

"I thought I was dying, and the nurses told me to be quiet," Zoe remembers. "They tied my hands down and strapped me to the gurney in the hallway. They never tried to calm me down. They just shaved me and gave me an enema and told me I was making too much noise. It was a long labor, and it was hours before they finally gave me a sedative."

Many birthmothers claim that the obstetrical staff became punitive, condescending, and cold as soon as they learned that a woman planned to relinquish. Nurses and doctors alike are described as indifferent to birthmothers' pain, slow with anesthesia, and simply unwilling to listen, smile, or talk.

"I kept screaming that my baby was coming," says Carolyn, who delivered in 1967. "The nurses ignored me. I was scheduled for a C, since the baby was turned feet down, and from my cot near the nurses' station I could see them chatting. They didn't even look up when I screamed for someone to come. One of them called back that I should quiet down and wait for my surgery. Finally, I felt what *had* to be the baby coming out and I was afraid he would fall out on the floor. I reached down and found a foot between my legs. I grabbed it and screamed that I was holding my baby's leg—*then* they came running."

Although attitudes have changed in the years since Carolyn's delivery, some relinquishing mothers still describe medical professionals as insensitive. While it is possible that these perceptions are accurate, it is also possible that some birthmothers, already feeling judged, vulnerable, and punished, interpreted impartial professional attitudes according to their own predisposed expectations. Whatever the reasons, many birthmothers remember childbirth as even more painful emotionally than physically, and few give credit to medical professionals for providing very much help.

"The whole process was hidden from me," Zoe continues. "They cloaked my lower body with a sheet. I couldn't see anything. My nerves were shut off by a spinal. I couldn't feel and I couldn't see. I was cut off from my body and my baby. When she finally was born, I heard her screaming and asked the doctor if she was healthy. His response was, 'What do you care? You're giving it away.' He wouldn't even tell me her sex. I only found out she was a girl when I had to name her. I wanted to hold her, but they wouldn't let me. They kept me sedated so I wouldn't get hysterical. My mother arrived, finally, and she insisted that I not hold the baby. Everyone decided things *for* me. I was drugged and not permitted to see my baby. When I begged, they told me to stop, to get a hold of myself, that it was 'for the best.'"

To See or Not to See

A number of birthmothers said that they had no conscious memories of childbirth, that they had blocked out most of the experiences associated with it. Those who did remember often described childbirth as "humiliating" or "infuriating," because of the attitudes of hospital staff. Even Lynne, who is herself a nurse and who delivered in 1986, when hospitals were supposedly "sensitive" and "tolerant," said that the head nurse in the operating room was hostile and snide. "I remember her holding the baby and remarking, 'This is such a beautiful child—how can you give him up?' I think I asked her, in a postpartum haze, if it would be better if he were ugly, but her comment stung, nonetheless."

One of the most common regrets of the birthmothers interviewed was that they did not spend more time with their newborns before relinquishing them. Many were not allowed to see or hold their babies until moments before they left the hospital. Others were discouraged from contact by well-meaning but controlling relatives, clergy, or friends who thought that seeing the babies would make it more difficult to give them up.

"I was put in a room at the end of the hall," Liz remembers, "so I wouldn't see the babies when they were brought to their mothers' rooms. When I went to the nursery to see my daughter, they told me I couldn't. I had to refuse to sign the papers in order to be allowed to see and hold my baby."

Toby complained to her pastor, after giving birth in 1970, that the nurses wouldn't let her see her infant. She pleaded with him to intervene on her behalf; he refused. "He took my hand and told me that my baby was dead to me, that I was no longer his mother and he was no longer my son. He spoke slowly, but I still couldn't grasp what he was saying. This concept was completely foreign to me. My son was *not* dead to me then, and he never has been. But that was what I was supposed to agree to believe, if I were going to be 'good.'"

Some birthmothers state that not being able to hold their newborn babies left them with the feeling that the birth process was unfinished. Some insist that this sense of being unfinished and of needing to connect with their relinquished children has haunted them ever since. Pam declares, "It was as if they were afraid I'd bond with him. What were they thinking? We were *already* bonded. He was my flesh! I'd been carrying him in my body for nine months! How could we be anything but bonded? It was cruel and unnecessary to keep us apart. We both needed to see each other as separated beings, to touch and hold each other and make our own good-byes in our own time and our own way. Worst of all, that longing to hold my baby has never gone away."

Seeing their newborns, however, did not necessarily make re-linquishment any easier for birthmothers. Although seeing a baby might have made the birthing process feel complete, it did not break the bonds between mother and child or ease the pain of separation. "When I saw her," Zoe recalls, "I felt like I was swimming upstream, against the current. I felt a magnetic pull to her. I cried from the depths of my heart to my mother. I begged her to help me, so I wouldn't have to give the baby up. But she told me to get control of myself, that my hormones would settle down and I'd realize it was for the best. I pleaded to no avail. She got the doctor to sedate me. Drugged, I did what she said, I signed the papers and stayed calm, but I've never trusted my mother—or really loved her—since. She, after all, was a mother! How could she advise another mother to give her child away?"

No Touching

Some relinquishing mothers were allowed to see their babies but not to hold them. "I went to the nursery," Jean says, "and some nurse was rocking her. I remember wanting to smell the baby's hair and to touch her little arms. I asked if I could rock her for a while, and the nurse told me that she was sorry, it was not her decision, but I could not."

In 1968, Sue stood outside the nursery window, silently saying good-bye to her baby boy. "I begged the nurse to let me hold him. 'Please,' I repeated, 'just one time, for one minute.' I remember her clearly, a round, black woman with a kind face and eyes that filled with tears as she told me, 'No, Honey. I can't let you hold this baby.' I felt I was a horrible person, that I didn't deserve to hold my own son. But I couldn't leave without touching him. My face was wet from crying and I clung to the window that separated us, as if I could reach through it and pick him up. They finally had to call an orderly and pull my hands off the glass to get me to leave."

Experiences like Sue's were common for decades. Although they varied from hospital to hospital, state to state, policy was policy and exceptions were rarely made, no matter how compassionate the staff or how compelling the birthmothers' pleas. In 1968, Cindy was allowed to spend one hour with her baby before she went home. Like many other birthmothers who were granted limited contact with their newborns, she felt detached and numb, as if she couldn't connect her emotions with a situation that seemed so unreal. "I felt I had to hurry up and absorb as much of him as I could in sixty short minutes. It was like holding a doll, a fascinating little toy. Or, maybe because I was so young, he just seemed like a doll to me. But I remember I held him and then I took off his clothes and dressed him again and took them off again and dressed him again and held him some more. I stared at his eyes a lot. But I don't know what I felt. Maybe I felt nothing. He wasn't mine, after all, to love. So, what could I let myself feel?"

In recent years, most hospitals have allowed relinquishing mothers to see and hold their babies without interference. Especially in open adoptions, when the birthmothers have a permanent role in their children's lives, postpartum bonding between birthmothers and babies is tolerated, sometimes even encouraged. Even without outside interference, however, such bonds can be difficult for birthmothers to manage.

Donna went home just hours after delivering but came back to visit each day until her baby was released to the agency and the adoptive parents five days later. "I held her and sang to her by the hour," Donna says. "I talked to her, explaining how much I loved her. I told her about women who'd kept their babies before they'd finished school, about how poor and unhappy the children were. I rationalized what I was doing in singsong tones, knowing that neither of us would ever really understand it. I rocked her, snuggled her, fed her, changed her, bathed her, and listened to her babble and coo. I tried to get all the mothering I could into those five short days. At the end, I didn't want to leave. I thought my heart was tearing apart, but I told myself: 'Be strong. It's the right thing to do. I'll see her again soon.'"

Unlike Donna, some birthmothers say that open adoption allowed them to minimize feelings of loss or mourning. Some, in fact, have found that their lives have been enriched through their relationships with adoptive parents. Lynne invited the adoptive parents, Audrey and Dan, to the hospital. They held, cuddled, and acquainted themselves with their new baby together. "They were hesitant to take her from me, at first. They didn't want to appear overly greedy for her, and they wanted to give me time to get to know her before they took over. But I really wanted them to be part of her first hours and for their faces to be embedded with mine in her earliest, unconscious memories. I felt, and still feel, that each of us has a different role in her life, that we each give her different gifts. My daughter, their daughter, has four parents, not two. I couldn't help but feel reassured about our open adoption when I first handed the baby to Audrey. Audrey took her, looked at her, and burst into tears. Her husband, Dan, began crying, too; so did I. The baby just gurgled and stared. Spontaneously, we all hugged. The four of us were a bundle of tears, fears, love, and joy.

We were all bonding, in a way, and setting out as an odd little 'family,' into unexplored territory."

A Kiss Is Just a Kiss

Among the most repetitious themes in interviews with birthmothers were low self-esteem and feelings of powerlessness in the face of overwhelming, multifaceted loss. Many insisted that they were damaged by their efforts to keep their pregnancies secret and claim that secrecy was considered more important than they were. In the frenzy to maintain the "hush" around relinquishment, the needs of both birthmothers and babies were often overlooked.

Birthmothers who were obstructed from seeing, holding, or caring for their babies often saw those obstructions as primary factors in their feelings of powerlessness and low self-esteem. Although those who were able to have contact with their newborns were not without such feelings, most did not attribute them to childbirth or the few days following. Instead, birthmothers who had time with their babies often described the first days of the babies' lives with savored sentiment; their frustrations focused on the decades of life *after* surrender. Unlike those who never spent time with their babies, they'd connected concretely and physically with the infants they surrendered. Those who had had no such opportunities were left with an unending emptiness, grabbing at airy fantasies of the children they brought into the world.

If contact with their babies helped birthmothers deal realistically with surrender, the promise of continuing contact through openness in adoption helped even more. Grief at childbirth was inevitable for almost every birthmother interviewed, but those who knew they would see their babies from time to time, or at least that they would be in regular communication with the adoptive families, felt less lost and abandoned. At least initially, the idea of open adoption and the promise of future relationships with their children minimized their senses of loss and softened their separations, sometimes marginally, sometimes substantially.

No matter what the terms of their adoptions were or how they had braced themselves to deal with the loss of their babies, few birthmothers were prepared for the broad spectrum of intangible losses brought on by relinquishment. The months that followed found many struggling and disoriented, unable either to define the causes or clarify their emotions. Without awareness of the full extent of their losses, many found it impossible to complete the grieving process and, therefore, impossible to proceed with the progress of their lives.

4

Getting Stuck
or Moving On

THE BUNDLE WAS DOTTED WITH TINY YELLOW BEARS. AMBER STRUG-
gled to identify the shape of the tiny body inside it. Her heart
raced. She was, after five long days, finally going to see and hold
her baby boy.

The nurse placed the bundle in Amber's arms and disappeared
behind her wheelchair. She said something about the agency or
someone waiting somewhere, but Amber wasn't listening. She was
absorbed in discovering a little face that looked familiar and tiny
hands that grabbed her fingers. She caressed her baby's cheek.
Newborn skin, like velvet. She had to remember it. Violet eyes
that drooped and fluttered, fighting sleep. She had to store away
the images. For the first and last time, she nuzzled him against her
sore, milk-swelled breasts. The baby dozed. Amber closed her eyes,
concentrating on the peace of feeling his body resting on hers.

Not noticing the elevator, Amber memorized the weight and
warmth of his body. Unaware of the ride down, her mind recorded
the sound of his breathing, his smell, the features of his tiny face.
Oblivious to the nurse's chatter, she learned the rhythm of his
heart and the lulling softness of his skin.

When the elevator doors jolted open, she was unprepared. The woman came right at them, saying words Amber didn't hear and reaching large, unmanicured hands toward the baby. Amber watched, stunned, as the hands took him from her. Jostled awake, the baby began to howl his protests. The woman walked off with him, without hesitating. Amber wanted to stop her and comfort his cries, but she couldn't find her voice. She stood up to go after them, but her feet tangled in the footrests of the wheelchair and she tripped, cutting her leg on the metal. Amber reached for the nurse, trying to steady herself, but the nurse pushed her back into the chair, exclaiming, "Listen to him scream! He *knows* what you've done!"

Unnerved, Amber sank back in the wheelchair and shivered. Without the baby's warmth, she was suddenly chilled and trembling violently. Blood trickled down her ankle. As the nurse wheeled her to the car that would take her home, the rage of tiny cries echoed all the way down the corridor and all along her spine.

Parting Postpartum

Some of the birthmothers interviewed had only dim memories of the days and weeks that followed the birth and surrender of their babies, describing that period as "blank" or "foggy." Among those with clearer memories are a few who felt peace or even relief after relinquishment. The vast majority, however, recalled unbearable isolation, depression, and longing. Many suffered intense guilt, frustration, or anger. Some experienced dramatic mood swings; others were so dazed, numb, or "zombielike" that they felt nothing at all. Many tried to bury their experiences, even to deny that they had ever happened. No matter what else they felt, however, most were surprised that proceeding with "normal" life seemed uninteresting, impossible, or both.

In general, birthmothers expected that, after relinquishing, they would simply heal and move on. In fact, many had been counseled that relinquishing was the only avenue that would allow them to do that. Most, however, said that they had no idea of *how* to "move on" and that they were completely unprepared for the difficulties they encountered when they tried. Even those who had expected to feel grief were often surprised that their losses were far deeper, longer lasting, and harder to overcome than they'd anticipated. Loss, anticipated or not, was inherent in the act of relinquishing. For this reason, every birthmother interviewed experienced the need to mourn after relinquishing. Whether they'd been active or passive in the decision-making process, whether they'd given up children in open or closed adoptions, whether they'd been traumatized or relieved—all had experienced losses that they needed to address. For some, the need focused completely on the loss of their babies; for others, it was more diffuse, including intangible losses such as the role of mother, self-esteem, or the sense of being "good" or even "normal." Although the particular losses that plagued them varied, each needed to be mourned. Most birthmothers, however, were unable to do that. Confronted by a wealth of external social contradictions, they were prevented from acknowledging their losses, blocked in grieving for them, and obstructed from moving on.

Paradox and Contradiction

"We were told," says one birthmother, "that by giving up our children, we were doing the noble thing. After we gave them up, though, instead of being rewarded or even supported for our 'nobility,' we were shunned by anyone who knew about our 'noble' acts."

The mixed message that relinquishing was simultaneously "good" and "shameful" prevented many birthmothers from seeking help or emotional support. Another common contradiction was that birthmothers were expected both to love and to be indifferent to their relinquished children. Many had been convinced, "If you really love your child, you'll give him up for adoption." After they relinquished out of love, however, they often found that their sacrifices were treated as trivial when they were told to move on, as if nothing of significance had happened.

"The people at the agency told me that my baby was too important to be raised by me alone, that she deserved two parents," says a birthmother named Cammy. "But if she was that important, how come she wasn't important enough for me to grieve over? How come they told me to just forget about her and go on with my life as if she'd never been born?"

The days and months following relinquishing were, for many birthmothers, rife with contradictions like these. Further, many found that the very theories that had solidified their decisions to relinquish led them to feel ashamed of their subsequent reactions. If, for example, relinquishing was "right," then were they not "wrong" to find it so painful? And, if they were supposed to be able simply to move on afterward, was not something the matter with them when they felt too paralyzed to try? Feeling wrong to grieve, yet overwhelmed by an array of perplexing and intangible losses, many birthmothers were thoroughly confounded in their efforts to move on.

Loss and Mourning

Every culture establishes techniques for helping people survive traumatic loss or grief. These techniques include formal rituals and structured practices that allow people to face their losses, grieve, and heal. Through these practices, victims of trauma and loss receive support and acknowledgment, opportunities to express their grief openly, and time to understand and integrate their losses. Further, society defines the duration of grieving periods, encouraging mourners to limit their isolation and rejoin the community.

In our society, for example, deaths of loved ones are recognized by bereavement periods, ceremonies, and symbols to guide survivors through crisis, loss, and grieving. Wakes, viewings, funerals, memorial services, and visitations at home provide social acknowledgment, opportunities to express open grief, and time to begin to integrate the impact of what has been lost. Formal mourning, with symbolic behaviors like wearing black, is limited to definite time periods, so that mourners condense their bereavement and prepare, even as they grieve, to move on.

Although the most universal, death is not the only loss recognized by our society. Methods for dealing with other personal losses are often less public, structured, and consistent, but they involve the same basic elements that pave the way for healing: social support and acknowledgment, opportunities to express emotion, and methods to help integrate loss.

"When my husband retired," a birthmother named Ida says, "he was given a party bigger than our wedding. Speeches were made and gifts were given, including the symbolic gold watch. Dozens of people got up to say how he'd affected their careers. He cried. They cried. Hugs all around. It was very moving. Even though he was devastated to end a forty-five-year career, he basked in the recognition of his peers and was sent off with a bang. It was a formal rite of passage and he was allowed to get drunk, cry, and get as sloppy as he wanted. I thought, 'What a nice way to say good-bye.' It wasn't until much later, after he'd looked at the party pictures for the thirtieth time, that I realized how jealous I was of the attention his retirement had brought him. By comparison, when I'd had to deal with *my* major loss, I'd had to hide it and nurse myself on my own."

When losses are socially acceptable, occurring within the basic guidelines of social structure, they evoke emotional support that assists the process of grief and, thus, the progress of affected individuals. However, when losses occur *outside* its norms, society withholds its mechanisms of comfort from those who grieve. Having broken society's rules regarding pregnancy and motherhood, most birthmothers found little support in grieving and healing. Ironically, many who endured the losses of their children in order to regain social acceptance found that society turned its back on them, denying them the very rituals and tools that might have helped them recover, afterward.

"When I lost my second baby in a miscarriage," says a birthmother named Paula, "my whole family grieved. I got flowers, and we had a small service at the church. It helped, to say good-bye that way. But I couldn't help resenting, by comparison, the total silence that followed the loss of my first child, the one I'd given up for adoption."

Coming Home

Unlike others who had endured traumatic losses, birthmothers were left without publicly acknowledged, formal periods of bereavement or mourning. Instead of supportive acknowledgment of their losses, they often faced stigma, shame, or condemnation. Because it was considered unacceptable to talk openly about their feelings, many were unable to work them through and achieve understanding or integration of their losses. Without rituals, routines, or concrete methods of actualizing their grief, they were often unable to express themselves at all. Left alone to "forget" and move on, many fumbled, unsure of how to deal with their feelings or even of what those feelings were. Often, however, their internal confusion was nothing compared to the hostility, ostracism, and cruelty that greeted their postpartum returns to "normal" life.

In 1965, a twenty-five-year-old photographer named Bridget fell in love with and become pregnant by a married man. When he asked for a divorce so that he could marry Bridget, his wife attempted suicide. Bridget ended the relationship and relinquished for the sake of their baby; she couldn't allow their child to grow up in the shadows of such pain.

While pregnant, Bridget developed toxemia so severe that she lost her vision. Her blood pressure rose dangerously, and her kidneys failed. During labor, her parents were told that she had a 50 percent chance of survival and that her baby might die. She was unconscious for three days after her baby was born. Twelve days later, she came to her parents' home to convalesce. Pillars of their church, they were charitable people. Bridget was, therefore, stunned by their reactions to her.

"They wouldn't speak to me," she recalls. "At the dinner table, they alternated between staring at me and avoiding my eyes.

Nobody'd given me anything to dry up my milk, so I was drenched all the time. My body was large and bloated. I was sore and wet and surrounded by hostility. The man I'd loved with all my heart and our child were lost to me. My inner pain was so profound that the physical discomfort didn't matter. I was alone, sore, and wrong. My family abandoned me. They were 'good shepherds' to strangers, but not to me. I'd lost all my illusions about my family. I had nothing left. In the hospital, the doctor had said he'd never seen anyone so close to death who didn't die. But he was wrong. I *had* died. Everything I'd valued in my life was gone."

Relinquishing mothers who were greeted with such icy post-partum hostility often felt, like Bridget, that their "real" lives stopped or froze at surrender. Although they subsequently went through the motions of relationships and living, they became detached and unable to connect emotionally with either people or events. Because they believed that they had suffered to make the best, most selfless choice for their unplanned babies, they were shocked by the punitive intolerance that impeded their postrelinquishment attempts to move on.

Another birthmother named Bea relinquished in 1971 at age sixteen. "When I came back to school senior year," she says, "nobody talked to me. People turned their backs, literally, when I walked toward them. I was persona non grata at my former girlfriends' houses. I hadn't even known that anyone *knew* about my pregnancy, and I'd come back to school full of anticipation and anxious to see my friends again after all those months alone in the home.

"Until then, I'd had no idea that people gossiped. But my boyfriend had told a couple of his friends, and, actually, I'd confided in my best friend, so before you knew it, the whole school knew. My boyfriend, the baby's father, wouldn't even come near me when I came back. My pregnancy embarrassed him. He punished me by dating my former best friend. Giving up my baby was like a kick in the stomach; coming back to school was like a punch in the jaw."

Even when their secrets were out many birthmothers, like Bea, were pressured to deny rather than to deal with the truth. Conspiring to pretend that nothing had happened was often considered more important than coping with what had. Jill was a junior in high school when she relinquished in 1970.

"My father went crazy because I got such bad stretch marks," she says. "My parents acted like, if they could *only* make my stretch marks go away, they could erase the whole experience. So, they got a note from my doctor, saying that, due to my recent bout with rheumatic fever, I should be excused from gym class, so I wouldn't have to shower with the other girls. And, in the summer, those stretch marks meant I couldn't wear a bikini like the other girls, so I was told to stay away from the pool. I went to consult a plastic surgeon, but he didn't think he could help. The stretch marks were permanent. But nobody, neither my parents nor myself, paid any attention to my other permanent scars, the ones inside my head."

The Mechanics of Grief

With or without the support of society, people who endure loss need to finish grieving before they can incorporate their experiences and effectively move on. Birthmothers are no exception. Despite massive efforts to disguise, ignore, bury, or forget their losses, the need to grieve has persisted and often dominated their lives.

The process of grieving has been divided by psychologists into successive phases of denial, anger, depression, and acceptance. In the first phase, people deny or reject the facts, trying to protect themselves from the truth of their loss. In the second, they protest the loss, expressing rage, frustration, and sometimes even violence. This anger eventually gives way to a quieter form of sadness or despair. Finally, resolution occurs when a degree of detachment from the lost object is achieved, the sadness eases, and the loss is finally accepted. Only after acceptance, according to experts, can new attachments successfully be formed and "normal" life be resumed.

Because their losses were not socially acknowledged, birthmothers often found that their needs to grieve were also unrecognized and unaddressed. Most were left to their own devices in managing their grief. Many claimed that they never experienced certain phases, skipping denial and anger and proceeding directly to depression. Others described their emotions as muddled, vacillating combinations of rage, sorrow, and guilt. Regardless of the order in which they experienced the phases of grief, however, most became stuck at some point in the process. Many were unable to complete their grieving; others were unable even to begin.

Denial: No Problem

"Everybody acted as if nothing had happened," Alexis says. "During my pregnancy, I wasn't allowed in my parents' home, but after I gave up the baby, they took me to Florida on vacation, as if nothing had happened. No mention was ever made of my pregnancy, delivery, or baby. Nobody asked how I felt about giving him up. It was as if there had never been a baby, and I might have thought I'd dreamed the whole thing, except that my milk was coming in. My body was acknowledging my sanity by performing all the functions, emotional and physical, that it was supposed to after giving birth.

"The truth was that I ached, I yearned to bond and connect. But, instead of screaming for my child, I tried to act like nothing was wrong. I thought my family was right, that I should simply bounce back. Everyone treated me not as a new mother grieving for a lost child, but as a person recovering from some sort of a malady."

Like many birthmothers, Alexis internalized the judgments of her family and society. Lacking acknowledgment for her feelings of loss, she had no idea whether she was *entitled* to grieve, much less of *how* to express, manage, or cope with grieving. Instead of grappling on her own with these issues, she dismissed her feelings, at first because she believed them to be "wrong" and later because she'd begun to deny them altogether, at least consciously.

"Shortly after I gave up my baby," she continues, "I volunteered at an adoption service through my church, counseling pregnant women to relinquish. I continued to do this for over six years. I married within a year and had four children in the next five years. All during that time, I enthusiastically encouraged other women to give up their babies. I told them, 'I did it; you can, too. You can be successful; you can marry and have more children. Look, relinquishing isn't so bad; it worked for me.' And I *believed* it when I said it.

"It never occurred to me, during those years, that the reason I kept having babies was to get my first, lost baby back. Or that the reason I'd married so soon was to have more babies that I could keep. Or that the reason I felt the need to counsel these women was because I needed to repeat the process of pregnancy and relinquishment again and again, to justify it over and over by convincing others that it was 'right,' because I was in such deep, confused pain and had no acceptable way to acknowledge or deal with it."

Eventually, despite her deliberate suppression and conscious denial of her feelings, Alexis became debilitated by inexplicable bouts of depression and anger. When she sought professional counseling more than eight years after relinquishing, she finally permitted herself to begin the process of grieving. Some birthmothers, however, denied not only the effects of relinquishing but also their symptoms of anger and depression. For many, such denial lasted decades and became entrenched in the structure of their lives.

What Daughter?

"My phone rang one day," says Wendy, who conceived her relinquished child in a 1964 date rape. "A young woman asked to speak with me and identified herself as the daughter I'd given up for adoption twenty-six years earlier. Without thinking, I did what I'd taught myself to do for a quarter of a century: I denied it. I said, 'You're mistaken—I have no daughter,' and I hung up. I went back to cooking dinner, and it was about half an hour before I began trembling. I couldn't stop. I went to my room. My heart was fluttering and I couldn't breathe. I was sweating, shivering, terrified."

Some birthmothers kept their relinquishments secret, even from their spouses and closest friends. Others told their husbands but no one else. A number confided the facts about relinquishing but hid their related feelings, sometimes even from themselves. Eventually, many were overwhelmed when both their secrets and the emotions connected with them unexpectedly emerged. Long-buried feelings often erupted when a similar event occurred, such as the birth of a subsequent child or even a grandchild. For Wendy, the trigger was being found by her adult daughter. The feelings she had successfully suppressed for decades stormed into her consciousness, finding her thoroughly unprepared.

"Even as I hung up the phone, I realized that time had stopped. My hand moved in slow motion—I wanted to drop the phone, as if it were burning hot, but I couldn't get my hand to move in real time. I wasn't thinking about my daughter, though. I wasn't thinking at all. I was panicking, but it was a panic I'd been awaiting, somehow, for years. Sometime after I'd hung up, it occurred to me that I had no way to contact her, no idea where she was calling from or why or even if I wanted to know. I concentrated on acting normal, slicing meat loaf—still in slow motion—and trying to listen to my husband talk about his day at the office and to make sure the boys ate their peas. But I couldn't stop trembling. The jig was up."

Many birthmothers, determined to move on after relinquishing, completely banished their feelings and unwittingly blocked themselves from completing the grieving process. By burying rather than experiencing their anger and depression, they became stuck in denial and set themselves up for delayed emotional crashes that were both unpredictable and uncontrollable. Like

Wendy, some denied their pasts to the point that they refused to acknowledge the truth, even when it directly confronted them as a voice on the phone or a knock on the door.

"Sometimes I wonder if I should have asked her where she was calling from, so I could find out what she wanted," Wendy confides. "But, most of the time, I hope she's going to leave it alone. Whenever the phone rings now, I'm afraid it's going to be her. When it isn't, I'm a cross between relieved and disappointed. Because I'm left with the dread of another unexpected contact. If she calls again, I've decided to answer her questions but insist that she not call any more. The past is the past and should be left alone, as agreed in the beginning."

Although women like Wendy insist that they have chosen to close the door permanently, the intensity of their reactions belies such uncomplicated attitudes. If the past *were* simply the past, the prospect of facing their relinquished children would undoubtedly be less threatening. Rather than emotions too resolved to be remembered, it is likely that such intense panic and rigid avoidance reflect feelings too deep to dig up.

Anger: The Quest for Vengeance

Relinquishing left a number of birthmothers seething with unappeasable anger. Some aimed their rage at society at large and vowed never again to give in to social pressures or the opinions of others. These women were determined to pay any price to express their fury, even if it meant making sacrifices by living in solitude or in outright rebellion.

"I saw the surrender of my son as just another round in my ongoing battle with society," comments Sylvia, a professional diplomat who relinquished at age thirty-seven. "Losing my child to social pressures was as violent as if someone had put a gun to my head and taken my baby. It alienated me forever."

Some women blamed society for forcing them to relinquish; others blamed their families, the birthfathers, their careers, or the times. Although their targets varied, their fury consistently protected them from blaming themselves. By concentrating on external enemies, these women were able to ease their guilt and avoid a degree of self-condemnation. In doing so, however, many blocked their progress in the grieving process and became stuck in anger that they could not resolve.

Commitment to long-term, uncompromising anger meant that women like Sylvia refused to rejoin society on *any* terms. Whatever was socially acceptable or "normal" was automatically unacceptable to them. Refusing to move on to marriage and more children, some remained spitefully single and never gave birth again. Others rejected traditional careers or female roles in zealous pursuit of the "abnormal," whether in romance, career, or lifestyle. Given any choice, these birthmothers opted for the nonconventional, the untested, the dramatic, or the defiant. Although they never moved beyond the anger and frustration they felt about relinquishing, many converted these unresolved feelings into motivation and energy. Some aimed to escape the bonds of society; others aimed to change them. Sylvia did both.

"I rejoined the diplomatic corps and ran away," Sylvia says. "I lived where values directly oppose those hypocrisy imposed on us here. I found living with *no* values preferable to living with false ones. I stayed away for sixteen years. I lived all over the world, anywhere as long as it kept me away from the society I blamed for the loss of my son. When I came back, I retired and joined NOW, Planned Parenthood, adoption lobbying groups. I'm an activist, committed to any social or political movement that might disrupt the priggish, narrow social values that robbed me and my son of the life we might have shared. I was not your typical birthmother. I saw myself and my son in an adversarial relationship with society from the very beginning. The enemy knocked me over and got my son, but I managed to survive and bide my time, and I *never* gave in. I never forgot or gave up the ongoing war I'd engaged in."

Sylvia's wrath generalized to the point where she considered marriage and family mere extensions of the enemy. In fact, she considered *any* participation in traditional society a betrayal of her cause. "The adoption counselors had tried to console me by telling me, 'You'll get married and have children of your own.' Imagine saying that, as if I'd given birth to somebody else's child! That child *was* my own! No, after that experience, I wouldn't get married, I wouldn't have another child. I wouldn't give them the satisfaction of conforming and joining the social ranks!"

Birthmothers like Sylvia, who so thoroughly generalized their anger, often went to the extreme of rejecting all aspects of society. For some, radical political and social activism provided acceptable excuses for avoiding the risks of further traditional intimacy. By rejecting traditional society and relationships, these birthmothers found not only a way to express their outrage and frustration but also a protective shield of isolation. Despite their fierce commitment to avenging their losses, however, many kept the driving force behind their anger—their relinquishments—secret.

"Why would I tell anyone?" one birthmother asked. "I'd only have to deal with other people's preconceived notions. I have enough to deal with, just with my own."

For Sylvia, silence was a practical way to conceal her vulnerability. Even if it interfered with her ability to grieve, it allowed her to maintain a protective distance from others. "I didn't discuss it," she says. "I did all my talking in a journal that I kept for years, counting the days, weeks, and months since I'd last seen my son. When he was about five years old, I cut a magazine picture of a little boy out of a magazine and kept it in a frame on my desk. People would ask who it was and I'd say, 'Nobody.' But it was a focus for me, a face, a boy. I did what *I* had to do to cope with my loss, like write to him nightly in my journal, or look at a picture that might have looked something like him. But I didn't tell others about him. Not because of their moral judgments; like I said, I was with people who wouldn't have judged. But because talking about it would have been like taking off an artificial leg and saying, 'Look at my stump!' I would have been too exposed. Besides, nothing would have been accomplished by talking about relinquishing. It's my actions that might, someday, politically make a difference."

Nowhere to Run

Some birthmothers felt no anger about relinquishing until they confronted social ostracism. Instead of buckling under to the judgments of others, these women focused on their own indignation and distrust. For many, these angry emotions blocked not only pain but healing as well.

Bea faced rejection and gossip when she returned to school in 1971, after four months at a maternity home. Almost two decades later, she is still screaming her anger. "People treated me like dirt," she shouts. "But who were they to judge *me*? Why was *I* bad? Because I'd had sex? I didn't and don't buy that idea. *Everyone* had sex. Judging me was ultimate hypocrisy. But, even though other people's attitudes said more about *them* than about me, I was still afraid of what people thought. So I dropped out of high school at seventeen. I quit. I was sick of the whispers and gossip. I said good-bye to the birthfather, who was still just a kid, and I ran away to California. I trained as a keypunch operator and went to work where nobody knew anything about me and wouldn't talk behind my back. I learned not to rely on other people, not to trust or confide in anyone. I learned to trust only myself. And that lesson has stuck; I'm still surprised when people are nice to me."

If running away in anger protected some birthmothers from devastating rejection, it also prevented them from working through the emotions that followed relinquishment. When they considered the treatment they received after relinquishing in the light of the advice they'd received beforehand, some developed attitudes that sounded almost paranoid.

"The propaganda at the home was that I'd go on, forget my child, and have other babies that would replace him," Bea declares. "That line was as absurd as telling someone that he could saw off his leg and still dance. I felt like there had been a conspiracy to get me to relinquish and that there would be another to judge and punish me afterwards, for my 'sins.' So, anyone who played a part, anyone who even *knew* about my relinquishment, became my enemy. I ran away from the people who would stare or gossip. And from my parents who were ashamed of me. And from my anger. I was angry at everyone. Even the baby, because his adoption, his future happiness required my misery. So I was angry at him, because his happiness mattered more than mine. And I was angry at *his* adoptive parents, who would see his first tooth, wipe his runny nose, and change his poopy diapers. The fact is, I'd have *bronzed* my child's dirty diapers, the way I felt."

Some birthmothers who ran away in anger began patterns of distorting or idealizing the past. For Bea, efforts to escape from pain, grief, and judgment by others only enhanced her need to romanticize her losses. Without people who could verify or affirm her memories, she lost not only her child but also her own history and sense of identity. Moving away, wiping out old relationships, and adopting aggressive new identities rarely helped birthmothers like Bea move ahead; external environments could not free them from internal trauma. More often than not, those who ran away remained emotionally inert, chained to the time and place of their relinquishments. No matter what romantic notions they held, no distance was great enough to separate them from their unresolved grief.

"I had nothing, no papers or certificate or document to prove I'd ever had a son or that he was alive or dead," Bea says. "Bronzed diapers would at least have given me something to touch, to prove that he had happened. But I had nothing, and nobody who knew or cared, so I got tough. I learned to count only on myself, keep apart from others, and hide my past and my feelings. Only once a year, like a ritual, on his birthday, I let it all out. I cry for a solid week and then I put it back inside and go on. I've become very tough, but through it all, almost twenty years, I still dread the last week of October because I know I'll fall apart, and I always do."

Dropping Out

Some turned their anger inward, onto themselves. Often, they found others who would encourage that. Annie's grieving went awry in 1969, when the people to whom she turned for help led her to further pain.

"I was depressed in the hospital," Annie says. "Maybe it was partly that I had a reaction to the medication they gave me during labor. Anyway, I was ranting and hysterical. The doctor concluded that I was suicidal and left orders for me to be taken to the psychiatric ward twenty-four hours after I gave birth. On the psychiatric ward, I couldn't see my baby. I kept trying to sneak out to see him, but I kept getting caught. Finally, a large, singularly unattractive doctor came in and told me that, if I tried to sneak out again, they'd send me permanently to the state mental hospital. Obviously, I didn't try to see my baby again."

Postpartum, Annie struggled to cope simultaneously with separating from her baby, obeying insensitive authority, and losing her relationship with Dave, the birthfather. She went to a therapist for help and became convinced that, as a single woman, she was unfit to parent her child. Discouraged from expressing or working through her feelings, she became trapped in her grief and fluctuated between states of despair and anger, neither of which were understood or tolerated by those she trusted.

"Dave sent me flowers at the hospital. The card said, 'Take care.' I was dead meat to him; he was living with his new girlfriend. I was a mess," Annie says. "I had nowhere to turn. I didn't care if a truck hit me, if I lived or died. I'd lost my boyfriend and my baby. I saw the baby once a month while he was in foster care, but I wasn't able to reclaim him. My life was over.

"Finally, I went back to live with my parents. Nobody talked about the baby. I wanted to go get him, but I never said it. I was convinced that I wasn't good enough to mother him and I didn't want to hear them say it. My parents acted as if I were depressed for no reason and sent me to a shrink. The shrink was a jerk. He wanted to hear about my sex life. What sex life? He wanted to fix me up with guys, to sign me up at a dating service. He didn't want to talk about my child. After a few months, when my depression continued, he prescribed shock treatments. After the shock treatments came drugs. He gave me every clinical procedure psychiatry ever practiced, short of lobotomy, and I was still depressed. In fact, I was worse. My problems got deeper, because I had no one I could trust. The people who were supposed to help me kept hurting me."

Although Annie's electric shock treatments were extreme, many of the other women interviewed said that their families were similarly intolerant, refusing even to hear about their feelings, their babies, or the process of relinquishment. A number saw therapists who overlooked or denied the impact of relinquishment. "My psychiatrist asked me if I was OK about relinquishing," one recalls. "I shrugged and said, 'Yes, I guess I am,' and that was the last time she ever mentioned it."

When their feelings were repeatedly overlooked, denied, or treated as unimportant, birthmothers who already felt bad about themselves felt their remaining self-esteem dissipate. Some felt unworthy of any indignation and, believing that they were being punished justifiably, either repressed their anger or aimed it inward. Like Annie, these women were so angry at themselves that they joined the ranks of their own tormentors.

"During the time that I saw that shrink," Annie says, "I hung out with sleazoids, hippies. I took drugs, whatever was going around. It was the early seventies, the time of 'free love,' and that's what I gave. I was used by men, by anybody. I didn't feel I had the right to say no, because I wasn't worth anything. After all, I was not even good enough to mother my own son. I felt I was garbage. I'd shamed my family, lost my boyfriend's love, alienated my shrink. So I went with creeps. I'd get drunk and cry and slobber to people about my baby. I was lost in the freakiness of the times, hiding my misery behind sex, drugs, and rock and roll. Everybody saw me as rebellious and free, but inside I was desperate, unfocused, and without hope. I was nothing and had no hope that I ever would be. Happiness, even life, seemed entirely out of my reach."

Depression: After the Numbness, After the Rage

It took the birthmothers interviewed an average of fourteen years to seek help for their depression about relinquishment. Many felt depression much sooner but were unable to confront it for years. Some buried or denied it; others became so devastated that they were unable to participate in their own lives. Those who sought professional counseling rarely felt that they received useful help. A few appeared to move through delivery, relinquishment, and the subsequent years calm, cool, and collected. However, what outwardly seemed to be composure or even indifference often *felt* more like hopelessness and despair.

"Before I could leave the hospital, I had to name the baby," Zoe recalls. "I'd put off naming her for as long as I could, to keep her name to myself. Finally, I told them I'd chosen 'Brooke.' But they said that Brooke was unacceptable; I had to pick something that began with my last initial. So she became 'Susan' and I lost even her name."

For Zoe, the events that followed delivery seemed distant, as if they were happening to somebody else. She went through the motions of naming and relinquishing obediently, as if she were not really there. It wasn't until she left the hospital and returned to her mother's home that her sense of protective distance fell apart and she exploded into desperate rage.

"My first night home, I became hysterical," she says. "I was ranting, throwing things, smashing mirrors. I was tormented. I wanted her. I wanted my baby and all I could think was, 'Uh-oh, what a huge mistake I've made by giving her up.' I felt primal things, things you can't make disappear with rational arguments. I'd been cut off from all these feelings during my pregnancy and labor and after her birth. Suddenly, at home without her, I reconnected and wanted her. I wanted to leave the house and physically go get her. My mom told me she'd called the doctor to talk about it, but when he came over, he gave me sedatives to prevent me from leaving. It's 'for the best,' they kept telling me. 'It's for the baby's benefit.' All the usual stuff they tell birthmothers. 'You couldn't do right by her; this way, she'll have *two* parents.' And they kept me drugged so I wouldn't do anything violent, like kill myself, or rash, like reclaim her. I was literally groggy with drugs for six or seven weeks. Every time the drugs wore off, I started smashing things again. I actually threw a lamp at my mother—it hit her in the head. She had to have stitches. She was sure I'd have killed myself—or her—if not for the drugs."

Birthmothers who were prevented from exploring their feelings about relinquishing prior to surrender often had difficulty dealing with those feelings later. Those who were actually stopped, as Zoe was, from acting on their feelings often reacted not only with guilt and frustration but also with fury and violence. For these women, even rationalizations by family and friends, months of heavy sedation, and decades of consistent psychiatric care rarely helped. Nothing could either replace what they had lost or erase the effects of having had their babies taken away without their full consent. When the fury abated, depression of equal intensity usually replaced it.

"I remained angry and depressed, basically forever," Zoe says. "For the next twenty-five years, anyway. I still see a shrink and take antidepressants. My life revolves around my relinquished daughter. Wanting her has been the theme of my life. Getting her back was all that could have helped. I married, but that didn't help. I divorced, traveled, and married again, but that didn't help. I wouldn't let myself have another baby for twenty-two years. I was doing penance and grieving, full-time. I denied myself the joy of having another child. And, when I finally gave in to my last husband and had another baby, it was a catastrophe. The longing for my first child became unbearable. What I'd lost became even more clear. It got so bad that I wanted to die unless I could find and touch and love my Brooke, or my Susan, or my whatever-name-that-baby-had-been-raised-by. The pain of losing her had stayed with me—no, it had grown—all these years."

Some who, like Zoe, suffered from long-lasting, sometimes debilitating, anger and depression believed that they had been predisposed to emotional conflicts prior to relinquishing. A few confided that they wondered if they had *used* the trauma of relinquishment as an excuse for not coping well and for allowing problems to dominate their lives. These concerns may be well grounded, but it is also possible that they merely illustrate the common tendency for birthmothers to feel wrong about everything they do—even about feeling wrong about everything they do.

The Judge Within

"When I left the home," Sue says, "I was determined to make up for everything I'd done wrong. I was obsessed with trying to be a 'good' girl again, to regain my self-image, to feel 'normal,' but I couldn't. Instead, I studied like a maniac because I felt I needed to be perfect, get straight A's, atone and make up for the past. But I couldn't be normal, couldn't get into the spirit of fun or football games. Normal life was beyond me. I wanted two things and only two things: my baby and Bob, his father."

Becoming "perfect" was the goal of many birthmothers who, unable to deny or suppress their feelings, tried to cover them up with acts of "wholesomeness" or "purity." In doing so, they exhibited extreme behavior and adhered to absolutes. They were to judge themselves as either horrible or perfect; there was no middle ground. Most, however, found that in seeking perfection by burying their pasts, they doomed their futures. Their determination to attain redemption by personifying goodness often impeded their abilities to cope with reality, much less to attain happiness.

"After a month or two," Sue states, "Bob got so worn out by grief, loss, and secrecy that he broke up with me. I was lost. I had no reason for living, anymore. Without my child, without Bob, I had nothing. I felt unworthy of success, unworthy of marriage or love. It sounds pathetic, now, but I actually tried to drown myself in the bathtub. I held myself under the water and tried to pull water in, to breathe, so my lungs would fill up, but I kept coughing and coming up and gasping for air. In the end, I gave up. My throat was raw, I was gagging and my chest hurt, but I was still very clearly alive. I hated myself; I couldn't even kill myself right. But I realized that death was actually the easy way. Not painful enough. I deserved worse—I'd have to live and endure the punishment of staying in a world where I'd lost everything I'd loved."

Although a number of birthmothers, like Sue, were so overwhelmed by postrelinquishment despair that they actually tried to end their lives, many others adopted subtler and more lasting methods of self-punishment by denying themselves any sources of joy in their lives. Abandoning suicide as a viable solution, Sue joined these women by embarking on a path that would guarantee that her existence would be, at best, miserable.

"I convinced myself that I had to be punished for having loved a man so deeply, that love was the source of my sins," says Sue. "As a result, I became afraid of my sexuality. It was the era of 'free love,' but I became frigid toward men. I wouldn't even kiss one. When a guy asked me to marry him anyway, even though I'd never had *any* kind of sexual contact with him, I jumped at the chance. Love wasn't my goal in marriage; forgiveness was. With Greg's proposal, I thought I was being given a second chance, a gift from God. So I abandoned my childish dreams of a college degree, a career, and a romantic marriage to Bob. Within a year, I married a dominant, controlling man who would make all my decisions for me and take care of me. I felt unworthy, undeserving of more. I was too busy covering up my sins, atoning and trying to be, or at least to appear, 'perfect.' I wore white. I did what I thought I had to, even though I had no sexual attraction to my husband and was still in love with Bob. I thought about Bob and my baby all the time, and I suffered in silence, agreeing to roles and relationships that felt, in many ways, like the terms of the punishment I believed I so sorely deserved."

Loveless marriages to the first men who asked them were common among birthmothers immersed in the depression phase of the grieving process. Many attempted to leap ahead and skip over their grief by attaching themselves to men through marriage. Some hoped to erase their pasts, attain acceptability and respectability, and even replace their lost children with new ones. In the context of secrecy, guilt, and despair, avoiding controversy and attaining the image of "the perfect woman" became the priority for many birthmothers, even at the expense of their own dreams.

The Quest for "Normal"

Birthmothers who tried to redefine themselves through marriage usually found that their unions provided poor escape and little relief from grief. Those who pretended to be "normal" or happy often found that their ability to keep up appearances soon wore thin.

Lisa relinquished in 1972. "My daughter was born May 31; I graduated from high school on June 6. My parents gave me a graduation party on the 14th. Nobody knew, and I had to go outside and act happy, like nothing had happened."

Because she was underage, Lisa's parents had forbidden her to marry the birthfather of her relinquished daughter. The son of a factory worker, Ted was not the son-in-law they had envisioned for their aspiring, upper-middle-class, college-bound daughter. Ted had furiously tried to prevent the relinquishment, to no avail.

"By the end of the summer, Ted forgave me enough to want to see me again," she says. "But, in August, I'd met my parents' definition of Mr. Right. Dwayne was in college, Protestant, handsome, and from a proper wealthy family. I agreed to marry him, but I couldn't stay away from Ted. I tried—I told him to stay away from me—but I didn't mean it. I saw Ted secretly, even as I accepted Dwayne's ring. And I was pregnant again with Ted's child even as I took my wedding vows."

In their determination to live respectably at any cost, birthmothers like Lisa only compounded their problems. Superficially, they may have appeared to be fine, but their actions often revealed deep inner conflicts.

"Dwayne was the first acceptable person who came along after I gave up my daughter. He was my ticket away from my problems, or so I thought. Two years later, we were divorced. He wasn't as 'right' as he seemed. Ted and I, on the other hand, have been seeing each other off and on for twenty-three years, through three failed marriages—two mine and one his. We won't ever get it together, but we probably won't ever be done, either. There's too much unfinished, from a time we can't either get back to or let go of. Without Ted, I'm lost. Without each other, we both fall apart."

Normal life continued to elude women like Lisa who hid within roles that made them appear to be "normal." Motivated by externally defined values, many prevented themselves from identifying their own goals and rejected anyone or anything that didn't fit the profile of the norm. Like Lisa, many became stuck in cycles of alternating denial and depression and sacrificed, along with their chances for healing, their abilities to choose their own directions in life.

Abandon All Hope

"The day I left the hospital," Donna recalls, "I went to the nursery and held my daughter for hours. I talked to her. I tried to explain to her what I was doing and why. Finally, it was time to go. I got in my car, but I couldn't drive out of the parking lot. I couldn't make myself leave. I couldn't see because my eyes were swimming in tears. Eventually, I forced myself to pull out. I drove blindly. I missed my turn on the expressway. Twice. I got lost coming back from a hospital less than five miles from my home. A ten-minute drive took me almost an hour."

After relinquishing, a number of birthmothers felt that they deserved punishment. Some allowed it; others sought it. A few created it themselves. With a wide array of potential sources, punishment took on many forms, including isolation and loveless marriages. For those who had taken control and personally arranged their children's adoptions, guilt and grief often became intricately interwoven and punishment, accordingly, took convoluted turns. Donna, who had relinquished in a private, open adoption, set about destroying her remaining chances for fulfillment, achievement, or self-satisfaction.

"It was ironic," Donna says. "The main reason I'd relinquished my daughter was so I could finish college, attend graduate school, and attain an independent, secure career. After I gave her up, though, I lost all interest in school and career. My life fell apart.

My plans seemed absurd and meaningless. I couldn't concentrate on my studies and took incompletes. I considered dropping out altogether, but even that—going to the registrar and filling out forms—seemed like too much effort. For months, for over a year, I was preoccupied with death. I was waiting to die alone in my room. I think, now, that I was *hoping* I would die. It would have ended my misery."

Like Donna, birthmothers who thought they could control their feelings and move on to pursue their former goals after relinquishing were frequently surprised that their lives did not go as planned. In the face of unending grief, maintaining independence, equilibrium, and secrecy became more than many could bear.

"During my last year of college," Donna says, "I worked two mindless full-time jobs, where I could put in hours and get paid just for being there. I couldn't bear to be alone and I couldn't bear to be with other people, so I worked all the time. I had less than four hours of sleep each night and stayed in a half-awake state for months. Somehow, I graduated, by the skin of my teeth. The day of my graduation, though, fourteen months after my baby was born, I fell apart. I couldn't contain my secret any longer. My parents wanted to take me out to dinner to celebrate and I actually collapsed onto the sofa. 'I can't go to dinner,' I told them. 'I can't go anywhere.' And I told them about the baby. My mother dissolved into tears and she cried all weekend. She was on the phone with attorneys and was devastated to learn that she had no rights, because she wanted to undo the adoption, get the baby back, and help me raise her. Everyone was angry at me. My sisters, my father, my mother. All they kept saying was, 'Why didn't you come to *us*?' They were hysterical, guilty, amazed that they hadn't known."

The life plan Donna had envisioned became irrelevant in the light of the all-consuming depression that followed relinquishment. Although she finished college, she dropped her long-term goals in order to work full-time on coping with her own and her family's emotional reactions to the loss of her child. Like many who relinquished so that they could realize their ambitions, Donna herself was so changed that her former goals no longer applied. Undone by her own decision, she vehemently defended the reasoning behind it when she realized that its ramifications touched lives other than her daughter's and her own.

"Telling my secret to my family, I suppose, was the beginning of dealing with my relinquishment," she says. "By doing that, I reached out and finally allowed them to help. But if I'd told them sooner, they'd have taken her back and she'd have become their baby, not mine. We'd have spent our lives fighting about how to raise her or about who was in charge. And my parents, in their fifties, didn't need another baby to raise. So, subconsciously, I guess I waited until the adoption was final before I let my family know. And then, when they couldn't take her back, I fell into their arms and said, 'Help me. I need help.' And that's when I began to grieve, to face the extent, the finality, the depth of what adoption, even open adoption, was going to mean, not only to me but to every one in my daughter's biological family, because she'd been not only mine but theirs, as well."

Penance and Punishment

In a desperate effort to survive depression, Donna finally reached out to her family. Some birthmothers, however, had no such recourse. Callie remembers her parents as being completely oblivious to her grief. "My mother came to pick me up, and I cried all the way home. 'What are you crying about?' she asked. 'It's all over now.' As usual, Mother couldn't have been more wrong. It was over for *her*. But for me, it had just begun."

Others had families who were not merely insensitive but actually abusive. These women found the period following birth particularly dire.

"My father wouldn't talk to me," a birthmother named Francine says. "He and I had been very close before I'd gotten pregnant. I was his only child and he'd spoiled me. Now, I was no longer pure; I'd had sex! He was enraged that he'd lost his little girl. Rage was all he could express. He lost his temper over *anything*. He didn't trust me, so if I was late for dinner, he'd accuse me of meeting a guy somewhere and he'd chase me around with his belt, trying to beat me. I began to stay away, to stop his attacks. I was broken-hearted, though, because I wasn't welcome in my family any-more."

Relinquishment was not always the cause of hostility from birthmothers' families; sometimes it was merely the *excuse*. In families with histories of abuse, postpartum birthmothers were often not merely depressed but actually uncertain of their own survival.

"I hid in my room," Cindy says. "I avoided people, especially my mother. If she saw me, she started beating up on me. She constantly taunted and cursed at me. I stayed out of sight. I had no one to talk to, no one. I couldn't eat or sleep. I lost weight, more than I'd gained from pregnancy. I thought I was abnormal—crazy, even—because I was so down. At the home, they'd said I'd forget about the baby and move on. But I couldn't. I cried all the time. I couldn't stop crying. I remember my cheeks were raw, from being wet all the time. I stayed by myself and didn't even know what day it was. I'd lost interest in life."

Birthmothers like Cindy, young, with low self-esteem and no emotional support from close relationships, often felt that, in giving up their babies, they'd lost their only sources of love and sole reasons for living. Many withdrew from normal activities and, like Cindy, cloaked themselves in protective seclusion.

"Before the baby," she says, "I'd felt unlovable. I'd been loose, promiscuous, always searching for someone to love me," she says. "But when I lost my baby, I lost interest in living. Boys, dates, the prom—nothing seemed important. I managed to go back to school, but I didn't care about it. I abstained from sex for years. I wouldn't let anyone touch me. I stayed in my room on weekends, crying or staring at the television. Truthfully, I don't know what I did. I was in a shell. I felt crazy."

Already scarred by years of family violence, some women found relinquishment a final blow from which they could not recover.

Surviving long-term abuse and hurtful relationships, these birthmothers had often developed tremendous resilience and inner strength. Relinquishing their babies, however, left many lost in a void, lacking the motivation to resume their lives, let alone to pursue intimate contact with other people.

"I knew I should get out and live," Cindy recalls, "but I had no interest in any part of life other than my baby. My baby was all I thought about, all I wanted. And my baby was gone."

Patterns and Cycles

Even many women with relatively strong egos and close-knit, supportive families became lost in postrelinquishment grief. In despair, they saw themselves as "bad," "undeserving of love," "not worthy" of raising their own children, as deserving punishment for "sinning," for having had sex, for having been pregnant, for shaming their families, and, most of all, for relinquishing their babies. In many cases, professionals encouraged this sense of culpability.

"The social worker at the agency counseled me one final time before I signed the papers," Pam recalls. "As I was about to leave, she said, 'Go, Pam, and sin no more.' It was her final chance to throw a rock at me, and she did. I was already in bad emotional shape, but she wouldn't give up an opportunity to reinforce the idea that I was scum, not good enough to keep my own child. She'd worked hard to make me believe that. Brainwashing me played a big factor in convincing me to relinquish."

Like others who suffered depression and guilt after relinquishing, Pam was further conflicted because she believed such feelings were wrong. Believing that relinquishing was for the good of her baby, she felt that grieving was nothing short of selfish. "I thought I was wallowing if I felt sad," she says. "So I forced myself to dismiss my feelings, snap out of it, and act normal. That would work, usually, for a while. But my emotions would eventually build up again and overwhelm me. *Anything* could set me off—a TV commercial about baby food or seeing a pregnant woman on the street—anything! And when my sadness began, it would knock me over completely. I'd be unable to get out of bed or stop crying, much less to go to class or study. For months—no, for years—I lived a cycle of bottle up and burst, bottle up and burst."

Birthmothers who struggled to suppress their grief often began patterns of strict emotional control that they maintained for years. Some, like Pam, alternately controlled and lost control of their emotions. Others tried to control their relationships and eliminated contact with anyone or anything that they could not keep in line. Having lacked control over their babies, they were determined to maintain tight reins over the remainder of their lives, often defying authority or rejecting both people and opportunities that represented risk. "I couldn't let anyone tell me what to do," says a birthmother who is a registered nurse. "The year after I gave birth, I was fired from my job because I wouldn't follow orders. They wrote in my personnel file that I had a problem with authority. And I did. I still do. I have to make my own decisions, all the time, and do what I think is right for *me*."

If their lack of control regarding relinquishment led some women to avoid situations in which they felt powerless, it was not without cost. For the nurse described here, the price was a job. For others, it was intimacy and the inherent risks. For Pam, it was a future with the man she loved.

"Jeff and I both had to sign the papers within seventy-two hours of birth," she recalls. "That was the law. Jeff flew in from college. I couldn't speak or even cry, I was in too much pain. Jeff stayed with me. We went to the lake and sat just looking at the water. We didn't say anything. We were both too raw. Before he left to go back to school, we held each other for a long time. When he was gone, I walked around, finally crying, for hours. I hadn't slept for days, but I was unable to rest. I had to get a hold of my life again, and that meant getting rid of Jeff, because he hadn't come through for me and our baby. It was a double loss, the baby and his father. But I couldn't afford anymore risk, so I wrote Jeff that I couldn't see him anymore. He flew back immediately to try to change my mind, but I broke off with him. I needed him out of my life."

The need to feel in control and to choose between "all" or "nothing" was common among birthmothers stuck in the despair phase of grief. Many clung to absolute judgments of right or wrong, black or white, one extreme or the other, in order to attain a sense of security and avoid threatening relationships and situations. Despite her love for Jeff, Pam eliminated him. If he wasn't "good," he was automatically "bad." Jeff had to be banished so that Pam could maintain strict control over her life and avoid any contact with the sources of her former "sins."

For some birthmothers, the need for control and absolute thinking extended beyond personal relationships to careers, long-term goals, and daily routines. This insistence on absolutes reflected a desperate need for protection from potential sources not only of pain but also of ecstasy. Women who had been badly hurt by the results of seeking happiness were not willing to take similar risks again. Rigid structuring of relationships, work schedules, and other external regimes provided comfort for some. For others, they provided survival.

"My *only* purpose," a birthmother named Debbie says, "was to keep my baby healthy during my pregnancy. But once the baby was gone, I became an empty shell, a zombie. I didn't dress; I stayed in bed. Or I scrubbed my mother's house, from floor to ceiling. I lived a cycle of feeling too bad to get up, of sleeping and dozing, or of getting up and wiping everything clean in a fury. After a few months, I dragged myself back to college and took a double course load. I knew I had to keep busy if I wanted to stay alive."

If scheduling every minute of their days shielded women like Debbie from pain, it also separated them from possibilities. In their determination to keep spinning, many became trapped in their own webs of depression. "I kept apart from others," she says. "I left myself no time for relationships. I went on a date once, but I was worlds away from him. He was a college senior. I was a mother. That's *all* I saw myself as—a mother minus her baby. So there was nothing to talk about. There was no way I could date, party, or do the bar scene. I had nothing in common with college kids."

Rigidity and Ritual

Another birthmother who relied on rigid patterns and routines of constant activity found that self-made rituals helped her deal with her grief. Jean was twenty-seven, divorced, and the mother of an adopted son when she relinquished.

"I completely structured my life," she says. "I left myself no time for emotions. I went back to my job as soon as I could. I followed a strict routine. I got up, I showered, I got my son dressed and fed. I worked all day. After work, I made dinner for my son, my mother, and myself, and then I bathed my son. I read to him every night. Finally, and most important, I wrote in my journal. I wrote private messages to my relinquished daughter every night. I found the mechanical, predictable nature of this routine not just soothing but life saving. Without it, I'd have been lost."

Without the aid of society's rituals for grief, some women, like Jean, invented their own. Homespun, private rituals like writing letters or journal messages provided regular, rhythmic outlets for their emotions. In the process of writing, some were able to examine their feelings enough to gradually work through their debilitating depression.

Others found it necessary to enact more elaborate, sometimes secret rituals that helped acknowledge both their relationships to their relinquished children and their grief. Mother's Days, Christmases, and the birthdays of relinquished children often found them conducting tearful ceremonies in solitude.

"I have a closet full of presents," Alexis says. "They're all wrapped and with cards and letters that give the date and occasion. From rattles to a wristwatch, for every year of my son's life. I bought Christmas and birthday presents for him every year, saving them in the irrational hope that, someday, I'd be able to give them to him. And I wrote long, impassioned letters, telling him how much I loved him, how I thought about him, and how sorry I was."

Women like Alexis, who purchased gifts for children they never saw, who wrote letters they never sent, and who baked cakes and celebrated birthdays, candles and all, by themselves, admitted that they were not always sure if these acts helped or hurt. They were certain, however, that they performed these rituals because they needed to *do* something tangible to express their feelings for their children and their grief. Although collecting cakes, cards, and presents may seem futile in the absence of the children, it nevertheless provided a vehicle for some birthmothers to share, in absentia, the occasions of their children's lives and to acknowledge, in a concrete manner, their own sense of loss.

Acceptance: In Touch, Out of Reach

Some birthmothers were able to complete their grieving and incorporate relinquishment into their lives. Abby relinquished in 1973 and describes giving up her child as an unhappy experience with which she has finally come to terms.

"If I had *not* relinquished my baby," she says, "I'd have been saddled, at the age of sixteen, with parental responsibilities and financial burdens I could not have handled. My grief would have been for *me*, not for the baby. I'd never have gone to college or met my husband. I'd never have had my career or my other children, at least, not *these* other children. It was hideously painful, at the time. I wanted to die, I really did. But I see—no, I *feel*—quite clearly, that relinquishing was right, both for me and for the baby. True, I wasn't able to go back to being a carefree kid again, afterwards. And true, I cried for years, and still do on her birthday. But it's also true that I wasn't ready to be a parent yet. *That's* the reality, and I've come to accept it. Relinquishment enabled me to have a good life, even if I still have a few missing pieces and my share of regrets."

Abby is one of several women interviewed who appear to have reached a level of peace regarding relinquishment. Accepting it philosophically and emotionally as an imperfect compromise to a problem for which there were no perfect solutions, she has been able, after twenty years, to quiet her anger and put her despair to rest.

Many of those who were able to accept relinquishment with relative calm had participated in open adoptions. Lynne, for example, said that she *never* felt any depression, loss, regret, or sorrow. "It's certainly not ideal," she says, "but I found it the best option available. No one can promise a perfect solution for every problem you face in life. But I was able to turn my problem into somebody else's blessing through adoption. I have no regrets about that. I can still see my child. I talk to the adoptive parents regularly. I get pictures on her birthday and send her letters twice a year. I can have as much or as little contact as I want. It's not perfect, but it works for all of us. Adoption was, for me, a workable compromise."

Although Lynne was convinced that open adoption spared her much of the difficulty experienced by other birthmothers, she was not certain that it would continue to do so indefinitely. She saw the eight years that had passed since her relinquishment as a relatively short time and still considered herself a newcomer to the birthmother experience. In fact, many agree and claim that those who have *not* experienced profound grief are still in denial, unable to identify or face their dormant feelings. They warn that denial can last decades and that birthmothers like Lynne should be prepared for the day, perhaps years ahead, when their grief will inevitably erupt.

However, even if open adoption *did* spare Lynne, some others in open adoptions have not shared her relatively painfree experience. Donna, for example, thinks she fooled herself about her relationships with her daughter and the adoptive family. "Open adoption," she says, "offers no immunization against grief. You may know where your child is and what her favorite TV show is. But, in a way, that can be *more* difficult than not knowing. You see your child as your child, love her as your child, but you are *not* her mother. She already has somebody she calls 'Mom'. You have to take whatever scraps of time, contact, and information her adoptive parents are willing to toss you. And that's tough. It's very tough."

Getting Stuck or Moving On

Almost all of the women interviewed reported that recurring depression and anger, often directed at themselves, dominated their lives. More than one in ten had been so devastated by relinquishing that, at some point, they tried to end their lives. About one in five completely abandoned the goals they'd previously been striving to attain. More than one in five became involved in abusive relationships after relinquishing, and many married their abusers and remained with them for decades.

Under the influence of anger and depression, some set out on paths of self-punishment and self-destruction; others attempted to embody "purity" and "goodness." Some rejected any semblance of "normal" life; others struggled to become the living definition of "normalcy." Some tried desperately to "replace" their relinquished children by quickly having additional babies; others refused to consider the painful prospect of another pregnancy and birth.

Most of the women interviewed believed that their lives had somehow become fixed at the point of relinquishment. In the months that followed, immersed in secrecy, shame, and guilt, they often developed patterns of living by extremes. Pursuing either perfection or punishment, having many children in close succession or having no additional children at all, seeking social acceptability or rejecting social norms altogether, and becoming obsessed with the relinquished child or denying the existence of that child completely—all were typical of postpartum birthmother patterns. Identifying their own particular patterns has been a slow, complicated, and critical step in the healing process for many birthmothers in both closed and open adoptions. Decades later, despite the pervasive effects on their lives and subsequent relationships, many had yet to discover either their patterns or the incomplete, suppressed phases of grief that led to them.

Among those interviewed, very few had attained anything resembling acceptance regarding their relinquishments. Often, those who had attributed their success to help from others: therapists, psychiatrists, their husbands and families, and, more than any other single source, the other birthparents they'd met through support groups. Most significant of all, however, was the fact that almost every woman who had found peace after grieving knew where and how her child was. With few exceptions, these women had either participated in open adoptions or searched for and found the children they'd given up. Without the knowledge that their children were all right, even the help of support groups, loving spouses, and battalions of psychiatrists was rarely successful in guiding them through their grief.

Knowledge alone, however, was not enough to launch birthmothers past their grief. In fact, without social recognition of their losses and acknowledgment of their reasons to mourn, the vast majority remained locked in various combinations of denial, anger, and despair. Those who had some success in coping were usually those who improvised their own techniques for expressing and examining their grief. They celebrated their children at birthdays and Christmas; they wrote unmailed letters, poetry, and journals that gave voice to their secret emotions. Fending for themselves in dealing with grief, they created private rituals that mimicked but rarely effectively replaced those denied them by the greater society.

5

Intimacies and Marriage
The Impact of Surrender

T HE CHIEF OF SURGERY CURSED AS HE SLID OFF OF HIS WIFE. THEN HE leaned over and breathed into her face, "You're nothing but a two-bit whore."

Bridget winced from the stench of his alcohol breath, clenched her teeth, and waited, silently, for him to fall asleep. She knew that, if she were just quiet, it wouldn't take long. He never stayed awake long after sex.

"How'd you like it, whore? Is that how your *boyfriend* did it?" The chief of surgery grabbed her left breast and squeezed hard. Bridget involuntarily gasped, but she lay still. After seven years, she knew better than to resist her husband when he was in the mood to rub the past in her face.

He pinned her down with his thigh over her stomach, his hand over her face, and shoved his mouth against her ear. "You gonna cry again, Bitchett? You gonna sob for your lost little bastard? Or are you gonna get mad and slam doors and wake up *our* kids? Go ahead! Start shouting! Show them what a piece of trash slut their mommy *really* is!"

Bridget closed her eyes and waited for him to get bored or tired enough to stop. She ached for other hands that had been gentle and loving. Other whispers that had caressed, not cursed. She tried to hide inside her mind, to shield herself with memories of being bonded body to body and soul to soul. Another bristly face that brushed her cheek tenderly, his close, musky smell . . . .

Searing pain tore through Bridget so suddenly that she couldn't breathe. Her eyes opened and stared ahead, alert and waiting for it to subside. It was a familiar pain. By now, she should know better than to tempt it. Those memories—that time was gone—that man, those hands, still married to someone else, would never touch her again no matter how much she longed for them.

Unable to get a reaction, her husband released her, shoved off, and rolled over. Immediately, he began to doze. "You're not even a good fuck. . . ." was the last thing she thought he said, but it became a snore before he finished, so she couldn't be sure.

For Better, for Worse

Nine out of ten women interviewed married after relinquishing, most within two years. Three out of five of these marriages have either already ended in divorce or teeter on the brink. In almost every interview, birthmothers linked their marital troubles to relinquishment. Even most of those with stable marriages had endured definite strains that they attributed directly to their experiences of surrender.

Although they could not substantiate their theories, most of these women were convinced that birthmothers' marriages have a higher rate of failure than others. Some thought that they had married the wrong men; others that they had married for the wrong reasons. About a third married the first man who dated them after relinquishing, in order to become "socially acceptable" and escape stigma. One in six married the birthfathers, with or without love, hoping that their unions would somehow make things right.

Many whose marriages were floundering avoided divorce despite severe problems. "I don't want to seek an easy solution to complex problems," one explains. "I *can't* do that again. I abandoned my baby in order to find an easy solution through adoption and it didn't work. I won't abandon my marriage the same way."

Whether they divorced or stuck it out, whether their unions were happy or miserable, in their marriages birthmothers often exhibited the same patterns of absolute thinking and living by extremes that they established soon after relinquishing. They tended to marry right away or not for decades, to have children immediately or not at all. They strove to cleanse their pasts by becoming perfect wives and mothers or to atone by becoming doormats for punishing, abusive spouses. They gave up careers and educations for marriage or sacrificed marriage for education and careers. They redefined their identities in terms of their close relationships with men or avoided intimacy with men altogether. Whatever paths they chose, most avoided middle roads and went one direction or the other, adhering to their particular extremes absolutely, without compromise, for decades.

Further, the marriages and intimate relationships of those who had not finished grieving often reflected the phases at which they had stopped. For some, marriage became an arena for denial. Marrying "ideal" men, they became "ideal" wives and suppressed any emotions or memories that might stand in their way. For others, stuck in anger at society, marriage became simply another institution of conformity that was to be rejected at any cost. Those who aimed their anger inward often selected dominating or punitive partners who encouraged their self-recrimination. For those who struggled with lingering despair, marriage was often a relationship involving neither love nor sexual attraction; many hoped that dull marriages would keep them safe from the passions that had led to their previous problems and unplanned pregnancies.

Regardless of their reasons for marrying or their feelings for their spouses, 94 percent of those who had *not* married the birthfathers confided the secrets of their relinquishments to their husbands, and three out of four of the husbands responded not merely with tolerance but also, to the best of their abilities, with outspoken support and sympathy.

Even when their husbands tried to provide help, however, over half of the wives were unable to accept it. Many, whose self-esteem had been destroyed during relinquishing, felt unworthy of either forgiveness or affection. Others, whose closest relations had let them down, felt incapable of further trust, intimacy, or love. Some felt so deeply tied to the birthfathers that, even if they were no longer in contact, they could not allow any other men, even their own husbands, to come close.

In marriage, some birthmothers found rewards, such as respectability, social acceptability, and the opportunity to have more children. Others, however, merely found additional losses: controlling, dominating relationships; physical or verbal abuse; sexual or fertility problems; trouble in self-expression and independence; and difficulties giving or accepting intimacy and love. Among the third who found loving, understanding, and supportive husbands, many discovered that even the most glorious "knights in shining armor" could not rescue them from the villains lurking in their own minds.

Crossed Fingers, Left Hand

Unable to grieve openly or to resolve their feelings after relinquishing, many birthmothers determined that conformity was their best route. Many hoped that by becoming perfectly "normal" and "ordinary" they could recoup at least some of their losses and regain acceptability and respectability. Accordingly, their primary goals were to attain acceptable roles, like that of wife, and respectable titles, like "Mrs." Privately, however, some had other, more pressing reasons for wanting to marry.

"I got married in 1979, six months after I relinquished," Alexis remarks. "But, as a condition of my marriage, I insisted that we have a baby immediately. I *needed* a baby. I'd lost my first one, so I thought I needed another. When that didn't help, I had another, and another. In five years, I had four more babies. I'd have had more, but the doctor told me I had to stop or have a hysterectomy."

For many birthmothers, marriage seemed to be the acceptable way to recover what they had lost by relinquishing. Along with new names, they hoped that marriage would bring them new beginnings, new identities, and new children. Many discovered, however, that, instead of replacing their losses, their marriages compounded them.

"The marriage, of course, turned out to be just more denial," Alexis continues. "My parents were delighted by it—it gave them the opportunity to completely deny the repercussions of my 'mistake.' They were gleeful about my engagement to a proper 'blue blood,' who was much more acceptable to them than the Eastern European who was the father of my surrendered baby. Nobody, even my fiancé, seemed to care about love, or even about why I was getting married so soon. But I knew that it wasn't out of love. It was out of pain. I married to rid myself of pain, to regain my baby through another birth, to run away from the past and to live a 'good' way. *Who* I was marrying wasn't important to me. The only thing I cared about was that he had qualifications that would make me a mother and satisfy my parents."

Brides like Alexis, who married without paying much attention to their grooms or their marital relationships, consistently faced disappointment later. Alexis became distraught when she finally discovered that even four new babies could not relieve her grief for her first. But by then she had other problems, as well. Her husband, whom she had never considered particularly important, began to demand attention that she was unable to give.

"I never gave my husband a chance, I guess. He'd always been there for me, but I never thought about him. I was caught up in *my* needs. He knew about the baby and married me to help make me 'OK.' He gave me everything I wanted—the house, the trips, the four kids. He paid for nannies and private schools and tried to be a loving husband and good father. But I never loved him. He was my ticket out of hell and, even though he was very supportive and loved me, we've never had much of a marriage. We *couldn't* have. I hated myself—how could I have loved anyone else?"

Others like Alexis felt that their husbands became unintentional victims of their premarital relinquishments. Most lamented their haste in marrying soon after relinquishing, when, consumed by grief or lost in denial, they'd been unable to understand their feelings about themselves, let alone about prospective suitors. Consumed by their own needs, they were unable to give to others. Marriage had been grasped, by many, as a vehicle for immediate escape rather than as a lifetime partnership. Consequently, even dedicated, sensitive husbands often faced rebuke or rejection from wives who loathed themselves so thoroughly after relinquishing that they were contemptuous of anyone who could forgive, much less respect and love them. In these circumstances, Prince Charming never had a chance.

Pretending
Forever After

A number of women who married men they met after relinquishing had not yet resolved their relationships with birthfathers. Some remained deeply attached to the fathers of their surrendered children throughout their marriages, often with disastrous results. "I felt I'd been punished for loving a man totally," Sue says.

"After twenty-three years of marriage, I *still* feel that my husband isn't the man I belong with. Bob, the father of my first child, is the only man I really ever loved. But we were so young and overwhelmed by stress and guilt that he dropped me. After that, even in the era of free love, I developed a sexual hangup. Bob was the only man I ever felt I belonged with sexually. I wouldn't even kiss anyone else."

Sue is one of several birthmothers whose love for birthfathers survived relinquishment, even though their relationships did not. Even after all hopes of reconciliation were gone, these women secretly carried torches of passion for their former lovers. Often, after they'd married, their husbands were scorched by the intensity of those flames. A birthmother named Lisa, who relinquished in 1972, was pregnant a *second* time by the father of her relinquished child when she married Dwayne less than a year later.

"I told Dwayne about Ted and the baby we'd given up for adoption," Lisa sighs. "My mother was furious that I told him. She was afraid he'd drop me and that I'd be an old maid. But I couldn't keep so many secrets, anymore. I had to let something out. And, actually, Dwayne wasn't as upset as I thought he'd be about the baby. What he *was* upset about was Ted. He was so jealous and resentful that I never dared to tell him that Ted was also the father of the baby I was carrying when we married. To this day, he thinks *he* was the father, even though the boy's the spitting image of Ted. Dwayne and I got divorced after only two years, and I still see Ted. I'll never *marry* him—But I guess I'll never be done with him, either."

Regardless of whether they remained sexually involved or broke off all communication with them, many birthmothers remained emotionally committed to the fathers of their relinquished children. Some retreated from intimacy with other men by not dating at all, others by plunging into loveless marriages. Sue went from one extreme to the other.

"I wouldn't date anyone twice," Sue continues, "because I didn't want to get physically involved. I kept in touch with Bob's family so I could hear about him. I went to college and went through the motions of going on with my life, but I fantasized about Bob all the time. When a law student who sat near me in the library asked me to marry him, I thought, 'This is a gift from God. A second chance.' I'd never even dated my husband before we got engaged. Yet, I gave up college after one semester to marry him. I felt compelled to get married, as if it were my only chance. But marriage felt like just another part of my cover up. I wasn't sexually attracted to my husband. I was still in love with Bob. But I thought I shouldn't love Bob and shouldn't *want* to be in love—I thought that love that intense was painful and sinful. So I wore white, as if I'd never loved, as if I'd had no baby, as if none of it had happened, and I did what was 'right,' to make it 'OK.'"

If Sue generalized her feelings of being "wrong" for having an unplanned pregnancy and relinquishing her child to include being "wrong" for being in love, she was not alone. After relinquishing, many women were reluctant to enter into relationships that offered any possibilities of love. Instead of romance or sexual attraction, they sought men who made them feel safe, who would take care of them, or who would, at least, provide them with protection from intimacy. Like Lisa and Sue, however, many who married images that seemed "right" on the surface later discovered that their husbands had deeper qualities that were not what they'd expected.

"Dwayne liked other women," Lisa explains. "He didn't like to work. He was *not* what he appeared to be."

Sue's husband turned out to be controlling and jealous. Like many birthmothers who lacked self-esteem and confidence, she married a dominating man who insisted on making all the decisions. As long as they obediently followed orders, wives like Sue enjoyed a certain sense of safety and security. However, when they disagreed or dared to defy their husbands' authority, many faced rage, cruelty, or verbal abuse. Some of these wives submitted to their husbands wills because their marriages and the acceptable roles they provided seemed so important. Others gave in because they felt guilty about not loving the men they had married. And a number let their husbands boss them around because giving in without exploring or expressing their own opinions had become a habit.

"When I got married," Sue recalls, "I felt unworthy to make my own decisions, so I instinctively found a husband who'd rule the roost and make all my decisions for me. He knew that I didn't love him—he even knew that I loved somebody else, and that drove him bananas. He didn't trust me, suspected me of having affairs, and demanded that I tell him where I was every minute of every day. I had to be fully accountable. I had to call his office whenever I left the house. If I was late coming home, I had to call and explain that the line at the supermarket was longer than usual. It got crazy. He wouldn't let me go anywhere. I couldn't get a job because he was so insecure about me being around other men. It sounds strange, but I didn't feel I could get too upset about any of this. After all, I'd used him in order to escape my problems, without much concern for his feelings. So I thought I *owed* him and, besides, I thought I was wrong to want anything for myself. So for years I obeyed whatever he said. Lately, now that our kids are older, I've become more assertive, and we've had to work a lot to keep our marriage going. At times, it's looked bad, but, amazingly, we're still together and he's actually trying to change. After all these years and all these kids, we must have something good going on between us!"

Ten Steps Behind

A number of women who married dominating men were much more timid than Sue. Having been deeply wounded by stigma and ostracism after relinquishing, they were so terrified of being rejected by their husbands as well that they gratefully accepted obsequious roles in marriage.

"I hemorrhaged after childbirth," says Rose, who relinquished in 1965. "I almost died, and that would have been fine with me. When I was strong enough, I went back to college and confided in my best friend—my roommate—about what had happened. She moved out, into her sorority, without even an explanation. I assumed that my being an unwed mother was the reason. I was very hurt and afraid of other people finding out and rejecting me, as well. I was afraid to date, too. I thought guys would assume I was 'loose.' Besides, I was still hung up on the birthfather, even though I wasn't seeing him anymore.

"After several months, though, a guy I'd been dying to go out with for years asked me out. I went, but when he kissed me, I assumed he'd heard stuff about me and I ran away. I asked someone else, his fraternity brother, to drive me home. I didn't go out with anyone, after that, for a whole year. When I did, I waited until we'd been going steady for four months to tell him about the baby. And then he broke up with me. I was heartbroken, again. Plus, I was thoroughly convinced that no one would *ever* date me or be my friend if they knew the truth about me. I was terribly lonely and worried constantly about gossip, my reputation, my future. I'd planned on going to medical school, but I never even applied—I was afraid of taking the physical to get in. I actually believed they wouldn't accept me if they knew I'd had a baby. I basically dropped all my plans and goals and became obsessed with proving to myself that a man could still love me. So, when I met a moral, upright, religious lawyer who wanted to marry me even though he knew I'd had a child, I grabbed him. He accepted me, so I accepted his terms: I was to forget about the past and never mention it again."

When women desperate to escape condemnation and ostracism agreed to terms like those imposed on Rose, they often hoped that they could forget about the past and never refer to—or think of—it again. To many, marriage appeared to offer not only fresh starts, but also the opportunity to erase everything that had preceded it. Along with their husbands, they wanted to believe that their relinquishments were over and done with and that their future lives together would not be affected. Often, however, they found that even their best intentions failed to wipe out unintegrated memories and unresolved grief.

"We socialized a lot," Rose continues. "There were dinners and sports events and invitations from other members of the firm. We gave dinner parties for the partners. I always felt as if I'd stepped into someone else's life, as if I was pretending to be somebody I wasn't. I was on guard publicly. As if I were someplace else, watching the scene, instead of really there. As if I saw myself on stage, playing a lawyer's wife. And that would have been OK, if at home I could feel more relaxed. But, many times in bed, when my husband would want to make love, I'd have the same feeling, of not being really there. I'd kind of go through the motions but have no pleasure or sense of participation. I'd see myself, as if from a distance, and feel as if it was somebody else he was loving, not me, at least not the real me."

Another birthmother, named Ida, described similar feelings of dissociation. When her husband proposed marriage two years after her relinquishment, he asked Ida to guarantee that her past would never intrude on their future together. She agreed, grateful to be chosen, despite her past.

"I used to sit at the kitchen table in the morning, waiting for my husband to leave for work," she remembers. "I'd pretend to be reading the paper, but when I heard the door close, I'd breathe a sigh of relief. I didn't have to pretend anymore. I didn't have to smile or have a cheerful lilt in my voice. I could cry, or stare at the wall, or write poems to my baby in my journal. Maybe, if he hadn't *insisted* that I forget, I would have forgotten. But by trying to forget, all I could think about was that I hadn't forgotten, and I had to keep that fact to myself. So there was a big secret separating us, and the secret grew with time."

Rose's marriage eventually ended in divorce; Ida's, with the help of counselors, is still struggling for survival. But both reflect the experiences of others whose marriages required that they deny relinquishment. By excluding part of their pasts, they excluded part of themselves from their marriages. With one partner unable to be fully present or participate completely, these marriages were often doomed from the start.

Jekyll's Wife

After relinquishing, a number of birthmothers were attracted to men who were not merely dominating or possessive but actually abusive. Many married their abusers, claiming that they had seen no indications of their husbands' violence until after their weddings, when they lacked the stamina to escape. Bridget, for example, married a doctor who provided her with a proper role and high social status as the wife of the chief of surgery at a major hospital. When she married him, however, his credentials were of secondary importance.

"I married him hoping that I could reclaim my baby," she says. "In our state, I had two years to change my mind about relinquishing. I thought that, by marrying Ray, I'd be in a position to raise my child, so I told him how I felt before we were married. He'd lost contact with his own two children through his divorce, so I thought he'd be sympathetic. And he seemed to be, until after we'd married. But after the wedding, when I brought up the subject of my baby, he ordered me never to talk about her again. In fact, his entire attitude changed towards me after we were married. He became cold and intolerant."

Most of the birthmothers who, like Bridget, said that their husbands changed after their honeymoons, later attributed these changes to their husbands' own insecurities. In hindsight, they saw that their husbands had been so unsure of themselves and of their own desirability that they had become obsessed with and jealous of their wives' former lovers, even of the children they'd relinquished. If these assessments are accurate, fears of *not* being loved ironically led the men to behave in ways that destroyed whatever love existed in their marriages. Some husbands became so frustrated that they expressed their rage physically, even sexually.

"Publicly, Ray would praise me," Bridget says. "In front of others, he'd talk about me like I was a saint. But, privately, he would either ignore me or hurt me. I'd lie awake at night, next to him, and need to be loved. I'd feel so lonely that I'd think about the past, about my baby's birthfather, about how I'd felt metaphysically bonded to him. Ray seemed oblivious, totally disinterested in me. Unless he'd been drinking, and then he'd attack me. He'd torment me about the baby I'd given up or tell me I was ugly or fat or old. But even though I was so 'fat,' he'd wake me up in the middle of the night and force me to have sex, whether I wanted it or not. He was very rough, even violent sexually. I believe that he was turned on by hurting me. We had five children together, but I *never* enjoyed sex with him."

Marriages like Bridget's found both spouses fantasizing obsessively about a past they'd idealized. With each partner lacking confidence and self-esteem, communication became blocked. Mutual distrust and fear of rejection reigned as each partner jockeyed for defensive position. Most wives, however, did not immediately see their husbands as insecure; for decades, they assumed hostile husbands were merely part of the punishment they deserved for their past sins and passively acquiesced.

"I didn't think I deserved good sex," Bridget continues, "or to stand up to Ray. After all, he'd given me social acceptability, the role of a doctor's wife. Living without love, without good sex or even tenderness, was the trade-off. It was part of my repentance. And, no matter how ugly things got between us, when Ray got up the next day, he went to the hospital where everybody respected him and he *seemed* the perfect husband, perfect professional, perfect man. I alone knew that there was another side to him, and I didn't dare complain or I'd bust my own cover."

For birthmothers married to men with similarly polarized attitudes toward them, displays of public affection and private abuse dominated their marriages and their lives. Like Bridget, however, many felt that they had no right to complain; their husbands had rescued them from social ostracism and given them the chance to move on.

"I was either the Madonna or I was a whore," says Sandie, who relinquished in 1985, married in 1986, and divorced in 1991. "My husband was like two different men, and I never knew which one would appear. Sometimes he seemed loving, understanding, and supportive. I'd always fall for that. I wanted him to approve of me. It was like if *he'd* forgive me, I was OK. An hour later, especially after we'd made love, he'd turn into a tormentor, taunting me, accusing me of having affairs with my baby's father or with any man we knew. He usually just used foul language, but sometimes he got so worked up that he'd slap me. For a few years, I thought that I deserved it, so I took my punishment and actually felt *thankful* that he put up with me at all, after the things I'd done."

When their husbands displayed such intensely divided attitudes toward them, birthmothers like Sandie and Bridget often protected themselves by separating emotionally from their spouses while maintaining the outward images of happily married, respectable wives. This dichotomy required constant secrecy and hypocrisy, which often became more difficult to sustain with time.

"I was empty," Bridget says. "I was there, at the country club or the charity ball. I was there at medical conferences and dinners. But I was separate, watching everybody else. Like a robot, I did what I was told, went where I was supposed to go. When I was near Ray, I felt publicly safe, disguised as his wife. But I was not present in my life. I was watching my life, not living it. It got so bad that when I won an award for doing community work, I didn't feel the award was for *me*. It was for the 'doctor's wife,' for the role I played, for my costume. I didn't feel that I deserved that award. The *real* me would never have been in the position to receive it—they'd never have awarded it to me, if they knew who I really was."

Dividing themselves and acting out roles that did not feel real usually took its toll on birthmothers like Bridget. Most could not sustain the strain indefinitely and eventually sought relief through divorce. With the help of therapists and support groups, Bridget finally regained enough self-respect to divorce Ray, after almost thirty years. Separating from punitive partners could not heal the wounds these women had sustained over the years, but putting an end to domestic abuse and to the strain of maintaining false pretenses was, for some, an effective first step.

Solitary Brides

For some women, loveless marriages seemed the most plausible and effective defense against the potential pain of intimacy. A number, however, were so threatened by the risks of close relationships that they broke off all social contact, literally isolating themselves from other people for months or even years.

After relinquishing, Cindy returned to the home of her abusive, mentally disturbed mother. "I was terribly lonely," she recalls. "My father was at work from 4:30 every morning to 5:30 every night. He was in bed by eight. My sister was away at college. I was in high school and managed to go to class, but except for that, I hid up in my room. I was afraid of my mother, and I had no interest in anything like proms or dates or hanging out with girlfriends. Now, when I look back, I can see that I was in mourning. But, at the time, it felt permanent, as if I'd simply lost interest in living."

Women who retreated as Cindy did usually stayed in hiding for two or more years. Most continued to function at a survival level, going to school or work but involving themselves in little or nothing else. They generally avoided not only romantic relationships with men but even close contact with women friends or relatives, withdrawing into feelings of depression, worthlessness, and guilt. Like Cindy, many went days without sleeping and ate abnormally, either starving themselves or binge-eating, off and on for years. Eventually, some began therapy and were assisted in working through their grief. Others gradually reemerged into the world without ever resolving their problems. A few, like Cindy, were pulled out of hiding by the gentle persistence and fondness of others.

"Three years after I gave up my baby," Cindy says, "a girlfriend asked me to let her fix me up. I hadn't gone out with anyone since I'd gone into the home, and I was afraid. I'd been promiscuous before, and I didn't want anyone to know about that. I'd changed and I wanted that behind me. I was afraid of getting near a man. I can't even say what exactly I was afraid of, but my stomach did flip-flops at the very idea of going on a date. But, at the same time, I was almost nineteen years old, and I knew I couldn't hide in my room at my mother's house forever. So, after putting it off for a few months, I accepted that date. And I became friends with the guy. We held hands. We talked. He was funny, and we laughed a lot. I felt good being with him, and he didn't seem to mind that I wouldn't have sex. He *liked* me. This was the first man who'd ever been my friend, and two years later, I married him, and we're still together."

Although complete self-imposed isolation was not uncommon after relinquishment, it could not be sustained indefinitely. Sooner or later, birthmothers had to come out of their hiding places and face the rest of their lives. Even those fortunate enough to find friends, boyfriends, or husbands to help them, however, usually retained fears that their secrets would be discovered and that they would be rejected. Trusting others by taking people into their confidence was one of the most prevalent and consistent difficulties that birthmothers described.

"I was scared to tell him," Cindy recalls. "But I knew I had to. He loved me, but I wasn't sure he'd love me if he knew the truth. My palms were sweaty, and I had butterflies so bad I thought I'd throw up. I was shaking. But I told him. I couldn't look at him, because I didn't want to see him walk out. But he didn't walk out. He lifted my chin and kissed me. And it would have been OK, then. Except I hadn't told him the whole truth about how I'd gotten pregnant by sleeping around. I told him the same lie I'd told my parents, that I'd been raped, because, first of all, I didn't want anyone else to find out that I'd lied and, more important, because I was afraid I'd lose him if he found out how loose I'd been."

For many birthmothers, the secrets of the past simply seemed too sinful and horrible to be forgiven. Many so thoroughly doubted their own worth and appeal that they envisioned their relationships crumbling instantly should the whole truth, whatever it was, be revealed. Confessions were made and trust was granted bit by bit, piece by piece. Friends, lovers, and husbands were tested, retested, and tested again to see how much of the truth they would handle, tolerate, or support. Even if they passed all the tests, however, birthmothers like Cindy, who had survived their ordeals through lies, hesitated to reveal all. Their choices seemed clear: there seemed to be no point in telling the whole truth when it might set everyone, including their lovers, reeling with revulsion and distrust. Bringing secrets to their marriages, however, especially when the secrets required outright lies, brought stress to birthmothers as brides and wives. Sustaining the secrecy and dealing with the stress only multiplied their problems.

"I was trapped by a lie I'd made up when I was fourteen," Cindy says. "I should have trusted my husband, but I didn't know I could. I thought he wouldn't love me if he knew how many boys I'd slept with. Now I know better. My husband accepts me. Not only that: he respects me. He told me he thinks I'm strong and that I went through incredible hell and survived it, all on my own, as a kid. He tells me I'm a good mom. He encouraged me to see a therapist to help me feel better about myself, but I know, I really do know, that if there has been any healing at all, it's been because of my husband. Because he's given me the feeling of being safe and the knowledge of what it is to be truly and unconditionally loved."

After the Party:
In Sickness and in Health

If isolation promised protection from intimacy, so did crowds. A few birthmothers avoided the risks of close relationships by moving quickly through casual sexual relationships, adopting aloof attitudes, or having several affairs concurrently. Some had been so deeply wounded by birthfathers, their families, or the professionals to whom they'd turned for help that they determined never to let anyone close enough to hurt them again.

After relinquishing, Annie didn't care if she lived or died. "For months, I saw nobody except the shrink, who gave me shock treatments whenever I admitted that I was depressed about my baby. Then, after about a year, I began to get stoned and hang out with hippies, sleazoids, scuzbags. I let them do whatever they wanted to with me. I had sex with anyone who wanted it. I didn't feel that I had the right to say no. I was garbage, not good enough to take care of my own kid or worthy of his father's love."

For women like Annie, the losses brought on by relinquishment involved much more than their babies. Some lost *all* their close relationships and felt betrayed by everyone in whom they'd confided. Accordingly, many became hesitant to reveal themselves, their histories, or their true feelings to anyone and sublimated their needs for intimacy with sex, drugs, or other equally self-destructive substitutes.

Annie credited her husband with her survival. But she remained aware that even his love did not provide a miracle cure for her problems; healing after relinquishing had to take place internally. At best, her marriage provided a safe environment in which healing could occur.

"I met my husband three years after I relinquished," she says. "I could have gotten hooked or overdosed on some drug. I could have ended up with some creep who'd beat or kill me. I had no self-esteem, and I'd have gone anywhere with anyone. But my husband saw something in me that I didn't see. It was pure luck that he met me and wanted me, and it's been a miracle that he's stood by me, trying to convince me that I am worth something.

"But, even though he loves me, our marriage has been rough. Because giving up my baby affected *everything*. It made me distrustful of everyone, all men, even my husband. My husband is honest and wonderful, but I have trouble letting go even with him. I hold back. Often, I feel numb in bed, as if I can't allow myself to experience any sexual pleasure, because I'd have to let down too many defenses. Actually, I don't expect, after what I went through, that I'll *ever* completely trust anyone again. My baby's father dropped me when I depended on him. My own parents sent me to have shock treatments when I relied on them. My psychiatrist electrified me every time I told him the truth. I learned that I was on my own. I can't count on anybody else, even my husband, because . . . well, you just never know."

Some birthmothers believed that their fear of trusting men became self-fulfilling and led them to marry men who would deceive them. Others thought that their constant suspicion drove their spouses away, eventually causing the very dishonesty and betrayal that they had dreaded. Whatever the sequence, however, a number were so concerned about betrayal that they double-checked everything that their partners told them. Zoe, who'd participated in only casual relationships until her marriage ten years after she relinquished, says she was so determined to protect herself that she looked for lies before they'd even been told. Her search eventually led her to shatter not only lies but also the backbone of her marriage.

"I used to go through my husband's wallet and pockets for matchbooks or receipts, to see where he'd been. I used to read his mail, check his credit card bills for unexplained expenses, call him three or four times a day. I'd surprise him at his office, just to see what he was doing. I wanted to know who he ate lunch with. I used to look through his daily diary, to see if he had women's names written down. I did this for years. I was never satisfied when I found nothing out of order. I never relaxed and began to trust him. Trust was out of the question. To me, it was a question of *when* he'd betray me, not if. Finally, I did find him with another woman, and I actually felt relieved, because I wouldn't have to wait and wonder anymore. I *knew*. Divorce made me miserable, but loneliness was familiar—I could trust it."

For many birthmothers, the inability to trust extended beyond men to family, professionals, and friends. For those like Annie, it included even themselves. These women were so defeated that they didn't trust themselves to accomplish, maintain, or merit *any* goal or relationship. Even when their marriages succeeded, they took none of the credit, attributing all success to their spouses. Accomplishments in careers, parenting, or other efforts similarly were credited to others rather than themselves. Annie believes that only her husband's efforts have been responsible for leading her, step by step, to situations that have helped her heal.

"I'd been an art student. But I abandoned my art when I abandoned my baby. Years later, my husband told me about a birthmother support group he'd heard about. I went. They needed someone to do their newsletter. That newsletter became my first artistic project since college. Now, after twenty-some years, I'm doing art again—not anything huge—I do display cases and bulletin boards at my kids' schools. People say I'm good and it surprises me. After all this time, I'm beginning to consider my old ambitions and dreams again. After I gave up my baby, my only goals were to feel lovable, find love, and have a family. Now that I've done that, I'm trying to find the way back to where I was to begin with."

Despite their difficulties with trust, women like Annie often admitted that it was their husbands' consistency and devotion that gave them the confidence to step out of their ruts and begin to heal. Despite the gratitude they felt, however, most felt that their husbands had been slighted in their marriages; as wives, they had themselves been so needy of love and so preoccupied with absorbing it that it often took years before they had been able to give love in return. Even then, these women believed that it had been luck or chance rather than their own personal worth or attractiveness that brought their husbands to them in the first place. And some qualified their claims of marital happiness, even long after their silver anniversaries, with disclaimers indicating levels of reserve, if not of perpetual, habitual general distrust.

Day by Day,
Till Death Us Do Part

After relinquishing, many women adhered to extremes that temporarily helped them elude close relationships with men. Loveless marriages, frequent changes of location, isolation, and promiscuity were only a few. Another frequent path was that of commitment to career.

Sonia buried herself in her work, leaving no time for men or even for herself. "I averaged eighty hours a week, I think, for several years. I worked weekends, brought work home to do at night. The only contact I had with men was professional, and I became extremely aggressive, partly, I'm sure, to scare them off. I was extremely depressed whenever I slowed down, so I didn't slow down. I bought things: cars, jewelry, a townhouse, clothes. I kept trying to prove I was successful and strong and resilient. I fantasized about having a baby on my own and keeping it as a single mother, and I promised myself that I would do that as soon as I saved enough money. I was sure that the only way I could ever have *anything* was on my own."

Those who hid their vulnerabilities behind bold and aggressive exteriors sometimes found that the fortresses they'd built for protection trapped them instead. Their powerful careers, militant independence, and expensive possessions intimidated some potential suitors who might otherwise have approached and comforted them. Like Sonia, who eventually married a man twenty-six years her senior, these women often longed for the very qualities of tenderness and caring that they pretended to shun.

Others who delved into work to avoid men ironically met their husbands at the office. While working, these women lowered their defenses and began relationships without even realizing it.

"My first impression of Neil was that he looked sadder than I did," Jean recalls. "Somebody told me he'd just been divorced and that his wife had taken his kids away. I thought, 'Here's a man who knows what it's like to lose a child,' but I never thought about dating him. He was just a sad man with an office down the hall."

Even when they began to date, women like Jean and Sonia often avoided sexual contact. Trusting men enough to let them come close was so threatening that some actually married before beginning any sexual relationships with their husbands.

"I married Neil, but I didn't sleep with him first," Jean says. "And we'd been married six months before I told him about the baby I'd relinquished. He was kind about it when I told him. And he never even asked about the birthfather. He seemed to understand and accept my pain."

Birthmothers like Jean, immersed in grief and mourning their relinquished children, were drawn to men who seemed to understand pain. Frequently, however, these women were surprised that their marriages became arenas for obsessive suffering. Husbands who struggled with their own grief were rarely able to provide their wives with either comfort or assistance in dealing with their losses. With both partners absorbed in their individual sorrows, most of these marriages eventually foundered. Some birthmothers who were still reeling from the losses of relinquishment, however, found the threat of another major loss literally too much to bear.

"My husband was drinking heavily," Jean recalls. "I couldn't count on him. I was sinking. Nothing was under control. I'd married, hoping that I'd feel better, but instead, my husband was brooding and drinking all the time, so I felt worse. The only time he brightened was when his daughters came to visit on the weekends. But when they came over, I was excluded. I was an outsider, watching them be a happy family, but not part of it. So I was lonely and needy, and when they'd leave, Neil would start drinking again.

"One weekend, I couldn't take it anymore. I was too depressed to face being excluded and alone for the weekend. So I begged Neil, literally begged him to change his plans. 'If you love me,' I pleaded, 'stay home with me.' But he left to go get them, anyway. I wrote a note and washed down 100 Seconals with some whiskey. The next thing I knew, I woke up in the hospital with needles in my hands and needles in my feet. My first sensation was of embarrassment, as if I'd screwed up again. Then I was even more embarrassed, because I was dressed in a ratty old bathrobe— I guess it had been the first thing he could find. After that, though, I felt sorry—not for what I had done, but sorry that I'd survived."

Although the circumstances were unique, Jean's suicide attempt was not unusual. About one in ten of the birthmothers interviewed attempted, at some point, to take their own lives. Many acted in anger or despair. Some acted in desperation, hoping to get either help or relief from suffering. Many felt unloved, unlovable, guilty, and hopeless. For some, attempting suicide was a way to let go of everything they'd been struggling with, so that they could begin again.

"Everyone who attempted suicide was required by law to get counseling," Jean says. "Only because I'd tried to die did I begin to receive the support and guidance I needed in order to heal. At first, I blamed my marriage, not relinquishment, for my anger and pain. I wanted a divorce and I separated from Neil after just two years of marriage. But, with time and support, I was able to realize that Neil wasn't the source of my problem. In fact, he was essential to my happiness. I'd expected Neil to fix me, to make me feel whole and lovable and to make the past go away. But, of course, he couldn't do that for himself or for me. And I couldn't love Neil until I loved myself; I'd married him before I was ready. But, with my therapy and the help he's received from Alcoholics Anonymous, we've been together happily for over twenty-five years."

Like Jean, others who were unable to complete their grieving sometimes became completely drained by trying to escape facing their losses. Ricocheting from career to marriage, abstinence to sexual involvement, secrecy to trust, total independence to complete dependence, they began to confuse the sources of their problems with their attempted solutions. Those who survived learned that there was no escape: the losses resulting from their relinquishments demanded to be dealt with. Otherwise, the cost of avoidance would escalate, threatening not only their relationships but even their lives.

Making It Right

One in six women interviewed married the fathers of their relinquished babies. Sometimes these unions manifested love strong enough to withstand the trauma of relinquishment. More often, they reflected less inspiring emotions, such as fear, shame, and guilt.

"I married the birthfather," says one woman, "to right our 'wrong.' I didn't love him. And I know he didn't love me. He didn't want to marry me anymore than I wanted to marry him. But it was like we were on a path neither of us could leave, and the only way we could see to redeem ourselves and overcome the stigma was by getting married. So we did. And we got divorced a year and a half later."

Over half of those who married birthfathers were divorced within five years. Among these women were many who believed their marriages failed more from the effects of relinquishment than from a lack of love. Some said that the birthfathers married them out of guilt and obligation, even though they were too immature to maintain the role of husband. Others felt that the stresses of relinquishing had changed the birthfathers, driving them to drink, take drugs, or run around with other women. When discussing their marital breakups, however, most made no mention of either their husbands or their surrendered children.

Instead, they discussed the ways relinquishment changed *them* and their abilities to relate to others.

"I'd spent four months in the home," Helen says. "I didn't see Hank, the baby's father, in all that time. I had nothing to do, so I fantasized by the hour. I made Hank into the man of my dreams, a romantic hero, a perfect husband and father. I fantasized about the other children we'd have later, about what I'd name them, about our wedding, about furnishing our home. Anything to escape. And the atmosphere encouraged me. Everyone there was living on fabrications and fantasies. There was a forty-year-old teacher who'd invented a husband and told everyone that she'd eloped but that, on their honeymoon, her new husband had died in a car crash, leaving her pregnant. And a little twelve-year-old girl who had no idea how she'd gotten pregnant and made up stories to explain it. There was no one there who had a link to reality, and everyone was transient so that I couldn't connect. I created an imaginary world and slipped into it. In my world, I clung to the image of Hank. And later, I married Hank, but not the real Hank, not simply a man. I married my fantasy, my idealization of Hank, and *that*, more than anything else, is what eventually led to our divorce."

Like Helen, many birthmothers blamed their isolation during pregnancy for the failures of their subsequent marriages to birthfathers. Separated for months from families, birthfathers, and friends, they found out too late that they had idealized their relationships and developed unrealistic expectations. Some spent years readjusting to reality and reexamining, redefining, and reestablishing their relationships. Others tried to reshape reality to match their fantasies.

"Mark joined the Navy," says Joannie, who relinquished in 1963. "Except for his letters, nothing was real to me. We'd promised to stay together, no matter what, and we planned to marry as soon as I finished high school. But I had trouble studying. All I could think about was Mark, our wedding, and having another son. And the son I envisioned, of course, was exactly like the one we'd given up.

"I had three more years of school. When he got out of the Navy, I ignored the fact that Mark was dating other girls, taking drugs, and even getting arrested and convicted of dealing drugs. I wrote him in jail the same way I'd written him in the Navy. I loved him and I'd never loved anyone else. Nothing interfered with my fantasy. Nothing, certainly not reality, was going to interfere with my dreams."

Joannie's plan, as she described it, seemed realistic enough. But, when compared to the facts, it revealed distortions of impressive magnitude. Like many birthmothers, she was unable to see the birthfather as anything other than her romantic ideal, and she remained committed to that image, even if that required her to disregard the facts. Often, birthmothers' steadfast commitments were so intense that they overpowered the objects of their affection, convincing the birthfathers to shape up to the best of their abilities.

"Senior year," Joannie recalls, "I got pregnant again. Mark married me that time. He promised to give up girls and drugs and I believed him, but I'm sure he took his time about it. I saw what I wanted to see, and that was that my dreams were coming true. I was marrying Mark and having a baby I could keep. All I hoped for was that it would be a boy, like the first."

Even when birthparents committed to each other and tried to overcome their problems, many found that their marriages were haunted by the past. No matter how much they loved each other, the loss of their first child tended to make their happiness incomplete.

"Neither of us ever forgets our first child," Joannie says. "We've had four others, but we still miss the first one. We've been through a lot and we've stuck together, and we both wish that we'd kept him. Because we made it, after all. And we think we've had a *harder* time because our family's been separated; the oldest brother's gone. Keeping him couldn't have been harder, even though we were so young. It might have been hard for a few years, but we'd have all been together now. As it is, twenty-nine years later, we don't even know where he is or if he's alive, and *nothing* can be harder than that."

Starting Over

Pam was in college in 1973 when she broke up with her baby's birthfather, just weeks after relinquishing. "Jeff was my first and only boyfriend, but I said we'd have to break all contact. I loved him, but I saw that it couldn't work, not after we'd let our baby go. But he kept calling all semester. The more I told him to get lost, the more he persisted. Gradually, I started talking to him again because he was the only one who could relate to me about relinquishing, the only one who'd shared the experience. So I felt a connection, and I agreed to meet him again during the summer. But, when I refused to date him, as if our baby had never existed, he proposed. I couldn't help thinking, 'Why couldn't you have done this eight months ago, before we signed those papers?' But I realized I loved him and needed him and that those feelings were mutual, so we got married."

Some women who married birthfathers had clear pictures of their spouses and of their situations. Unlike those who idealized their boyfriends and immediately tried to replace their relinquished children with new babies, these women went the opposite route and tried to assess and control every aspect of their marital relationships, so that they could avoid further losses and additional pain. Like Pam, many tested birthfathers, resisted their advances, and made them prove their commitments before continuing their relationships. Most were determined to avoid any risk that might endanger them or their future children and built marriages that served as fortresses for familial protection.

"I planned everything, to the *n*th degree," Pam says. "All I cared about was stability. We both worked and saved all our money so that I could plan on staying home when we had another child. We planned our family, determining not to have another child until we'd bought a house. Once we had a home, we had a baby ten months later. But *that* baby would be secure and safe."

After three children and almost twenty years of carefully planned marriage, Pam and Jeff remained devoted to each other, but the relinquishment of their first child continued to take its toll on their marriage. Many birthparent couples felt stress from maintaining their secrets; some also suffered from unresolved grief.

"I'm still angry," Pam says. "I'm angry at the twenty-one-year-old Jeff and the twenty-one-year-old Pam. We didn't take the right steps or say the right things. We made a serious mistake—one of the most serious mistakes people can make—when we gave up our child. It feels as bad to me, as morally wrong to me, as if we'd planned and carried out a murder. That's how evil it feels, and we live with it every day; it's part of our lives."

Many birthmothers who married birthfathers expressed similar rage, often admitting that their marriages had suffered from mutual blame and regret. "I tend to beat myself up about the baby," says one birthmother. "But sometimes I get tired of that, so I beat up my husband, instead. When he gets tired of it, I start on myself some more. Being aware that I do this helps us, but it doesn't tell me how to stop."

In addition to guilt and blame, these birthmothers often suffered from recurrent feelings of generalized helplessness and impending loss. Even the most careful planning and cushioned bank accounts could not relieve the sense that they and their families were in danger.

"We're very affluent," Pam admits. "But I can't quit working. I never feel secure. I still remember not having enough money to keep my baby, and I keep thinking, 'What happens if...?' So I keep on working, saving, padding our accounts. I work part-time, so I can be with my kids, but I'm always petrified of not having enough."

Although the specific issues that plagued them varied, marriages between birthmothers and birthfathers were often speckled with scars and unhealed wounds from relinquishment. Even those who were deeply in love, highly educated, and professionally successful tended to feel helpless and unassertive when confronting the lingering issues of their pasts. Many sought professional help in coping with their marriages, sometimes with positive results. Often, however, the reticence that inhibited their progress in healing resurfaced and prevailed, even in the context of therapy.

"I went to a therapist, early in the marriage. Jeff listened to me, but he couldn't *talk* about my problems. I felt I was a lousy wife, a worthless mother. I was depressed, so I sought help. I told the therapist that I'd given up a child. She asked, 'How do you feel about that?' and I said, 'I don't know.' That was the end of the discussion. She went on to other topics. So I thought, it must not be a real problem, after all, and I tried to go on. Years later, an adoptee friend of mine took me to a conference on adoption. There were other birthmothers there! I found out other people had felt the way I did, and I went to meetings and learned about loss and grieving and acceptance. *That* was when I began to begin to continue my marriage and my life."

Islands That Cry, Rocks That Feel Pain

About a tenth of the women interviewed had never married. Some consciously avoided men, fearful that intimacy would only mean further pain. Among these were some who went out of their way to avoid attracting the opposite sex.

"I never lost the weight I gained when I was pregnant," Donna says. "In fact, during the first year after I gave up the baby, I gained another thirty-five pounds. That was a total of over seventy pounds. I was obese. But I was afraid to lose weight, because then I'd feel vulnerable to men, you know, that I'd have to deal with them again."

A number of birthmothers who developed weight problems after relinquishing agreed that their added pounds served as disguises to hide them from potential suitors. A few who had been in therapy believed that their obesity symbolized even more.

"If I lost the weight," says Sally, who went from a size twelve to a size twenty in two years, "I'd feel like I was giving up my baby all over again. I realize how sick that sounds, but I can't bear to lose the *feeling* of being pregnant, even after seven years."

Donna also admits that her added weight literally cushioned her physical sense of loss, since her body still felt some of the symptoms of pregnancy, like "bigness," swollen feet, and aching back. But she recognizes that, if being overweight helped her feel pregnant, it also decreased her chances of ever becoming pregnant again.

"No one was attracted to me," she says. "I was too fat. And that was how I kept my distance from people, by keeping myself unattractive. In fact, I hid from *everyone* for two years. Then I began thinking that, some day, I'd meet my daughter again, and I thought about who I wanted to be when that happened. I wanted her to be proud of me, so I began to apply more energy to my work and tried to get promotions. But, even then, I wouldn't go near men. I abstained from even friendships with men for over six years. I couldn't let anyone be close or intimate. The thought of anyone touching me was too much to bear. I have begun to see someone, finally, but he's someone I grew up with, someone who was my friend way back before I relinquished. He loves me despite my weight and wants to have a baby with me. But I've had trouble conceiving, and the doctor's advised me to lose weight. So I'm trying, but it's very scary. Losing the weight feels like losing more than weight—it's like losing my protection. My boyfriend's patient. He tries to make light of it, suggesting that I lose the fat and get protection by taking karate lessons or carrying mace."

Some who were afraid of intimacy hid by altering their physical appearances: applying heavy makeup, wearing loose and shapeless clothing, or gaining or losing weight. Others escaped intimacy through quick changes and mobility. Sylvia moved to a new location every two years, largely to protect herself from forming any potentially painful, deep, or lasting attachments.

"I went to Africa eight months after relinquishing. I was angry and determined to defy society in any way I could. Marriage was merely part of society, so, obviously, I wanted no part of it. Marriage was just a vehicle by which society manipulated people, just another construct designed to prevent people from thinking for themselves and acting independently. Marriage meant yokes and chains, cleaning house and taking orders. I was *not* about to let anyone push me around again, not after I'd been pushed into losing my son!

"Even if I avoided marriage successfully, I still wanted human contact. So, I stayed with the diplomatic corps, where everyone was transferred every other year. Whenever I arrived in a new location, I began dating the guy who was the next to be transferred. After he'd leave, I'd move on to the guy who'd be transferred after him. Within two years, every man I dated would, by sheer logistics, get ditched. The potential for genuine intimacy was nil. And I'd move through the lot of them, without pain or remorse. I lined them up and, when I was ready, I moved along. After relinquishment, the men in my life were interchangeable, like soldiers in a parade."

Sylvia's career provided her the perfect opportunity to avoid the commitment, conformity, and intimacy of marriage, while it allowed her to sustain herself with serially monogamous relationships, companionship, and sex. Even birthmothers with less ideal careers, however, sometimes established similar routines of short-lived, superficial romances in quick sequence. By dating many men in succession, women like Sylvia prevented men from coming close enough either to consider marriage or to threaten the often flimsy and not too transparent "invisible shields" that protected them from the anguish of intimacy, whether remembered or imagined.

Happily Ever After

A third of the birthmothers interviewed were happily married. Many, failing in their first, found happiness in their second unions. Even when their marriages were successful, however, most felt the repercussions of relinquishment.

"I tested my husband for years," says Paula, who relinquished in 1971. "I wouldn't believe that he could accept the fact that I'd had a baby with another man, let alone how I felt about it. But, after twenty years, he's never let me down on this. He's been supportive and understanding and patient, and he's gone along with whatever crutches I've leaned on, from psychiatrists to psychics, astrologists to adoption groups. He's paid the bills for all this 'help,' and he's stayed up listening to me cry when it hasn't worked. I guess, until this interview, I've taken all that for granted. Relinquishing was there before we married, and it's hung over us ever since. But, it's amazing—I've really never thought about what that meant to our marriage, or how it's affected us, until now."

Like Paula, many birthmothers were so wrapped up in their own reactions to relinquishment that they were unable to consider the effects it had on their spouses. Even those who did realize its impact on others often felt powerless to do anything about it. Some, on the other hand, didn't *want* to mitigate anything; in fact, a number became rather militant in their insistence on keeping relinquishment a central focus in their lives.

"I divorced my first husband after eighteen years," says Barbara, who relinquished in 1956. "After all those years of pretending that everything was just fine, I wasn't able to pretend anymore. I wasn't going to keep relinquishing a secret anymore, either. Relinquishing became a sort of litmus test for anyone who wanted to get close to me. I'd tell women about it before they became my friends, men before the first date. If they couldn't accept it—if they even had *any* judgmental attitudes or hesitations—they were out of my life. It was that simple, that definite. My second marriage has worked, and I know it's because I can be who I am: I can admit what I feel; I can talk to my husband and trust him to love and respect me. I was unable to do this thirty-three years ago, when I married the first time. It took lots of time and lots of work, but I came out of the darkness and demanded that the people around me look at me and at my secret, and that they accept me as I am, or reject me. Either way, I'm better off than I was, pretending to be somebody else, hiding in the shadows."

Birthmothers who are happily married usually attribute their happiness, at least in part, to their husbands' unreserved acceptance of their pasts and support of their efforts to cope with their feelings. Some, however, feel that their marriages work primarily because their husbands have helped them "forget" about the past.

Mary, for example, believes that her husband's lack of attention to the past has encouraged her to concentrate on the present and on their family.

"I was raped," she says. "I don't want to spend the rest of my life dwelling on that. I went through enough, just carrying the child and going through the legal process of relinquishing rights. I suppose I could ponder the situation and feel sorry for myself. But why should I? I have a couple of healthy sons and a loving husband, and I think it's just as well that we live our lives without looking back and dwelling on a cruel twist of fate lurking in the dim, faraway past."

Others who were not raped sometimes share Mary's vehement determination to ignore relinquishment and its effect on their subsequent intimate relationships. Clinging to their current roles and relationships, some are so deeply stuck in denial that they have built their marriages and families around it.

"Forgetting isn't really possible," Lynne says. "But the fact is that I owe my marriage and family to the act of relinquishing. If I'd kept that child, I'd never have returned to college and met my husband. I'd have based my life on a mistake, an accident, and I'd have become a bitter, lonely, single mother, struggling to make ends meet. Relinquishment was the smartest and the best thing I could have done, the happiest for everyone. The most important way it has affected my marriage is that it permitted it to happen. When I think of relinquishing, I think, 'Thank God.' Because everything good that has happened to me since—meeting my husband, marrying him, and having and raising his children—could never have happened without it."

Intimacy After Relinquishment

Most of the women interviewed believed that, because of their relinquishing experiences, they had many more problems with intimacy than other groups of women. Most felt that relinquishment had been a pivotal point in their lives, after which everything changed, including their abilities to relate to others. In general, these women saw their marriages and other intimate relationships as extensions of their inner realities regarding relinquishing. Most agreed that their problems with intimacy were not limited to marriages or relationships with men but extended to friendships with women and interactions with their parents and siblings as well. Many became emotionally estranged from everyone who had been involved, however remotely, in the process of surrender. Those whose trust and self-confidence had been casualties of relinquishing felt that, without these qualities, their subsequent relationships were, from the start, destined to be impaired. And, even if prerelinquishment relationships survived surrender, they often changed irrevocably because birthmothers felt differently about others and themselves. Relationships formed *after* relinquishment were often built on secrecy or false pretense, based more on function than emotion, and limited in intimacy or trust.

The difficulties these women experienced in their close relationships, of course, might have occurred even if their unplanned pregnancies had never occurred. Some wondered if their relinquishments were not the symptoms of their relationship problems rather than the causes. Most, however, believed that, no matter what prior problems they'd had, relinquishing was the single traumatic experience that pushed them over the threshold and set their lives on a downhill course. Some who tended to have problems with close relationships prior to relinquishment were convinced that relinquishment had cemented these tendencies, locking them into depression and anger or demolishing their self-esteem and abilities to trust.

Among those interviewed, more than one in ten had attempted suicide. More than one in five had entered abusive postrelinquishment relationships. Over half had been divorced. About one fifth developed eating disorders, becoming either emaciated or obese. More than one in five developed secondary infertility. Most, regardless of their marital status, remained permanently incapable of trust and intimacy.

Whether or not relinquishment *was* the single, critical factor leading to their subsequent problems with intimacy and marriage, birthmothers generally saw it as such. Desperate to break out of grief and isolation and to succeed in marriage and other close relationships, birthmothers often sought help from a battalion of sources, including relatives, clergy, literature, psychotherapists, psychiatrists, astrologists, psychics, friends, husbands, and each other. From each, they found varying degrees of help, but more than any other single source, the support they found the most effective came from other birthmothers. Having evaluated the available resources, most concluded that *only* other birthmothers could understand their feelings or problems; many were unable to trust or confide in anyone else.

Those who were the most happy and successful in their intimate relationships were those whose partners encouraged them to address openly the issues that haunted them and to seek contact with others who could provide understanding and support. One woman, however, married for the second time, pointed out that, because marriage and, in fact, all close relationships were actually "reflections of her inner life," the integration of relinquishment experiences was required before she—or *any* birthmother—could achieve success in marriage. If her theory is correct, no intimate relationships with others can be truly successful until birthmothers achieve and succeed with a certain level of introspective intimacy, facing the truths of their feelings, and loving, trusting, and forgiving themselves.

6

Parenting

Raising Kids After Relinquishing

THE SCHOOL BUS VEERED SHARPLY TO THE LEFT TO AVOID THE STRAY
dog. The driver of the van, speeding through the intersection,
never saw the dog and noticed the bus too late. The impact of the
crash sent the bus spinning onto its side. Children screamed.
Shards of glass splattered the asphalt. Bloody hands, then heads
poked through the rear emergency door. There was a smell of
gasoline, and suddenly, as Carla ran from her house to retrieve her
children, the bus exploded in a ball of orange flame. . . .

"Mom!" Timmy was tugging on her sleeve. Carla turned from
the kitchen window to her youngest son. "Please, Mom? Just
one?"

Carla had no idea what he was asking for, but she was so glad
he was safe that she couldn't say no. "OK. Just one."

"Thanks!" He spun around to go get whatever it was, but she
pulled him back.

"Not so fast," Carla tried to sound calm, but she needed to
touch him. She grabbed a damp cloth and wiped his face, an
excuse for detaining him. Then she rechecked his hands and

retucked his shirt. When she began to rearrange his hair, he squirmed. "Mom, I gotta go—The bus is coming."

Before she could kiss him, he sped off to the cookie jar. Carla checked the clock. The boys would leave in minutes. Her stomach knotted. She considered keeping Timmy home from school. How much, after all, would he miss in one day of first grade? Maybe she could declare an impromptu holiday and keep them all home—take them to a museum? Maybe she could pick them up early? Maybe . . . .

"Timmy, let's go!" Stevie, the eldest, flipped his bookbag over his shoulder and held the door open. "Bye, Mom—bus's coming!"

Carla ran to him, heart racing. "Wait! Stevie?"

"What?" He was twelve, a young man, impatient. The bus chugged up the hill, nearing their corner. Carla searched for an excuse, something important to delay him. As usual, though, she was too panicked to think and, besides, Jeff thundered down the stairs and flew past her. "Later, Mom!" He was ten and felt too big to kiss her anymore.

"What *is* it, Mom?" Stevie was waiting.

Carla flushed awkwardly. "Uh, uh . . . do you have your lunch?"

"Naw, Mom! I'm eating in the cafeteria! Gotta go!"

Shouts of "See you, Mom" trailed after the boys as they stampeded down the hill. Carla stood at the door, watching the bus drive away. She stared at the empty street until she couldn't hear the motor anymore. Still listening, she went to the kitchen and paused next to Timmy's half-eaten cereal. There were no sirens, no crashes, no phone calls.

Unsteady hands piled Timmy's dish onto Jeff's, Jeff's onto Steve's. Wrist-deep in soapsuds, Carla saw recess, the playground, broken legs, and crushed fingers. Concussions. Baseballs flying into heads. Accidents on slides, on monkey bars. On seesaws. Strangers. Drugs. Needles. Kidnappings. No!

Carla dried her hands and checked the clock. In seven hours they would be home. Nothing would happen to them. They would *not* disappear, not die. She would *not* sit and study their photographs. She would *not* call the school, *not* go over there. She would keep busy. She would function for another day. Already, just by washing dishes, she'd gotten through a full fifteen minutes.

Having Kids

About four-fifths of the women interviewed had children after they relinquished. In parenting, as in their other intimate relationships, they manifested a tendency for the extreme. Most either had babies right away, within two years, or waited at least a decade. They had either just one more child or, like over half of those interviewed, more than three. They either sought to be perfect mothers or felt unworthy to parent at all.

As mothers, many were overprotective and clinging, haunted by fears of danger and impending loss. Some overcompensated for these feelings and, determined not to overprotect, actively pushed their children away. A number vacillated emotionally between smothering overinvolvement and aloof distance, surprising even themselves with the contrasts. Those who adopted the role of "perfect wife" usually extended their ambitions to become the "perfect mother" as well. Some "perfect" wives, however, found that revived motherhood sent them out of denial and into explosive confrontation with their losses and suppressed grief.

As their families grew, some women hid their relinquishments, concealing their first child's existence from half- or even full siblings. Others told their younger children about the relinquishments, adding absent, ghostlike brothers or sisters to their family circles.

Those who did not have additional children tended to idealize the role of mother in general and their relinquished children in particular. About one in five developed secondary infertility, which many attributed to the trauma of relinquishing. A few who were later unable to conceive wanted to parent so badly that they adopted the children of other birthmothers. Others, presumably able to conceive, were simply too afraid or angry to try and abstained from motherhood altogether. Some had abortions rather than give birth again.

Whether or not they actually had more children, regardless of when, why, or under what terms they had relinquished, the topics of motherhood and parenting stirred up relinquishment issues for *every* birthmother interviewed. Relinquishing, they were convinced, had either profoundly affected how they parented or been a critical factor in determining that they never would.

More Is Not Always Better

"I had four more babies in the next six years," Alexis says. "I had the first three hoping to replace the baby I'd relinquished. Only the youngest was born after I'd abandoned the illusion that I could. He's the only one who was born because I wanted a different child than the one I'd given up."

Soon after surrender, many birthmothers felt a longing to "reconnect" with their babies. Unable to reclaim them, however, many attempted to replace them and connect with new babies instead. Because the "replacements" were not the originals, however, their longings remained unsatisfied and persisted, often leading to further futile attempts at reconnection through additional births.

Sometimes giving birth again actually enhanced rather than diminished birthmothers' feelings of loss. Bridget had four children during her marriage. "I'd been told by the adoption authorities that once I had another child, I'd forget all about relinquishing. But the other babies didn't make me forget—they only magnified the loss of my firstborn. The emotional pain associated with each birth was terrible. I relived the loss each time. 'Where is my *other* beautiful baby?' was all I could think or feel."

Some who were desperate to replace their first babies were devastated when their next ones were of the opposite sex. "I cried when I found out we'd had a son," said one birthmother. "I wanted a girl just like the one I'd given up the year before." However, even some whose next babies were the same sex as those they'd relinquished felt that they had lost the "perfect" child when they surrendered.

"I married the birthfather," Jill says. "We had another son within two years. But, while I was pregnant the second time, I had German measles. The baby was born with cataracts. He was deaf, retarded, and had a heart murmur. He's twenty-seven years old now, but he's needed constant care and repeated operations just to survive. We had three more children after that. They were all girls. I know how weird it sounds, but I believe that I've been punished by God for giving up my firstborn healthy son. My second son's merely an innocent victim of God's judgment for what my husband and I did wrong. My daughters are healthy. But God never let me have another healthy, normal son."

Although most birthmothers did not interpret their children's problems as God's punishment for relinquishment, many shared Jill's frustration at being unable to satisfy their longings for the babies they'd given up. Even years later, "happy" occasions like Mother's Days, birthdays, family vacations, or holidays found these women feeling melancholy and incomplete, yearning to include their surrendered children in the celebrations. Those whose spouses insisted that they keep silent about relinquishment found their longings and frustrations especially difficult to bear. "I'd promised my husband that I would never mention the child I'd given up," Bridget recalls. "So I obediently kept all my thoughts and feelings about the baby to myself. But, in doing so, I lost my former identity. A blank new persona, that of wife and mother, was created. And these new roles required that I bury my former self, avoid controversy, avoid exposure, avoid truth."

Although the births of new babies could not relieve their grief or soothe their longings, birthmothers like Bridget found that the role of mother brought new bonds and demands that dominated their daily activities, if not their emotional lives. Even those who had largely suppressed their relinquishment experiences, however, often saw the shadows of their buried former selves reflected in the patterns of their parenting.

Perfection and Grace

"I had to be a perfect mother," Bridget says, "as well as a perfect hostess, housekeeper, and wife. I had to be perfect at every traditional, 'normal' role in order to cover up the imperfect woman hiding underneath. I saw to my children's educations, religious training, and discipline. But, more than anything, I was always affectionate. I loved, appreciated, and enjoyed them from the depth of my being, because I knew how lucky I was to have them."

The need to be perfect mothers was described again and again by birthmothers. Like Bridget, many were driven not only to raise their children well but also to atone for their pasts, hide their secrets, and even acquire, through motherhood, new identities. For some, however, perfection was too vague a term; they often had trouble distinguishing between keeping their children happy and being "good" mothers.

"I had an intense need to be the best of all possible mothers," says Sue, who had three children during her marriage. "I never let a baby cry. I always picked them up and held and cuddled them, all night if necessary. I was easy on discipline. I let them talk back to me. I never was comfortable making them unhappy or angry with me. I guess I was afraid they'd stop loving me. Or maybe I was punishing myself, giving in when I didn't want to because I felt that they were more deserving than I was. I'd sacrifice sleep, time, money—whatever *they* wanted counted more than what *I* wanted. Now that the youngest is a preteen, I can see that I've spoiled them. But I wanted to please them—I needed them to see me as perfect."

When perfect parenting became confused with keeping children perfectly happy, mothers often left their children without consistency, limits, or structure. Those who, like Sue, tolerated behaviors that they wanted to discipline and indulged whims that they wanted to stifle ironically became more perfect at pandering than at parenting. Instead of acquiring new self-respect and stronger identities as mothers, they repeated behavior patterns they'd exhibited during relinquishment, such as avoiding assertiveness and denying their own feelings. Further, because they were afraid to test it by setting limits, these women never learned that the love they felt for their children *was* reciprocated. Instead, they tiptoed through motherhood as through other relationships, doubting that anyone—even their own children—could love their "real" selves, complete with imperfections, tempers, and needs of their own.

For some, striving to be perfect mothers became a fundamental part of their overall penance for relinquishing. "Guilt and self-sacrifice has dominated my parenting," Sonia says. "I loved my children, but I hated being stuck at home. I'd loved my professional life and felt frustrated, isolated, and lost without it. But I gave it up for my kids. I felt I *had* to stay home with them—I'd already abandoned one child; I was not about to abandon the others, for even a few hours a day, no matter what personal price I had to pay."

Mothering and Secrecy

"I married my baby's father," says Callie, "and we had four more children together. We never told them, for twenty-five years, that they had another brother. We kept it secret. I never talked about it, even with my husband. I kept my feelings to myself all this time, until three years ago. It's something that I thought about and felt every day, but I was afraid to face. It was as if I'd lose everything I had, as if the ground would fall out from under me if I talked about it. Finally, I saw a television show, a talk show. They showed a birthmother meeting her thirty-year-old daughter on daytime TV, and I started bawling. And right there, in front of three of my kids, I let the truth out. They were surprised. And they wanted me to calm down, but nobody stopped *loving* me. I was still their mom. One of them, who was fifteen at the time, even started to cry with me, because she was so overwhelmed and thrilled to have an older brother."

A number of birthmothers were reluctant or afraid to reveal the secrets of relinquishing to their other children. Some, like Callie, feared the judgment of or even rejection by their children; others were afraid of alienating their spouses by rekindling issues of the past. Many saw secrecy as merely one of many "motherhood" issues, as just another requirement for perfection, acceptability, or success. Having idealized the role of mother, they felt obliged to hide any aspect of themselves that did not measure up to their own images of maternal purity.

"Before I relinquished," Sheila recalls, "I'd been told by the adoption authorities that I wasn't 'fit' to parent a child on my own, that I wasn't 'worthy' to be a mother. Having been convinced of that made me want to prove, when I had kids later, that I was worthy—no, that I was *better* than worthy—that I was the best damn Supermom in the world! There was no task too great, no car pool too crowded, no Cub Scout pack too wild for me to tame. I cooked on campfires. I went fishing. I slept in tents and hiked and did whatever my little boys wanted to do, so that I could prove I was a good mom. Of course, there was a flip side to that. Because, if I proved that I *was* a good mom, I was left with no excuse for relinquishing my first child. If I was fit and worthy, then *why* had I given him up? So, to avoid this question, I've preferred, most of the time, to buy into the idea that I *am* secretly unworthy, that I'm really no good deep down, and that I have merely pretended to be a capable PTA president, room mother, and swim team chaperone so that no one would find out the truth or expose the real me."

For women like Sheila, motherhood after relinquishing felt unreal or unattainable, requiring a series of disguises to mask the past, hide the truth, and replace the label of "birthmother" with that of "good mother." Unfortunately, by concealing the facts, they condemned themselves to living with fears and anxieties about what would happen if their secrets were ever revealed.

"Every time I see one of those articles about adoptees who search for their birthparents," Sheila remarks, "I break out in hives. My daughter is in her twenties today. I don't know what I'd do if she ever showed up here. I couldn't go through all that, exposing all my shame to my other children, who see me as just a regular, 'normal' mom."

Women like Sheila preferred the stresses of secrecy to the stigma they believed the truth could cast over their families. Others, however, found that secrecy was imposed on them by others. Rhonda's immediate family resented the openness with which she informed her younger children about their relinquished half-brother. "My brothers-in-law and sisters told me quite explicitly that they did *not* want their children to know about 'my mess,' which is how they referred to my relinquishment. In fact, they said that unless I guaranteed that my kids would never mention it to their kids, they didn't want our kids to play together, and, for years, they wouldn't let their kids come over to my house unsupervised, for fear that they'd find out about my secret 'mess.'"

Even when women like Rhonda managed to be truthful and incorporated relinquishment into their family lives, the judgments of others often inhibited them. And sometimes the sources of these judgments lay within rather than outside their homes.

Mothering by Paternal Decree

"I'm always afraid of upsetting my husband," Sue says. "He's always been so threatened by the fact that I'd had a son with somebody else that secrecy about relinquishing was never a decision in our marriage; it was just *assumed*. But, as our children grew older, I felt more and more torn about that secrecy. I became sure that our sons had the right to know that they have a half-brother somewhere, but I hesitated to tell them. My husband's feelings were only partly responsible—I was also afraid that my children wouldn't feel the same about me anymore, if I told them. I was afraid they'd have contempt for me or be disillusioned about their mom. But then, one day, my twelve-year-old son was home with the flu and *Splendor in the Grass* was on TV. We watched it together. I cried and he asked me why. Without planning to, I told him that the movie touched me because, when I'd been a teenager,

I'd had a baby and given him up for adoption. It was a spontaneous admission, truthful and unrehearsed. It brought us closer, but I had to ask him not to tell the other boys or his father, so secrecy continued to dominate our family. But there had been a change. Because I knew that I *would* tell the others one day, and that they would *not* stop loving me or think I was 'unfit.' And, at last, I knew that my lost son—and the truth—would, eventually, become part of all of our lives."

Several birthmothers' husbands insisted that their children not be informed of their relinquishments. Other husbands demanded control of how, when, and exactly what the children were told. These conditions often enhanced birthmothers' feelings of shame, insecurity, and unworthiness. For some, the judgments implicit in forced secrecy impeded the resolution of their grief and acceptance of their losses. For others, the secrecy itself was so damaging that it contributed to the dissolution of their families.

"My husband ordered me not to tell the children about relinquishing," Bridget says. "He insisted that *he* have complete control over what our children knew about me, and he created an image of me as a 'perfect' woman. He said that *he* would decide when the time was right for them to know the truth and that *he* would tell them in the way *he* saw fit, in order to spare them any shock or disillusionment. I see now, after we've divorced, that he used my shame as a means of controlling me and that he used secrecy as a means of degrading me. I'm not proud that I relinquished a child. But I am who I am, not a statue, not a goddess, and my children can accept my mistakes, just as I accept theirs. It was not my relinquishment that was a secret; it was my humanity. Now that I've revealed it to them, I can breathe without fear. I can be a whole person, not just an image."

Most who kept their relinquishments secret from their other children feared, like Sue and Bridget, that the truth might destroy their children's trust, affection, or respect. Some, however, had even greater fears regarding their children. To them, revealing their secrets was just one threatening possibility on a seemingly endless list.

Mothering in Fear

"If they went to the pool," one birthmother says, "I *knew* they'd drown. If they went on a car trip, I *knew* there would be an accident. If they were late coming home, I'd drive along the road, searching ditches for their bodies. I was quiet about it, but I was always afraid that I'd lose them. No, not afraid—I was certain that something would happen to take them away."

More than half of the birthmothers interviewed had, at some point, been plagued with fears of losing their children. Although their relinquishments were, at least legally, made voluntarily, many compared their emotions to those of mothers of kidnap or murder victims, who see their surviving children as unusually vulnerable. Even those who had positive attitudes about relinquishing often felt exaggerated concern and grappled with unreasonable fears for the safety of their other children.

For some, the fears were specific to infants. Until their children had grown beyond infancy and no longer resembled their relinquished babies, these women were unable to relax and enjoy motherhood. "My husband was delighted when I went into labor," Gloria says. "But I couldn't think about labor. I was terrified of afterwards. I was afraid of losing the baby. After he was born, I wouldn't separate from him for an instant! I insisted that he room-in with me, and this was 1970—years before most hospitals did that. I held him in the recovery room. That was also unheard of back then. He was vomiting the day we were to leave, and they wanted to keep him another day, but I wouldn't allow it. I insisted that he leave with me. I was sure I'd never see him again if I let him out of my sight just once."

Rhonda found the birth of her second postrelinquishment baby even more difficult than that of the first. "My first baby in marriage was healthy, and I doubted that God would allow me to have *two* healthy kids. I expected some punishment to be exacted on me through my children, because of relinquishing. It was like waiting for a shoe to drop—I didn't know what to expect or when, but I thought punishment would come. So, while I was pregnant with my youngest, I was constantly afraid I'd miscarry. Or that something would be wrong with the baby. Even when my baby was born healthy, I couldn't stop worrying. I nursed him constantly. I couldn't stand to go out or to be away from him, even to go to dinner or a movie with my husband. I checked six or eight times each night for crib death. I listened to him breathe all night long. I couldn't relax until his first birthday, when, for some reason, I accepted that he'd be OK. Even today, fifteen years later, I don't like to hold infants or even to be around them. I teach preschool and love children. But I'm uncomfortable about newborns and babies up until they're about ten months old, when they can stand up and look like kids, not babies."

Smothering Mothering

For birthmothers like Rhonda, mothering became less threatening as their children grew. For others, however, the role of mother meant maintaining a constant state of alert. Anticipating retribution or loss, many unwittingly or unwillingly became overprotective and clingy.

"I didn't let them go *anywhere*, unless I was there," Lisa admits. "I made up excuses to prevent them from going to play at their friends' houses. I had their friends come to our house, so I'd be able to see my kids or hear their voices. I was uncomfortable whenever I couldn't see, hear, or touch them."

Many overprotective birthmothers claimed to be unable to identify the source of their feelings; some denied that they stemmed from relinquishing. However, those who suppressed or denied the significance of their relinquishment experiences had particular difficulty finding other explanations for their clinginess and fears.

"I had problems with my kids," Cindy says. "I was protective to an abnormal degree. I didn't connect this to what happened when I was fifteen, though. All I knew was that if they went to sleep over at a friend's, I'd panic and cry all night. If they went to camp or skiing, I'd not eat or sleep for days at a time. I'd stay in my room, hiding, until they came back. I wanted them with me, home, all the time. My husband was generally supportive, but when it came to this, he was unable to understand and told me I was hurting our kids by not letting go. I went to psychologists and therapists, but that only wore me out—it didn't help. Nothing helped, even talking with therapists about relinquishing. The only time I finally began to feel better and relax about my kids was when my twenty-two-year-old relinquished child found me and we were reunited. That's when, suddenly, it all came together and I didn't feel clutchy or fear separations anymore."

Like Cindy, many birthmothers were able to overcome maternal overinvolvements and fears only after they had confronted their feelings about relinquishment. For some, those confrontations were precipitated by reunions; for others, by therapists, support groups, spouses, or their own maturity and initiative. For many, however, the source of their neediness and fears remained obscure. These women often continued to grasp and clutch at their children for decades, unable to control or overcome the haunting terrors that dominated their motherhood.

"I try not to be as overprotective in reality as I am in my mind," Annie says. "Even now, when my youngest is a teenager, I'm *always* afraid something will happen to one of them. There is a constant undercurrent of fear, a threat of loss. I had each of them sleep in my room for the first two years of their lives. I was afraid of accidents. I was afraid of falls, diseases, parks, bikes. Later, I was afraid of motorcycles, cars, and sports. I was even afraid to say no, because they might reject me and leave. I *expected* them to leave, actually. I was certain that I would lose them, as I'd lost my first child, one way or another."

Mothering on a Seesaw

"After relinquishing, I was unable to trust anyone," Liz admits. "I was always afraid of being hurt. Loving anybody seemed like risking more pain. And my children, well, I was *afraid* of them. Because I loved them so much, I was always waiting for them to bring me pain. For me, motherhood was just another arena where I could be hurt. That seems clear to me now that my kids are both grown. But, when they were little, I reacted to the fear without understanding it. I went up and down. I had bouts of drinking and bouts of abstinence. Bouts of ambition when I'd take college courses, and bouts of depression when I'd stay in bed all day. I was super stable or I was a mess. And I mothered the same way. I was either completely involved in my children's lives, or I was completely removed. If got too close, alarm bells went off and sent me reeling. It took years of therapy and support from others to help me identify this pattern, let alone to deal with it. And I still can't separate maternal love from fear."

Vacillations between intimacy and distance, between embracing and rejecting their children, were frequent among birthmothers. "I felt like I was nothing, not worthy of my children's love," one says. "And I was so afraid that they'd reject me or that I'd lose them that I protected myself by pushing them away before they could push *me* away."

Some of the birthmothers who alternated between emotional extremes were able to control their behavior enough to protect their children. Others, however, admitted that the children they have raised have ridden their emotional roller coasters alongside them. "I tend to be either overinvolved or totally detached," Peg says. "I can't feel too close. I shut down. Yet, when I shut down, I become afraid that my children will drift away from me, so my detachment triggers my overinvolvement, which triggers my detachment, due to fear of getting hurt by overinvolvement. The whole cycle is clear to me, but I can't control it. After fourteen years of parenting, I'm still unable to reach any equilibrium and function steadily or consistently as a mother."

Jill says that the emotional extremes she's endured with her children have been reflected in other ways as well. "I'm emotionally uneven with them. It's difficult for me to sustain closeness with them. I love them, but I get moody and depressed. When I'm depressed, I overeat. So my weight goes up and down with my moods. I punish myself for feeling distant, especially from my handicapped son. I punish myself for wishing my girls were boys, like the baby I gave up. I punish myself for punishing myself. And my kids feel the effects of my mood swings. I feel guilty about it, but I can't seem to control it."

Although some had problems with maintaining consistent intimacy prior to relinquishing, most birthmothers saw the surrender of the babies as the origin of their emotional seesaws. Many felt permanently imbalanced, impaired in their abilities to maintain consistent love or trust. Accordingly, they found parenting to be a series of emotional swings and switches, up and down and on and off. Some were so haunted by feelings of unworthiness that, periodically, they defensively warded off their own children's unquestioning, unconditional love and fell into recurring bouts of despair. Often, the younger they were at the time of relinquishment, the more they blamed it for the problems they faced in their subsequent maternal roles.

"I was not fifteen yet when I relinquished my son," Jill continues. "After that, I never grew up. I wanted my baby back, so I had another baby and then another and another. *I* wasn't important— only my babies mattered. So I never finished school. I never went out in the world and worked. Instead, I was caught up in heartaches for babies, for one that was gone forever and for another that was retarded and needed operation after operation. I stopped developing as a person, when I relinquished. In many ways, I'm still fourteen and not ready, not developed as a person, not complete enough myself to be a confident mother. I guess the part of me that wants to grow up is the part that tries to get free of the children by pushing them away. But I love them, so I can't."

Mothering by a Map

Some birthmothers reacted to the lack of control they felt about relinquishing by taking strict control of *all* their subsequent experiences, including parenting. As mothers, these women often held particularly tight reins over issues that had played parts in their relinquishment decisions.

For Pam, a lack of money had been a critical factor in her decision. When she later married the father of her relinquished child, she was unable to rid herself of concern about finances, even after the couple had acquired substantial savings and assets. "I've planned every step of our marriage," she says. "And it's all been about security, about making our family safe and keeping us together. At first, I worked and saved every penny, so that I'd later be able to stay home as a full-time mother. I had to give up my first baby because I didn't have money, and I wasn't about to run into similar problems again. So I worked and saved and saved and worked. We bought a home—with cash. No mortgage. It took seven years of saving everything, but we had a home and, after I knew my baby would be safe, I gave birth within a year."

Often, once their families were started, mothers like Pam eased up on their careful planning and lost their tight control amid baby tears and diaper changes. However, some birthmothers applied their techniques of control not only to the creation but also to the management of their families. Pam claims that she and her husband carefully planned the process and philosophy by which they raised their postrelinquishment children.

"We are, you might say, 'gung-ho' parents," she says. "We do scouting and camping, and my husband's a Little League coach. We both go out of our way to be active parts of their lives. We touch, show physical affection, and we communicate. For us, parenting is a very conscious process. I love my kids, but I don't react to them emotionally as much as rationally. I *think* about what a 'good' mother would do and then I do it, especially when I'm upset, especially when I'm tired. I don't let emotions rule our family. It's controlled, it's calm, it's a place we can let our guards down and feel safe."

Like Pam, many birthmothers needed to create environments of security and safety before they would again attempt motherhood. Often, relinquishing had left them with generalized, sometimes unconscious associations between parenting and danger, parenting and loss, or parenting and threat. These feelings, in turn, led them to change the ways that they built families and parented.

"More than anything, I want my children to be secure," Pam says. "I want a stable home. I want money in the bank. I breast-fed all three of my kids for a year, so they'd feel secure from infancy. I give them whatever I can—time, affection, or material things. They never lack for anything. I was unable to afford a crib for my first child, and I don't want my others ever to worry about having things. To some, that may seem like I'm spoiling them. To me, it's a statement about security. About protection. About *having*, instead of not having. I want them to know that they *have*."

Mothers who planned their lives and families in order to achieve security or protection for their children often achieved some additional *un*planned results, including spoiled children. Further, many learned that not even their most determined efforts could assure that they would feel secure or keep their families safe from the effects of the past.

"I'd saved so that I wouldn't have to work after my kids were born," Pam continues, "but I couldn't let myself quit, and, when they were small, I moved my office into my home and continued to work. No amount of money in our accounts, no stocks or bonds or real estate was enough to make me feel safe. I've always needed more. It feels as if I could lose my other children, or that they'll be in danger, if we don't keep bringing in cash. Money, to me, means protection. So, there's never too much—you can't be too safe. But even with all our assets and all the love I feel for my children, there is something else that I can't control in our family: I still feel the pain of losing my first child, almost twenty years later. And the pain of missing *that* son separates me from the other kids sometimes, so much so that I feel I can't be there with them. So the bottom line is that I've built this big, expensive fortress to protect my family and keep us all together, but I'm locked out by my own past. No walls can keep out my pain."

Mothering Under Thunderclouds

"I was seventeen when I relinquished," Zoe says. "I was forty before I dared to have another child. I see now that I was grieving for all those years. I was doing my penance by denying myself the pleasures of having a child. But, once I finally went ahead and had another, everything fell apart. I couldn't *look* at my second baby without crying and longing for my first."

A number of birthmothers put off having more children after relinquishing, often for reasons similar to Zoe's. Some were punishing themselves; others could not repeat pregnancy and childbirth because their memories were too painful. Those who gathered up their courage and had other children often waited at least a decade to do so. Time alone, however, was rarely enough to prepare them for motherhood. When they gave birth again, many, especially those who had kept their relinquishments secret, found that they released not only a child but also a torrent of pent-up emotions.

"I fell into acute depression after my second child was born," Andrea says. "I'd waited seventeen years, but I still wasn't ready. I cried constantly, without even knowing why I was crying. I was afraid of the dark. I was afraid to be left alone. I developed all kinds of physical symptoms—vomiting, skin rashes, breast infections. I couldn't eat. I either slept all day or couldn't sleep at all. I lost fifty pounds in the first six weeks—much more than I'd gained while I was pregnant. I went to a specialist about the weight loss, and, without planning to, I blurted out, 'I gave up a baby for adoption when I was seventeen.' He referred me to a psychiatrist, and, for the first time in almost two decades, I began to *talk* about relinquishing. And once I began to talk, there was no stopping the flood of tears, sorrow, and anger that came pouring out."

After they gave birth again, birthmothers' unresolved grief sometimes revealed itself through physical symptoms. For Andrea, antidepressant medications, eight months of intensive therapy, and a careful regimen of rest and proper diet were sufficient to allay the acutely physical manifestations of her grief. Not every birthmother was as successful, however. Cindy spent years in therapy without noticeable results.

"Fourteen years ago, after my youngest son was born," she says, "I knew I couldn't bear my depression alone anymore. I needed help. It had gotten worse with each new baby, to the point where I was physically worn down, actually ill. With my youngest, it got so bad that I wanted to be put away. I felt worthless, unlovable. I felt like a fraud. I loved my kids and my husband, but I never knew if I'd get through the day. So I went to a shrink. I told him about relinquishing. He said nothing. Not a word. Silence. I felt rejected by his silence, but I went to him for a year, hoping it would get better, but he never said a single sentence that would help me. So I continued to fight depression on my own and to try to hide it, so it wouldn't affect my family. After another year, I saw an ad about a depression clinic. My therapist there talked to me, but she didn't think relinquishing was as significant as my early childhood and my relationship with my mother. So, after another year, I stopped going. It didn't seem to be helping. For ten more years, I struggled on my own to control desperate unhappiness while being calm on the surface, taking care of my kids, and being good to my husband. But all the time, and I mean *all* the time, I was upset or depressed. I hid my emotions and pretended to be OK. But I had no self-confidence, no self-esteem.

"Finally, my kids got older and I was alone all day. Without them, I didn't know how to keep going. I felt sick. I had no protection from my feelings anymore—no kids to keep me too busy to think. I had no confidence to look for a job. No sense that I could do anything or matter to anyone. So I tried again and went to a new therapist. For two years, relinquishing is all we've talked about. And she's helped me face it, all I've been holding in for all these years."

Although relinquishment was not the sole cause of their depression, birthmothers like Cindy saw it as primary in a series of traumatic events that left them emotionally scarred. As mothers, later in life, these women lacked self-assurance and confidence.

Some managed to protect themselves for years from facing their emotional problems by busily playing the role of mother. Like Cindy, they suppressed their depression and fears until some unpredictable event or their children's gradually increasing independence blew the lid off their facades of calm domesticity, exposing their simmering emotional states.

"I lied to my husband and to my kids," Cindy says. "I lied about what happened in the past, about how I'd gotten pregnant, about who I was inside and about how I felt about the baby I'd given up. Each lie weighed me down until I hit bottom. I felt unlovable. I had no self-respect and no idea how to be a woman. I was faking all the time. I was unable to trust anyone and sure that I was no good. I could have started drinking or taking pills. Or I could even have tried to kill myself, I felt so bad. But my kids kept me going. My kids have been my salvation. They needed me, trusted me, loved me. So I hung in there for them and my husband and tried to be whatever it was that they expected me to be, no matter how hard it was or how bad I felt inside."

Some birthmothers who endured similar depression believed that they would have suffered these bouts even if they had *not* relinquished. A few referred to family histories of postpartum blues or chemical imbalances. Many, however, were convinced that their depression had originated with relinquishment, which irrevocably changed their lives.

"I was never allowed to grieve," Andrea says. "I had to keep my relinquishment secret, so I carried it with me, inside. I married, probably for the wrong reasons, to escape stigma, and my husband encouraged the secrecy. I tried to deny my feelings and to move on, and, on the surface, I managed. But when a new baby came, the sky fell. I felt crazy, lost, completely unable to care for an infant. But the doctor said I was only 'mildly' depressed. So I took the pills he prescribed and began to talk about what happened in the context of therapy, and, gradually, I became able to take care of my second child, to feel deserving of her and capable of caring for her. But it's hard to describe how deep that self-doubt goes. I'd been convinced that I was incapable of caring for my first child—

so incapable that he'd be better off with strangers than with me. It was hard to overcome that when I had a new infant depending on me. All that self-doubt had been festering inside, and it resurfaced every time my baby cried: Was I good enough for him? Did I know what to do? Could I trust myself? Was I deserving enough to mother him? It was awful. I fell apart from the guilt, the fear and the strain."

The desire to parent their children effectively finally gave a number of birthmothers the impetus to seek the emotional support and help they needed. Even counseling, however, was too little too late to help some feel confident as parents. "I wish," Zoe says, "that I'd gone into therapy with someone who understood what I was going through *before* I'd had another child. It's important to resolve your guilt first and to come to your children strong. They need you to be strong and to like yourself from the beginning. I don't think you can be a really good mom, no matter how much you love your kids, if you aren't comfortable with yourself."

Empty Wombs and Compromised Cradles

A fifth of the birthmothers interviewed had no more children after they relinquished. Some felt so guilty about relinquishing that they found pregnancy and childbirth too painful to repeat. Others, who had felt pressured or even forced into relinquishing, were too angry to try again. And a few found that a viable opportunity to have more children never arose.

"I relinquished the child I conceived in a rape," Savannah says. "After that, I wouldn't let a man near me for five years. I was in therapy and weighed just eighty-eight pounds. I felt I had no control over my life, and food was the only thing I could control. Eventually, I started to eat again, but I didn't date for another three or four years. When I did, I wouldn't let anyone touch me. It took a long time for me to realize that I'd been raped by *one* man, not by *all* men. Even then, I was known as 'frigid.' I'd panic if a man touched me. One guy told me I'd be a better nun than a wife.

Another called me 'Ms. Untouchable.' I didn't tell anyone what had happened until a man from my church proposed to me, several times. Finally, I told him about the rape and the baby I'd surrendered. I was overcome—a lot of welled-up emotions came out with the secret. He said he was sorry for what had happened to me, and he held me while I cried. After that, I never heard from him again. Ten years later, I'm married to a man who was a good friend of mine in high school. We have a good marriage, but I'm forty-three years old and I doubt that I'll have more kids. The violence of the rape and then of relinquishment—well, together they robbed me of my chances for a normal life, a normal sense of sexuality, and a normal marital relationship during the years in which I could have had a family."

Other birthmothers faced less traumatic but equally effective obstacles to motherhood. "Seven years after I relinquished, I fell in love with a man who'd had five children in his first marriage," one says. "He didn't want more children. Five was enough for him, so what *I* wanted didn't occur to either of us, at least not then. Now that I'm almost fifty, it seems tragic that neither of us ever addressed my feelings about becoming a mother, and now it's too late."

Some who *were* outspoken about wanting children were blocked by difficulties that included their husbands' infertility or even, surprisingly, their own. A number of birthmothers attributed their secondary infertility or repeated miscarriages not to quirks of nature but to the deep and pervasive effects of relinquishment.

"Birthmothers have twice as much trouble conceiving again as other women," Donna asserts. "I've heard that a lot at various support group meetings. I myself have had four miscarriages in three years. I think about getting pregnant all the time, even though I know I need to relax about it. The thing is, the doctor can't find any explanation for my miscarriages. I have normal hormones and no trouble conceiving. They've done every test there is to my uterine lining, and they can't find a thing wrong. I'm beginning to believe it's psychological, that I don't feel I deserve to be a mother, that, because I gave up my first child, I'm not worthy of having a child I can keep!"

Whether or not Donna's infertility statistics are correct, birthmothers as a group *believed* that they experienced significantly higher rates of secondary infertility than the "normal" population. Most were also convinced that the trauma and psychological aftermath of relinquishment were linked to this phenomenon. Among those who were unable to bear other children were a few who took on motherhood through other means, including, ironically, adoption.

Mothering in the Mind

"Two years after I relinquished," Alice says, "I developed cancer. When I married six years later, my husband and I adopted a child through the same agency that had arranged my own relinquishment. I've pondered this irony for years, and all the implications. But I have a message for birthmothers who've had no children after relinquishing. And that is: get a dose of children in your life. Babysit. Visit your brother's kids. Be a foster parent. Volunteer at Girl Scouts or the nursery school at church. Whatever—just to see that *real* kids are *not* the way we envision them. Real kids vomit, talk back, and cry all night when you're tired. Real kids are not always intelligent or pretty or clean. They do not put their toys away. They spill, stain carpets, and draw with magic markers on wallpaper. They are tiresome, demanding, rude, and they interrupt all the time. It's a trap for us birthmothers to idealize the tiny babies we gave up when most of us were too young or vulnerable to make a valid choice. But, if you realize that the baby you carry in your mind is *not* the child you—or anyone else—really had, you might have an easier, more grounded time. Kids *are* great. Spend time with some. You'll value your time away from them more."

Jean, another birthmother who adopted a child, thinks that relinquishing has given her a broad view of adoption that includes a place for every parent in the triangle. "Because I am a birthparent, I'm sensitive to my adopted child's birthparents. I am not threatened by them, nor do I confuse my role in his life with theirs. And because I know what it is to relinquish a child, I appreciate the chance to raise one even more deeply than I would have otherwise. I see the unique preciousness of each child more clearly. No matter what his or her biological origins are, the child's needs, not the adults', must come first."

Even if they did not have other chidren—biological, step, or adopted—most birthmothers had clear images of how they would have conducted themselves in the role of mother. Often, these images were idealized; usually, they reflected the same extremes exhibited by birthmothers who did parent children.

"I know I'll be overprotective," says one who still hopes to have children. "I'll be terrified to let my kids out of my sight, for fear I'll never see them again."

"I'd love them to death," another remarks. "I'd hug them all day long. I'd never deny them anything, I'd be so thankful just to have them."

"I wouldn't ever let them know how afraid I was. I'd make them be independent, just like kids with 'normal' mothers, even if I was dying inside. I wouldn't let myself cling—I wouldn't let my problems affect them."

For those birthmothers who had no further children, relinquishing provided the sole experience of motherhood. Whether or not their lack of children was deliberate, their concepts of parenting were formed around and framed in the memories of surrender and of the children they had already given up.

Child Surrogates

Birthmothers who had no other children sometimes sublimated their maternal energies by passionately pursuing other interests. Some nurtured their careers, achieving substantial success and acquiring impressive wealth. Many joined helping professions, such as nursing, social work, or teaching and cared for others instead of the children they'd relinquished or never had. A few took more sinister paths, addicting themselves not to success and service but to drugs, alcohol, or shallow relationships with men. Regardless of how they spent their time, these women shared a determination to build lives around the avoidance of motherhood.

"As soon as I finished high school, I ran away to Hawaii," Audrey says. "I didn't want to face stigma or my breakup with the birthfather. Today, I'm thirty-seven and I'm still running away. Oh, I still hope to have a family—I *want* children, but I'm afraid. I doubt myself. I doubt that I'd be a good parent. I have an 'addictive tendency'; I've used drugs and I used to drink. I'm afraid I might slip into that again. And I doubt men. I doubt that you can trust them, but I don't want to parent alone. I run from men when they get serious, and I *know* that's because I'm afraid to get anywhere near a situation that would offer children. I still don't trust myself with the simplest things, like diapers and feedings, on a regular basis. And yet, I'm not a kid anymore. I've supported myself, finished an associate's degree. I have plenty of reasons to think I've changed, but I'm afraid to risk a baby's welfare by testing my abilities to stay put and not run away when it gets too tough. I hope I'll meet someone who inspires me to have children, a guy I can trust enough to stick with. But, so far, after twenty years, I'm still on the run."

If fear of failure prevented women like Audrey from having children, it motivated others to prove their success in every other area. Fed up with running away from stigma, some took on the challenges of defining and living by their own rules. Toby's parents insisted that she surrender the child she bore at sixteen. "Back then, I wanted to raise my baby, but it was considered wrong to keep an out-of-wedlock child. Today, it's considered wrong to give one up. Society can't make up its mind what's morally right, and people like me get caught in the swing of the pendulum. I gave up a baby to make things 'right.' I married the birthfather to make things 'right.' But when we got divorced, I faced even more stigma, so I was done doing what other people thought was 'right.' I decided to do what *I* wanted, instead. Having kids isn't everything! I went to college and grad school and got an M.B.A. I've got a fabulous career, a great car, and a nifty townhouse in the center of town. I travel all over, eat out, and dress the way other women dream about. Frankly, I've never considered having another child. I want to call the shots in my life, and I couldn't if I had kids."

Although some birthmothers shared Toby's disillusionment with society, most rejected her pursuit of the single life, material goals, and free-wheeling lifestyles. Rather than a source of freedom, most saw the commitment to lifestyles free of children as penance, self-denial, or social alienation.

"I wouldn't have another child," Sylvia declares. "To do so would be to say that I had survived relinquishing as an intact woman, that I'd bought into the 'proper,' socially approved rituals for reproducing. Well, I hadn't. I was *not* a whole, healthy person after losing my son. And I was not about to bring another poor soul into this messed-up world, as if it had never happened, as if my first child had never even existed."

Many who, like Sylvia, adamantly blamed their relinquishing on others, nevertheless exacted punishment on themselves. Withdrawing from social convention, refusing to conform on any level, denying themselves the opportunity to mother, these women often sentenced themselves to permanent isolation and mourning, even while they achieved monumental success in other areas, such as their careers.

"Wherever I went after giving up my son," Sylvia continues, "I thought about what he and I were missing. I lived all over the world. I wanted to share it with him. But he never savored sweet tea in the desert with the Bedouin. He never saw the canaries in the palm trees outside my window in West Africa. He never learned to speak French, Spanish, Arabic, Bengali, or Serbian. I could have offered him a broad, many-textured background. But my experiences never went to my son; they simply went to waste."

Like Sylvia, many women who had no children after relinquishing idealized the children they'd surrendered. Others idealized not only their own children but motherhood in general, seeing both as magical and ephemeral and always out of reach.

Motherhood After Relinquishing

Although many were certain that they had been successful at parenting, every birthmother interviewed declared that relinquishing had had a tremendous impact on her ability to mother later children. For most, however, motherhood offered little or no relief from the losses of relinquishing. Although new babies brought them renewed acceptability and the esteemed position of mother, nothing could replace the children who had been lost. In fact, motherhood often rekindled the pain of relinquishing, overpowering denial and releasing stored-up, overwhelming emotions that demanded, at long last, to be acknowledged.

No matter how much birthmothers loved the children they had later, raising them provided constant daily reminders of what had been lost. Particularly for those who married the birthfathers, additional children tended to become living symbols of how precious their first, surrendered children had been.

Whether or not they had other biological, step-, or adopted children, most birthmothers, unfinished in their mourning, stubbornly idealized not only their long-absent babies but also all children, motherhood, and all the lost possibilities of their lives.

$$\boxed{7}$$

Connections

Dreams, Flashbacks, and Coincidences

CINDY SAT UP STRAIGHT, STARTLED OUT OF SLEEP. SHE BLINKED, trying to unblur her eyes and figure out what had awakened her. The baby—the baby was crying. Howling. She jumped out of bed and ran into the hallway. Her nightgown caught on something—a hook in her doorway?—and she felt a rip, but she tugged her body away and kept going, desperate to get to the baby. It was difficult to see in the darkness. The door to the baby's room glowed unnaturally in the shadows, and, even though she was running, Cindy had trouble getting to it. Her body dragged, so heavy with sleep that she had to *will* it forward, to argue with her legs to hurry. The baby's screams grew frantic. Cindy reached for the door. Her hands trembled, fumbled with the knob, but finally she pushed the door open in a clumsy rush. Something was wrong; she sensed danger or evil. Her only thought was that she had to save the baby. Cindy lunged through thickly sweet air, past fluttering curtains, and pulled the squalling infant, swathed in blankets, to her breasts. It was all right! She'd saved him!

The crying stopped and the baby lay quiet and still in her arms. Cindy sat down on the rocker, winded and breathless. Looking down at the baby, she was puzzled to see blood streaming over her torn nightgown. She'd have to put the baby down before her blood could stain him! Cindy leaned over to kiss him before putting him back in his crib. She pushed the blanket back but, instead of kissing him, she gasped and recoiled in a soundless scream. Mouth wide open, Cindy sat in frozen horror, staring at her baby who inexplicably, horribly, *had no face.* . . .

Theater of the Mind

The daily lives of birthmothers interviewed were often riddled with recurring nightmares, dreams, flashbacks, preoccupations, premonitions, and anxieties that were linked to relinquishing. Some, in fact, had these experiences so often and found them so disturbing that they avoided contact with any people, places, or things that they associated with relinquishing. Many tried to dismiss their dreams or other psychic episodes as "tricks of the mind" or as the psychological scars of unfinished emotional business. Others interpreted them metaphysically, imparting symbolic meaning and spiritual significance to the images or emotions that haunted them.

The dreams that recurred tended to fall into two main categories: those that frightened and those that comforted. Each category, in turn, could be further divided: they reflected either relinquishment itself or the troubled periods of grief that followed.

The Stuff Dreams
Are Made Of

Nightmares about relinquishment typically portrayed themes of violence and pain, often replaying the same troubling scenes: losing babies and finding them bloodied, injured, or dead; trying in vain to rescue infants from dangers such as floods, abuse, or nameless brutalities; watching helplessly as infants were kidnapped by couples without faces. Powerlessness and lack of control were dominant themes. In their nightmares, birthmothers repeatedly experienced total and inexplicable paralysis or moved with horrifying sluggishness.

"I know, whenever I have my dream—I call it my 'stolen baby' dream—that I need to get to the hospital nursery pronto," Pam says. "Someone is taking my baby. I see my dark-haired, newborn infant, and, incredibly, he's forming a word—he's calling, 'Mama!' I try to scream, but I can't make a sound. I try to run for help, but I can't move. I look for the baby's father, but I can't find him; sometimes I can't even remember who he is. I see the baby's face peering over the shoulder of the perpetrator, but I can't get to him. I wake up panicky, lost, and shaken."

Zoe's recurring nightmare presented variations of birth and loss. "One particularly troubling dream took place in what seemed to be an airport, only it was round and soft and pink inside. Through the windows, I could see bright sunlight. People were riding an escalator down to what I assumed were the gates to the planes. I was waiting there, watching, present and not present until I saw somebody—a man—get on the escalator carrying a baby. I watch him descend and disappear out into the sunny tarmac. I'm troubled at the sight of him, and gradually I realize that it's my baby he's taking, and I run to the escalator to catch them. No matter how I hurry, I can't get to the escalator fast enough. Time seems frozen. Somehow I manage to get on and ride down but, when I get to the bottom, I exit not into the bright sunshine that I'd seen out the windows but into a sea of dark mud. Then I notice that the mud is moving, that it's *alive* and crawling with rats, thousands of rats, slimy, squirming, ugly rats. I look behind me, to go back into the airport, but the entrance is closed. In fact, it's gone. There's no sign of anyone, not planes or people, not the man or the baby. I'm stuck there, alone, amid rats."

Some recurring dreams were exceptionally violent, graphically illustrating the pain, horror, and guilt birthmothers felt about surrendering. "My father orders me to debone a chicken," Sonia says. "He's the dean of my college, so I have to listen to him. I take a sharp knife and hold the chicken upside down, by its feet. But, as I make the first incision, the chicken stops being a chicken and becomes a limp infant instead, and I know I've done something ghastly, something unforgivable. Something I can't undo."

Images of butchery, carnage, and bloodshed appeared again and again throughout birthmothers' horrific sleep encounters, reflecting not so much the wrenching process of birth as the violence of the process of relinquishing.

"The location changes a little, or my methods of trying to retrieve the baby may vary from dream to dream," Joanie says. "But basically, I dream that I'm on a road or a highway and I leave my baby in the sink at a rest stop. Somehow, I just *forget* her there. I'm miles away when I look in the back seat to check on her and realize that she's gone! I spin around and speed back through the darkness. Each second seems like hours, but I finally get to the rest stop and race to the bathroom. When I find her she's filthy, lifeless, and spattered with blood."

Whenever I Want You

Although nightmares about relinquishment tended to be gory and brutal, those about postrelinquishment focused more heavily on loss than on blood. Dreams became the vehicles through which many women achieved a sense of connection with those they had surrendered, a sense so vivid that it often seemed more like reality than dream.

"I'm at a park with two of my sons," Sue says. "I turn for an instant and one is gone. I look all over and see him across the park, near a tree. His back is to me. I run to him and turn him around, but when he turns to me I see that he has no face. I wake up trembling. In other dreams, I'm with the birthfather; in fact, we're having sex. These dreams are steamy. I'm on the verge of orgasm. Just when I'm about to climax, I look up at him and see with horror that *he* has no face. I reach to touch the place where his face should be and he disappears altogether. I wake up cold, shivering, still able to smell and feel him, and bereft, with feelings of self-recrimination, since I should have *known* not to love him again, that I should have known better, by now."

Some birthmothers dreamed of alternate outcomes to their unwanted pregnancies; in slumberland, anyway, they could temporarily change history. More often, however, their dreams mercilessly teased them, offering outcomes they would have preferred, only to whisk the happy endings away into the night. "The birthfather is sleeping on my sofa," Bridget says. "I see him lying there and I'm overwhelmed with joy. '*This* time,' I think, '*this* time, he won't go and I won't send him away!' I feel my belly, swollen with child, and I'm slow and clumsy walking over to him. I can't wait to reach him, to lie down and be with him, because I know that this time nothing will separate us. But, just as I get to the couch, he's gone. Like a mirage. The couch is empty and I am somehow not surprised. There is a familiarity to this impossible event. I am neither frightened nor shocked; instead, I'm immersed in a sorrow so profound that I can't find words to describe it. And, even in my sleep, even as I begin to recognize that I'm, once again, caught in this dream, I remember with dread that his disappearance from my sofa means not only the loss of the man I love but also, inevitably, of his *baby*, the child that I'm still carrying in the dream."

Many recurring dreams forced birthmothers to relive pain and loss; others, however, brought comfort. Some women actually found, in sleep, a reality that they preferred to that of their waking hours. "As my marriage got worse," Rose says, "I looked forward to dreaming, as an escape. Often, I would see my little girl in my dreams. Or, even better, I would see her *and* her father, the man that I had really loved. Sometimes, I'd go to bed with him in my dreams and I would wake up still feeling all the closeness, all the healing that I needed to get me to start the day. Of course, by breakfast time, I had to face reality and the truth of my unhappiness again. But at night, some nights, I felt that my dreams were truer and more real to me than my waking hours. In my dreams, I found a private, temporary sense of satisfaction or peace."

Nightstalkers

Some dreams were comforting because they offered solace, others because they brought a sense of empowerment. In a number of "empowerment" dreams, birthmothers took control and enjoyed the ability to change the past. A birthmother named Barbara revised the outcome of her stay in the home, taking her newborn home with her or forcing herself to wake up just prior to relinquishment. "The dreams would begin to run into nightmares, but I *knew* what was coming, so I stopped it from happening. Sometimes I'd sneak into the nursery and sneak out with my baby. Sometimes I'd grab her right after she was born and run from the delivery room. All the time, though, I was running in the home, unable to find the doorway or to know how to get out, but I had the baby, so it was OK."

Others empowered themselves in dreams to reunite with former lovers, reclaim surrendered children, or even reverse the events that led to their unwanted pregnancies.

"I call them my 'Germany dreams,'" Alexis says. "For years, I dreamed about turning back the clock and *not* going to bed with Peter, the birthfather, whom I met when I was studying abroad. In these dreams, I'd turn him down, push him away, even shove him out of buildings or out of cars or trains. Or I'd dream that I'd keep the baby. I'd walk the baby around the park, but the park was still back in Germany, not in America. Most of my dreams, though, weren't about the birthfather or the baby. The ones that were most frequent were simultaneously the happiest and the most disturbing. They were simply about being free, back in Germany, traveling or moving around the countryside before I'd even met Peter. In dreams I went back to a time when I was unencumbered by guilt, responsibility, or sadness, when I was free to be a young woman on my own in the world. They gave me brief glimpses of what life might have been like if I could only have retained my innocence, if I hadn't gotten pregnant and lost my youth so suddenly and prematurely. Because, once I became pregnant, there was no turning back. From that point on, my road took a sharp turn, and I've belonged to the past, to guilt, penance, and children ever since."

Although many birthmothers savored their dreamland power to change the events of their pasts, the forms that their power took sometimes left them with disturbing aftertastes. Some women found dreams to be their best—or only—outlet for pent-up rage and frustration.

"For years, I dreamed about losing my baby" one says. "Over and over again, I lost her. I'd wake up crying and feel like I'd relinquished her again, just that night. Lately, though, my dreams are different. I dream that I stop the nurse from taking her away. But it's pretty gruesome, because the way I stop the nurse is that I stab her. In fact, I usually stab her repeatedly, enthusiastically, with an abandon, delight, and uplifting sense of release that feels rather joyous. It sounds sick, but this is what I dream. Sometimes my victim is not a nurse, but some other woman, maybe the adoptive mother, or even my own mother, who influenced me to relinquish. But, whoever the victim symbolizes, she's always the woman who's taking my baby away. And I feel *good* doing this, as if I'm protecting my child from something evil. Or as if I'm getting even. When I wake up, though, all that elation disappears and I'm left feeling abandoned, dirty, exposed, and ashamed."

Dreamlessness and Delays

Recurring dreams and nightmares associated with relinquishment were not experienced by everyone interviewed. A number of women denied dreaming anything that could be even remotely connected to surrender. Others said that their dreams had not begun until several years after relinquishment and had been triggered by specific and clearly identifiable events, such as the birth of another child.

For Alexis, the dreams began after the arrival of her second baby and intensified with each of her three subsequent births. "In my dreams I relived the loss of my first child. Each baby made that loss more real, both when I was awake and when I slept. In fact, the emotional differences between my nightmares and my waking life diminished as time went on, until there was virtually no difference and I finally was compelled to get some meaningful help through therapy."

Many birthmothers described similar periods of "psychic numbness," in which they had no dreams of relinquishment what-soever. Then, when some new experience jolted them and ended the numbness, these dreams burst disruptively into their sleep night after night. One birthmother's dreams began after she wit-nessed a birthmother/adoptee reunion on television. Another's began after her twenty-two-year-old relinquished daughter found her. A third had dreams only after the birth of her first grandchild, nineteen years after she'd surrendered. Relinquishment dreams were triggered by marital crises, deaths in the family, and mile-stones, such as weddings, graduations, retirements, or births. Whenever birthmothers experienced a major change, stress, loss, or gain, unresolved emotional and psychological issues reawakened and relinquishment dreams were likely to appear.

Some women, however, claimed that they had *never* had any such dreams and doubted that they ever would. A few never dreamed at all. Others did, but not about relinquishing. Some occasionally dreamed about relinquishing but didn't consider these dreams any different from, or more significant than, those concerning other life experiences. Lynne, who participated in an open adoption, maintained regular communication with her relin-quished child and the adoptive parents. "Of course I dream about my child sometimes," she says, "but so do I dream about many other acquaintances and family members. I don't consider it a 'relinquishment dream' just because I see my child in it. There's no regret or remorse in these dreams—no sense of danger, anger, or fear, like in a nightmare. If she's in my dreams, it's because she's included in whatever it is I'm dreaming about, playing in the grass or eating in a restaurant. But so is my sister, so is a friend I met in third grade. My daughter's not the focus of the dream; she's just a member of my troupe."

Some who never dreamed about relinquishing believed that they were still experiencing psychic numbness, suspecting that it might be permanent or last indefinitely. "I've had no dreams," Rhonda says. "I *think* about him all the time, though. I fantasize about him and wonder what he's doing, how he's growing, but I don't have dreams. I wish I would, in a way. Because that might feel real, like I was seeing him. But maybe my mind won't let go enough to let me dream about him. Maybe I'm too realistic, too grounded in the tangible world to let him come out in my unconscious—maybe I'm just wrapped too tight to see him in my dreams."

Others rejected the idea that relinquishing had left them with any lingering issues to dream about. Mary, who became pregnant as the result of a rape, admitted to nightmares of sexual violence, but she associated these with the rape rather than with relinquishment. Gail, who had put relinquishing behind her years ago, doesn't usually remember her dreams, but was sure they were not about relinquishing. "Why would they be? That simply isn't part of my life. I have a family. I made a mistake, but that was a long time ago, and I relinquished to solve it. I did the best I could. I don't dwell on it. Other people may think I should, but, sorry, I don't. It was a long time ago. I've no need to look back. Nor, I might add, do I have the desire."

Flashbacks and Phobias

Many birthmothers experienced dreamlike phenomena related to relinquishment even during their waking hours. For some, these sensations were so vivid that they seemed actual, interrupting birthmothers' lives and leaving them feeling as if they had traveled through time to moments from the past. For others, they involved sudden surges of sadness, anger, or panic that occurred whenever some apparently innocent trigger, even remotely associated with relinquishing, set them off.

"I'll be folding laundry," Sue says, "and suddenly I'm sixteen again, packing my clothes for the maternity home. Minutes later,

I'll pull myself back into the present and stop crying. Or, just recently, I was at my son's school as room mother. They were fixing macaroni and cheese in the cafeteria. I was no longer in his school, but back at the home where, every Friday, we got macaroni and cheese. It even smelled the same. These flashbacks happen to me all the time. I'll hear an old song from when I was a teenager and, suddenly, I'll *feel* the baby kicking me so hard that I have to massage my ribs, even though I'm not pregnant! Or something will set me off, like seeing a newborn baby or driving by a hospital, and next thing I know, I'm reliving the moment that I left the hospital and came home. I mean, reliving it. It's like replaying a tape. The scenes happen again and again. This happens to me unpredictably, only sometimes—not all the time. But one flash-back occurs pretty often. I'm writing checks—paying the bills, but instead of signing checks, I'm suddenly signing relinquishing pa-pers! It's embarrassing—I've voided more checks that way, by messing up my name in the middle and ruining the signature before I come back to the present, control myself, and see what I'm really doing."

Flashbacks like Sue's were commonly accepted by birthmothers; some seemed to expect them as part of everyday existence. Others, however, were so disconcerted by the sudden and uncontrollable intrusion of the past into the present that they avoided contact with *anything* that they associated with relinquishing, in order to minimize the likelihood of flashing back.

Unexplained Fears, Mysterious Monsters

Some women who practiced avoidance, though, were not entirely certain that flashbacks were what they were avoiding. These women knew only that there were items, places, or activities that seemed too menacing or frightening for them to be around. Often it took years of therapy or a particularly poignant experience to shake their psyches enough to discover the root of their fears.

"I was afraid of milkshakes," Amber says. "I couldn't bear to be around them. The thought of them made me sick, nauseated. I was also terrified of cancer. I never knew why. There was no real history of cancer in my family. I thought it was just all the publicity about cancer or something. Through therapy, I've uncovered the reasons, though. When I gave birth, they didn't put me on the maternity floor because I was relinquishing. They put me in a room with a woman who was dying of cancer. I didn't even remember this for years. She was so sick that she couldn't eat, so they gave her milkshakes full of drugs. She was zombielike, just as I was. The two of us lay in bed, miserable, and to me, relinquishing became confused with cancer. Milkshakes became confused with loss and death."

Some phobic reactions were unlocked through therapy, but others remained obscure until some crisis or unexpected event brought them out. A birthmother named Celia, a librarian with a normally calm and rational disposition, had an intense fear of having anything close to or covering her face. Halloween masks, for example, made her frantic and dizzy, but she had no idea why. She was often nervous when offered cups or wide-mouthed glasses, preferring to sip from straws. At her wedding, to avoid arousing these fears, she'd refused to wear a veil.

Celia and her family accepted her avoidances as quirks of her personality and considered them manageable until the night she first met her adult, relinquished son. After years of searching, she had found him and they'd arranged to meet at a restaurant. During their dinner, Celia experienced dizziness so severe that she felt as if she were about to faint. The waiter offered her a glass of water but, as he held it to her, Celia's phobic reaction took over and she pushed it away with flailing arms and knocked the glass out of his hand. Her vertigo was so profound that she had to be rushed to the hospital. There she became hysterical at the sight of the curtains in the emergency room and wouldn't let anyone put anything near her face, even medications or water. Eventually sedated, calm, and embarrassed, she was released hours later, unable to explain either her physical or her emotional reactions.

A few weeks later, Celia was still disturbed by this experience and described it to another birthmother at a support group meeting. The other woman thought for a while, then asked what kind of anesthesia Celia'd received during childbirth. As she answered, Celia believed that she had found the explanations for everything that had occurred.

Anesthesia had been administered by masked doctors through a facial gas mask. Celia's last memories of delivery were of dizziness and vertigo and of trying to push the cuplike mask of sleep-inducing, nauseating gas away from her face. Reuniting with her son had apparently awakened her anguished, locked-away memories of childbirth, with results so intense that Celia actually reexperienced some of the physical symptoms, linking them to objects that resembled those used in the hospital: a glass of water held to her mouth, for example, became a mask of sleep-inducing gas forced onto her face.

Although Celia's experience was extreme, it resembled those of many who associated the traumas of relinquishment with the otherwise neutral objects, people, or places that happened to be present at the time. For women like Celia, these associations aroused fear; for others, however, they provided different emotions, even comfort.

"The only place I felt peaceful was in the hospital," Claudia confides. "My first time in a hospital was when I gave birth to my relinquished child. For years afterwards, though, I developed one medical problem after another. I had surgery almost every year for, oh, a dozen years. Nothing serious, mind you, but I always had something that would take me back to the hospital. I understand now that the hospital was where I'd been *happy*—it was where I'd been with my little baby girl. It was where I'd been able to see her and hold her. I treasured those days, and being in the hospital somehow brought them back to me. I felt a special kind of safety or calm whenever I smelled the antiseptics, felt the sheets, tasted the food, saw the nurses. It was the closest I could come to getting back my daughter."

Some birthmothers, through therapy or other means, unlocked the sources of their avoidances, phobias, and flashbacks. Many explained that these phenomena resulted from relinquishing experiences too traumatic to be consciously remembered. For some, forgetting had been crucial, even necessary for survival. Even if they had consciously repressed or forgotten details, however, their unconscious minds had not. Pieces of memory, glimpses of emotions too intense to be reckoned with surfaced indirectly through reactions to milkshakes, paper cups, and medicinal odors, objects and experiences that were certainly easier to control than the memories of relinquishment buried beneath them.

Posttraumatic Stress Syndrome and Birthmothers

"When I first met Danny, the man I'm engaged to now," Donna says, "he was having dreams about Vietnam. He'd wake up sweating, screaming, reliving God-knows-what in his sleep. I began to dream with him, only my dreams incorporated what he'd said about Vietnam into my *own* trauma. I'd dream that my daughter was in a one-room hut in Vietnam. I opened the door to get her, knowing that the house was about to blow up. There were lots of babies inside, rows of them on shelves and benches. I stood there, immobile, not sure which baby was mine. Before I could think or move, the house blew up, right before my eyes."

Even though Donna participated in an open adoption, she was subject to the same kinds of dreams and flashbacks as women who relinquished with closed terms. Her relationship with a Vietnam veteran, however, led her to information that provided some insight as to their meaning, as well as how to cope with them.

"Danny's dreams and flashbacks were so disruptive and out of control that I began to get books about posttraumatic stress disorder. What I learned was helpful to our relationship, and, unexpectedly, it was also helpful to *me*, independent of the relationship.

Because I learned that I, too, had the symptoms. I, too, as a birthmother, was a victim of posttraumatic stress disorder. And, though there is no definite cure, just knowing what was wrong with me gave me a sense of being more grounded or better oriented about what to expect. It gave me a framework for dealing with it."

Posttraumatic stress disorder is a term that, as Donna said, has commonly afflicted populations such as survivors of war, rape, child abuse, violent crime, and disasters. It occurs among people who have experienced events outside the range of normal human experience, events that would be vastly distressing to anyone, such as life-threatening situations, harm to children or spouses, or destruction to home or community. Because their experiences have been extreme and outside the frame of reference of "normal" society, victims of this disorder have often found that "normal" society has provided them with little effective support, help, or even understanding.

"Just like some Vietnam vets who found themselves doing things they'd never thought themselves capable of—blowing up villages or whatever—birthmothers have done the unthinkable," Donna explains. "We've given up our babies—what could be more alien to the experience of 'normal' society? What could be more traumatic? But because what we've done is so outside the range of common acceptable experience, we don't know how to incorporate it into the framework of our lives, and we're left with fragments, remnants, wounds that show up again and again in our minds in the form of hellish recurring nightmares and dreams."

Symptoms of posttraumatic stress disorder typically include not only depression, anger, guilt, and lowered self-esteem but also recurring dreams, daydreams, preoccupations, and flashbacks. Frequently, sufferers experience acute distress when exposed to places, people, or objects associated with their original traumas; some avoid distress by eliminating contact with such stimuli. Other typical symptoms include feelings of emotional numbness or detachment, the inability to recall pertinent aspects of the actual traumatic event, and a sense of a doomed or foreshortened future. Further, those who suffer this syndrome often survive in overly alert states of arousal. They often experience difficulty in sleeping, are subject to emotional swings or outbursts, and are unable to concentrate or relax. Many react to events or objects associated with their traumas with physiological conditions like dizziness, sudden sweats, or stomachaches.

Although birthmothers commonly experienced the symptoms of posttraumatic stress disorder, most were unaware of their significance. Plagued with seemingly irrational fears, recurring nightmares, flashbacks, or inexplicable physical symptoms, many simply felt alone, frightened, and embarrassed.

Psychic Reminders

Although posttraumatic stress disorder offered a framework through which to view a variety of birthmothers' psychic distresses, it offered no guaranteed cure. Even after years of counseling or psychotherapy, many birthmothers found that the symptoms of this disorder persisted. Even if they couldn't end it, however, some felt that understanding the sources of their fears and distresses provided them a significant degree of comfort.

"I avoided parks," Cindy says. "I avoided seeing children playing, even after I had other kids. Whenever I passed a park, I felt the darkness and doom that I felt before I relinquished. Sometimes, I'd get crampy, as if I were about to go into labor again. Until I attended a meeting where someone talked about posttraumatic stress disorder, I never thought about the reasons for those particular fears. Actually, it was obvious: My window in the home I'd been in while I was pregnant looked out onto a park. But my fear reaction wasn't limited to parks. It could be set off by almost anything: the sight of a baby in a carriage, the birthday of my relinquished child, driving through the neighborhood where I grew up, seeing a TV commercial for baby shampoo—anything. Panic would begin unpredictably, so I was always on the lookout, always afraid that something would make me afraid."

The birthmothers interviewed also described phobic or avoidance reactions to stimuli as varied as childbirth, intimacy with men, contact with newborns, children of a particular gender or hair color, birthday parties, baby powder, milk, fish sticks, Jell-O, surgery, hospitals, nuns, nurses, neon lights, birth announcements, pregnant women, toys, children's stores, baby carriages, religious statues, and elevators. Contact with these stimuli, which they had linked to some aspect of pregnancy, delivery, or relinquishment, triggered varying symptoms of physical discomfort, including clamminess, sweat, diarrhea, dizziness, shakiness, and headaches or emotional responses of fear, rage, and sorrow.

"For three years after I relinquished," Bridget says, "I began to hemorrhage at the time of my relinquished daughter's birthday. For three years straight, I had to go into the hospital to have a D & C, to stop the bleeding. At the time, I didn't associate the bleeding with delivery, but now I'm convinced that I was physically reliving the experience of giving birth, even without a conscious awareness of what was happening."

If Bridget experienced physical symptoms of labor when exposed to emotional stimuli, others relived emotional experiences when exposed to physical stimuli.

"With each new baby," Alexis says, "it got worse. Labor, the contractions, brought it all back to me, and I relived relinquishing. I had four more children and I went through it again, every time. The emotions came back more intensely each time. Terror began and increased as the contractions became more frequent and intense. Then the smells of the hospital, the smells of the baby, the smell of the food they served. The bathroom smells, the disinfectant smells. The smell of the linens on the beds. Smells brought things back to me that were so real that I was truly unsure, at times, that the relinquishment was a memory and not an upcoming event. With each new birth it got worse, so that, by the third child, I was afraid of being in the hospital and by the fourth, I was afraid of the pregnancy itself, because that would lead me to the hospital, where I knew I'd have to go through it all again."

Symptoms like those of posttraumatic stress disorder occurred to birthmothers of all ages, regardless of when they'd relinquished or under what circumstances. Whether they'd relinquished at fifteen or at thirty-five, in 1955 or in 1985, with open or closed terms, most experienced at least some typical signs.

"I have an open adoption," Donna says. "So I know what day my daughter goes to art class and I know what size dress she wears. I talk to her family on her birthday every year. Yet I still have dreams of a lost baby crying, and I wake up positive that it was real. I have nightmares that my boyfriend will die if I get pregnant or that some great loss will follow if I have another baby. Open adoption allowed me to know that my child is healthy and what she looks like and that she likes to dance. But it didn't allow me to escape the results of the trauma of giving up my baby. I have the same kinds of dreams and recurring fears as my boyfriend does about Vietnam, the same hauntings as birthmothers who participated in closed adoptions."

For some birthmothers, therapy was helpful in allaying symptoms of the disorder. "Once I found the right therapist," Alexis says, "I gradually accepted that I couldn't *change* the past. I stopped fighting it, stopped trying to reverse time and to erase my relinquishment. After I finally accepted my relinquishment, the dreams stopped. I didn't have to go back there anymore, in my mind to rescue the infant I'd left behind in the past. Once I accepted that *that* infant was no longer an infant, that the past was gone and irreversible, I could stay in the present and deal with things as they are."

Other birthmothers, however, had less success with therapy. From the onset of her treatment, Donna's psychiatrist warned her that it was difficult to eradicate the symptoms of posttraumatic stress disorder successfully through traditional psychotherapy. "He told me that only about 50 percent of the patients got better through psychological counseling. Unfortunately, I wasn't one of the lucky ones. My dreams and nightmares, my distresses and panics have all remained alive and well. Even though therapy helped me understand them better and learn how to deal with them, it couldn't make them go away."

Intuition, Commonalities, and Coincidence

If posttraumatic stress disorder explained a number of psychic phenomena common among birthmothers, it could not explain them all. Coincidences between relinquished children and their biological mothers, premonitions, and intuitive impressions were prevalent but could not be explained away by disorders resulting from trauma or stress.

"These are just *some* of the coincidences we discovered when we finally met," says Liz, whose grown daughter searched for and found her twenty-two years after relinquishment. "She'd moved into my neighborhood when she moved out of her parents' home at eighteen. She hung out in the same crowd as my other kids—they all knew each other and were friends. But there's more. I was fifteen when I had her. When she was fifteen, she'd gotten pregnant and her parents had her get an abortion. Also, I'm a waitress. Her parents wanted her to go to college, but she refused. All she ever wanted to be was a waitress. In fact, she told me she never understood why. But she'd always known that was what she wanted to be. She'd played waitress all the time as a kid. One of our biggest coincidences, though, is that when I met her, she was working in the same building as I was—I worked in a restaurant on the ground floor; she worked in the one up on the roof."

Career coincidences between birthparents and relinquished children were frequently discovered after they'd been reunited later in life. "My son's pre-med," says Annie. "He doesn't know this, but his birthfather's a doctor. His adoptive family's got a retail business, but he wanted no part of it—he knew he wanted to be a doctor from early childhood. He looks just like his biological father, and he has the same temperament, the same interests, even the same impatient, intolerant reactions to *me*. It's weird. When I've talked to my son, I've seen his father, whom he's never even met, in his gestures, expressions, and attitudes. They're like clones, not just physically but in personality, too."

Some birthmothers had radarlike impressions whenever they were in physical proximity to their relinquished children. "I was *drawn* to Cape May every summer," Nancy says. "It was the only place I felt calm. I felt connected to my daughter there. No matter where my family lived—Connecticut, Massachusetts, Maryland—I brought the kids back to Cape May in the summers. I felt pulled there, as if by a magnet. I walked the beaches, looking for a child who looked like me. Of course, I never saw her, but I felt her presence and knew, somehow, that she was nearby. It turned out, when we met, that she'd been not in but right outside Cape May, with her adoptive grandparents, every summer of her childhood."

Nancy found another way to feel connected to her relinquished daughter: poetry. For years, she wrote poems expressing her love and hopes for her child without realizing that, from the time she was old enough to write, that child was writing poems expressing her feelings to her birthmother. Years later, they discovered that some of their poems seemed to answer each other.

On her birthday, Nancy's daughter once wrote:

> Every year on August first
> I've wondered if you knew
> Another year had come and gone,
> and were thinking of me, too. . . .

On one such August first, the birthmother, in nearby Cape May, wrote:

> How often I stop, along my walks
> Beside that silent sea,
> Hoping to find a little girl
> that might resemble me. . . .
> I long to find my Summer child.
> In my heart she'll always stay,
> And if it be the will of God,
> our paths will cross some day.

Like Nancy, others felt the presence of their relinquished children, even when they had no conscious knowledge of their whereabouts. Jean was positive that her daughter lived near a lake in New England. It was years before her intuition was verified, but she never doubted it. "I could visualize a park where she played that overlooked a lake. There were green, lush mountains all around. I also knew that she had dark hair and dark eyes, even though I'm fair. Don't ask me *how* I knew these things. I've no idea. It's just what came to mind when I thought of her."

Some coincidences were too odd to bear explanation. Rhonda, for example, had named her son Steven at birth. His adoptive parents had changed his name to William. All through school, however, with no apparent knowledge of his original birth name, William asked his friends to call him by the nickname "Steve."

History Repeating

Physical and emotional coincidences were not limited to those between biological parents and their children; sometimes they extended to their partners, as well. "When I met my son," Sue says, "he stared at me so intensely that I felt uncomfortable, but I thought it was because he was trying to get used to me. He was the spitting image of his father, the man I had loved so deeply in my youth, and he was the same age when I met him as his father had been when we broke up, so it was jarring for me. I felt as if I'd met my boyfriend again, except that I was old. The next time we got together, my son introduced me to his girlfriend. I nearly fainted and I understood why he'd stared at me with such amazement. She looked just like *me*! Or, rather, like I looked in college. She's my size, my weight. She has big hazel eyes like mine and her hair's the same style, same length, same color. It gave me the chills. It was like meeting myself and my boyfriend, twenty-six years ago.

"But that's not all. The reason he wanted me to meet her was that she was *pregnant*. They were trying to decide what to do— whether to get an abortion or to have the baby. Whether to get married. He'd wanted her to meet me so that she could talk it over with me. We talked, we cried. I finally told her that, no matter what else she decided, she should never consider relinquishing. But the irony of all our similarities was not lost on any of us, and we felt bound together by some quirk of fate, some unending loop of history. It seemed to me that for some reason they had the chance to do it over, to make up for the mistakes that Bob and I made years ago. And they did, by the way. They got married."

Similarities in careers, personalities, and predicaments were discovered again and again by birthmothers who met their relinquished children later in life, as adults. "My son's a maverick, like me," Sylvia says. "He's a loner, strong-willed, uncompromising. He stands apart from people, like I do. He's small and introspective. He's got a great, sarcastic, wry sense of humor—same as mine. He uses it to entertain people and manipulate them, the same way I do. But his adoptive family is boisterous and rowdy, not subtle. They're gregarious, athletic, big people. They didn't know what to *do* with him. But personality may be inherited, so it's no real surprise that he's so similar to me. Our resemblances may be due to twists of DNA. No, the real coincidences that I see are about other things.

"For example, when he met me, my son asked if it had been snowing the night he was born. It had. In fact, I'd been more than a little afraid that the taxi wouldn't get to the hospital in time, the storm was so bad. He'd had a recurring dream of a violent snow-storm, that snow had endangered his birth. Also, some of our dreams were connected. I'd had a recurring dream of taking him to a park or playground and losing him there; he'd had one of going with me on a ride at an amusement park only to turn, at the end of the ride, to see that I was gone.

"But the coincidences went on and on. The strangest, I think, was what we found when we shared letters that we'd written to each other over the years. We were both surprised—and somehow *not* surprised—when we realized that several of the letters not only had the same dates on them, but also addressed the same issues. I wrote him about his father about the same time he wrote to ask me who his father was. I wrote him about how I wanted to show him the wild canaries the very week that he wrote to ask me if I ever thought about him. Stuff like that. There's no way to explain it. It just happened."

Reflexes, Reactions, and Riddles

The intuitions birthmothers described often involved more than benign sensations of proximity or appearance. Many were sudden, dramatic, and rife with impressions of urgency, danger, or emergency. Without knowledge of the whereabouts of their children, most were unable to discover whether their concerns were justified.

"For the last four years," one birthmother says, "I've been certain that the child I relinquished is dead. I can tell you the date, the hour, that I felt that she had left this earth. I have no idea what happened to her, or even if anything happened. All I want to do is find out that she's OK, that I'm mistaken. But I have no way to know."

Some women *have* been able to verify or dispel their extrasensory impressions concerning their children's safety. "In 1983, I began to worry about my son," Pam says. "I actually thought he was dead. I was sure some tragedy had occurred, and I thought it was a car accident. Gradually, the feelings calmed down, but five years later, I woke up in the night sweating, certain, this time, that something dreadful had happened to him. I began searching that very day. I was frantic, relentless. I hired a private investigator who found him in a matter of months. I learned that my fears had been well grounded, although I'd been wrong about their cause. In 1983, when I'd begun to worry about him, my son had, indeed, been in trouble. His adoptive mother had walked out, abandoning the family without warning. I also found out why I'd awakened sweating in the night: my son had just attempted suicide. In fact, his adoptive father had initiated a search for me at the same time I'd begun to search, because he hoped that I could help our son survive by dispelling the idea that he was unlovable, that he'd been rejected by both of his mothers."

Psychic warnings were not limited to birthmothers. Some who searched for and later met their relinquished children as adults learned that the children had had strong, unexplained feelings of concern for them at times of crisis, as well. When one birthmother was nearly killed in a car accident, her relinquished daughter became distraught about her and decided to initiate a search. Another began her search just about the time that her birthmother, coincidentally, had been diagnosed with cancer.

The list of coincidences is endless. Rhonda fell into a deep depression at the same time, as she learned years later, that her relinquished child's adoptive parents were divorcing. "He was on my mind constantly during the time that his family was breaking up. He later told me that I was on his mind, then, too. He fantasized about me, made me into a fairy godmother type, and he kept wanting me to rescue him from his pain. I had no idea, though, that anything was wrong with him. I was just, suddenly, unbearably depressed."

A few birthmothers were so aware of their inexplicable metaphysical or spiritual ties to their relinquished children that they sought help from psychics. Those who did so often maintained a certain cynicism about these consultants but went because they did not know to whom else to turn. Paula was told by a psychic that her relinquished child played on a Little League baseball team in a city that began with a *P*. "I paid $100 for that piece of information," she laments. "And I've never even found out if it's true."

Others took precautions, however odd, against being misled by these professionals. "I consulted three different psychics simultaneously, independent of each other," Bridget said. "If I went to one, I made subsequent appointments with the others. I listened only to what all three agreed upon, because I knew they might be charlatans, but if they *all* came up with the same ideas independent of each other, I thought that there must have been something at work other than greed.

"Originally, I went because I couldn't explain why I'd been hearing a woman's voice calling, 'Mother,' outside my bedroom window for weeks. I'd wake up, hearing the voice, positive that it had been real. I'd check on my kids. They were all asleep. Besides, they all called me 'Mommy,' not 'Mother.' I was certain, from her intensity, that the woman was my relinquished daughter, who was now grown. And I had to discover what she wanted. Without a way to find her, I went to psychics. I was worried about her to the point of desperation."

In addition to a voice at the window, Bridget heard knocks at the door and a woman's voice saying, "Mother, I need you." Her three psychics cost Bridget hundreds of dollars and suggested that Bridget, her husband, and the birthfather of her relinquished child had been involved in unresolved rivalries and love triangles for centuries, but they did not explain the frightened young woman who awakened Bridget and frantically called for her mother. It was not until years later, when Bridget successfully searched for and found her relinquished daughter, that she found the startling truth. At the very time that she had heard the voice at her window, her newlywed, pregnant daughter had been standing at her own bedroom window, silently calling for her. Her new husband had not wanted a child so soon and had been trying to force her to get an abortion. Unwilling to abort, she had yearned to consult with her birthmother, to ask her how to deal with this crisis, to learn why she had chosen to carry and give birth to her, when she could have obtained an abortion. The woman's voice had, in fact, been calling Bridget for help.

Further, when her daughter had first become pregnant and later given birth, Bridget had, without knowing why, experienced physical symptoms of pregnancy and labor. Her breasts had swelled painfully and remained uncomfortable for months. Then, on the morning her grandchild had been born, she'd experienced stomach cramps so severe that she had to cancel her luncheon plans and lie down. "These incidents didn't stop when my grandson was born," she says. "Two years later, on Thanksgiving, he scalded his hands by reaching for a pot of boiling water. He had to go to the hospital and have his hands bandaged. I hadn't yet found my daughter and had no idea that her son had even been born. But that same day, I had to stop cooking because my hands hurt so badly. I took pain pills and we ended up going out to Thanksgiving dinner. That was the first and only time I haven't served Thanksgiving at home."

SOS or PMS?

Because of the closed nature of many adoptions, most coincidences were not discovered, most premonitions not explained, unless and until either birthmothers or their relinquished children successfully searched for and found each other. Many women who were *not* in communication with their relinquished children, therefore, were unable either to verify or dismiss their feelings of urgency or concern. Most, in fact, were left wondering if these feelings were the products of their imaginations or of something more dire.

"I'd get a feeling or a vibe," Cindy says, "that he needed me, that he was calling for me. I'd pray for him for hours, until it seemed like I'd only imagined his cries. But I never knew what had caused the feeling or if anything was really wrong."

"Whenever I think of the son I surrendered," Jill says, "I wonder if I'm thinking about him because he's thinking about me. Every so often, I'm overcome with emotion about him and wonder if it's mutual. I wonder if he's searching for me and if that's why I think about searching for him. I attach meaning to everything where he's concerned. I hear songs from the year he was born, and I always think he's listening, too. But there's no way to know."

Some impressions expressed themselves in concrete manners. Annie was compelled at times to sit down and draw violent, scary images of a child in pain. "It was as if my hand was possessed," she recalls. "I'd be doing something else—laundry, reading—and all of a sudden, out of the blue, an image would come to me that I had to draw. I wondered where these images came from. They were ugly, jagged, full of bloody purples and reds. I was afraid that my son was in pain, or being abused. Or maybe that he was feeling emotional rage or pain. But I've never found out. I've found him, but he won't talk to me about the past, his childhood, or any of his feelings. So I can't find out if the anguish I drew was his or mine, real or imagined."

Posttraumatic Stress Disorder, ESP, and Connections of the Mind

Although some of the dreams, flashbacks, and other phenomena experienced by birthmothers could be explained as symptoms of posttraumatic stress disorder, others defied such tidy explanation. Even if these coincidences and intuitive impressions were distorted by time or exaggeration, they were reported so frequently, similarly, and intensely that they were difficult to dismiss. Most birthmothers interviewed, in fact, were convinced that they had experienced both extrasensory perceptions and posttraumatic stress disorders and saw no conflicts between the two. Many believed that the trauma of relinquishment was so severe that it could never be completely healed, that the biological bonds of birth were so strong that neither the passage of time nor the distance of oceans could sever them altogether. Only a few denied the possibility that, in times of their children's distress, some primitive, instinctive response *could* come into play, regardless of relinquishment, alerting biological mothers to their children's needs. Although some sought relief through therapy, hypnosis, or consultations with psychics, many who experienced these phenomena accepted them without question, seeing them as ongoing, inevitable parts of their everyday postrelinquishment lives.

8

Choices

To Search or Not to Search,
To Be Found or Not Be Found?

ALL ZOE HAD TO DO WAS ANSWER THE DOOR. AFTER TWENTY-THREE years, the wondering and waiting would finally stop. Time had quieted the terror of Jack's threats; the degradation of their relationship had faded years ago. Today, she was going to retrieve the only part of that nightmare worth saving. She was finally going to meet her baby, her relinquished child, now a fully grown woman.

She'd anticipated flying to the door, flinging it open, and throwing her arms around her daughter. But now that the door-bell had actually rung, Zoe could not fly. She couldn't even walk.

What was this hesitation? Zoe told herself to get moving. She bid her legs to go, but they were not legs anymore; they were oatmeal, soggy, stuck to the floor. What was she afraid of? A thousand times, ten thousand, Zoe had envisioned this moment. Of rushing to meet her daughter somewhere, sometime, of find-ing a petite brunette, a younger, prettier, more delicate version of herself. Sometimes her daughter had been sophisticated and refined; other times, sporty and playful. Occasionally she'd been softly serene, swathed in silk. Always, though, regardless of her style, the daughter in her mind had been beautiful. Always she and Zoe had rushed to each other, hugged, kissed, and bonded instantly. Always her heart had lurched and her eyes had flooded when she'd imagined their long-delayed, two-decades-pent-up embrace.

But now, when her daughter was waiting on the other side of the door, Zoe froze. Icy fear, or something like it, took her by surprise. What if her daughter didn't like her? What if Zoe couldn't live up to some idealized "birthmother" image? Could she deal with rejection? Could she bear to lose her child again?

Zoe tried to dismiss her doubts as she forced her feet toward the door. This was her *daughter*, after all. This was the child of her body, the girl she had dreamed of and longed for for so many years. Her alter-ego. The lost part of her past, of her very self. Probably what she was feeling was normal prereunion jitters. She approached the door cautiously, hesitating every few steps to reassure herself, rechecking her manicure, smoothing her skirt. Finally, she held the doorknob in her hand, drew a deep breath, and opened it.

At first, she thought it was a mistake. Then she thought it was a joke. Then she thought that it was Jack, the birthfather, in drag, come back after all these years to fulfill his threats and kill her. Finally, she asked the creature what its name was, to check. Its voice sounded female, and it gave the right name.

Elizabeth was the image of her father, the greaser from hell. She was the female version of Jack, except that her head had been partially shaved and what remained of her hair had been dyed neon magenta. She stood six feet tall, just like Jack. She smoked a filterless cigarette, the same brand as Jack's, and she held it the way he did, between her thumb and forefinger. She wore leather pants and boots. She had even arrived on a Harley. And, though Zoe hadn't seen Jack in twenty-three years, she still shivered when she saw Elizabeth's long, strong arms, decorated with tattoos, just like Jack's.

Zoe blinked, but nothing changed. Nothing went away. In fact, the creature extended an arm to hold the open door and enter the house.

The arm, unbelievably, was covered by a coiled purple serpent, just like Jack's.

Zoe felt dizzy. She swooned into her foyer and sank onto a chair. Elizabeth followed her, casually flicking ashes onto the cream-colored carpet. "Hey, Mom," she grunted, "got any beer?"

The Question of Search in Closed Adoptions

In a recent Harvard University study, about 96 percent of women who relinquished later contemplated searching for their relinquished children; over 60 percent actually undertook search at some point. In addition, tens of thousands of adoptees initiate searches for their birthmothers each year. The world of closed adoption is apparently swarming with networks of lost biological relatives combing the country in search of each other. Many searches have led to successful reunions; others have not. Most reunions were less shocking than Zoe's; nevertheless, many brought surprises that shook up everyone involved. A number of searches led not to reunions but to further, seemingly endless searching. Some went on for so many years and required such intense expenditures of emotions and finances that they were conducted in spurts, alternating between active pursuit and exhausted abandonment.

Why They Search

Three-fourths of the interviewed birthmothers with closed adoptions had searched for their children. The reasons they had been driven to search varied. A few said that television talk shows featuring birthmother-child reunions had compelled them to launch their own searches. "I watched a reunion on 'Oprah' and I thought, 'If *they* can do it, why can't I?'" Joannie recalls. "A day or two later, I got up the nerve to call the number they gave on the show, and I began my search. But it never would have occurred to me to do that if I hadn't seen it on TV. Because I would have thought I had no right to search, since I'd signed my rights away when I was seventeen."

The vast majority, however, admitted that they'd had pressing motivations for search that had begun long before the mass media promoted such efforts. "I have an addictive personality," one birthmother says. "Years ago, I learned that tendencies to addiction can be hereditary. My father was an alcoholic. His father was, too. As am I, although I no longer drink. For years after I relinquished, I was dependent on drugs. I want to warn my son and his family, to have them be on the lookout for symptoms so they can seek help early, in case he turns out like my family. It could be tragic if they ignored his tendencies and worse if they blamed him, as I blamed myself, for being 'a bad kid,' instead of realizing that the origin of the problems might lie in the genes."

Medical concerns, ranging from addictive tendencies to genetic heart disease, were among the most prevalent reasons birthmothers gave for their searches. A woman who had later married the relinquished child's birthfather initiated her search when her husband learned that his heart condition was rapidly deteriorating. "I wanted to find our son before it was too late," she says. "I wanted him to have a chance to meet his father and knew that we might not have much time. And, of course, we wanted to warn him that he might have genetic heart problems, to make sure he takes good care of himself."

Nonmedical, intangible reasons for search were also frequently cited. Many women ached to let their children know that they had been relinquished out of love, not out of rejection. Some regretted their relinquishments and longed for knowledge of or contact with their children. A number were plagued by guilt, generalized worry, or unexplained feelings of emergency concerning their children. Some experienced recurrent dreams in which their children were in danger, and the mothers felt compelled to discover whether these dreams were factually based. Others, even without nagging dreams, were plagued by uneasiness concerning their children's well-being and hungered to know that their children were well and thriving in their adoptive families.

"Think about it," Ida says. "Most of us parents are very careful in selecting babysitters even for one evening. Yet when we had to find caretakers for *life*, many birthmothers were expected to entrust our children to complete strangers, selected by others. How can we permanently, blindly be required to adhere to those agreements? We *need* to know that our kids are, at the very least, happy and healthy."

A number of women were encouraged to search by therapists or psychiatrists helping them deal with postrelinquishment depression, low self-esteem, or incomplete grief. Search, for these women, was often a critical part of integration and healing, requiring them to overcome denial, reject passivity, and confront and act on their feelings.

"I was literally obsessed with my lost child," Zoe says. "My therapist beamed when I finally mentioned searching. All these years, I'd felt like a victim, but by searching I allowed myself to take action and *do* something to change that pattern. My mental health was at stake. Personally, I *had* to assert my feelings—I had to express my right to be known and recognized as a legitimate person, as the woman who brought my daughter into the world. If I hadn't taken charge and searched, I believe I'd have given up and eventually lost my will to live. That's how serious and how important it was for me to stand up, speak out, and search for my child."

Jean's motives were similar. "I have more self-esteem because I searched. I'm happier and less anxious than before. I'm not less angry that I gave up my child, but I feel better about myself because I finally stopped holding in my grief and took action. I stopped being silent and obediently invisible. I *did* something to relieve my misery and declare my presence in the world."

Other women searched because they felt personally responsible for their children, even after relinquishment. Some wished for an escape clause to relinquishment, allowing the adoptive parents to raise the children only as long as they remained accountable to the birthparents for the quality of their care. If that quality became unacceptable, these women wanted the right to intervene.

"It took me a few years, but I finally overcame the problems that led me to relinquish," Alexis says. "I needed to know—for myself—that if my child were not being well cared for, I could step in to help him. I needed to let his adoptive parents know that if there were an emergency in his life where I could help, I was available. I had no intention of reclaiming him or of interfering in their family. But I felt the responsibility both to check up on him and to make the offer."

Horror stories drove a few to undertake search. "You hear all kinds of rumors," Sylvia says. "I'd heard about a birthmother who searched and learned her son's address. She drove by the house several times, hoping to catch a glimpse of him, but she never saw a bike, a ball, or a toy. She became worried—she thought he might be dead or something, so she got up the nerve to call his home. It turned out that not the son but the adoptive mother had died. The father remarried but his new wife didn't want children. So the eight-year-old boy had been sent off to boarding school, year-round. The child *never* came home. The father was overjoyed that the birthmother had called and offered to let her take the boy back. Without hesitation, she agreed to take him and went to the school to bring him home."

Despite such tales, which may be apocryphal, not one of the birthmothers interviewed searched with the goal of reclaiming their children or of breaking up adoptive families. They were generally appalled at the thought of disrupting their children's family lives or bonds. Even when their own anguish and despair were extreme, most put their children's interests before their own. With few exceptions, they remained on the sidelines of their "found" children's lives, watched from afar, and revealed themselves carefully, gently, and only after their children had reached maturity.

The Risks

Some who searched never found their biological children. Many eventually gave up. Others continued their searches relentlessly, unwilling to accept defeat.

Even when they succeeded in their searches, a few birthmothers met with failure in the forms of disappointment or rejection. "My son has no use for me," one remarks. "He's thirty-three, married, and a father, but he refuses to see me and wrote me to stop trying to contact him. Still, I feel better than I did before I found him. Because now I know who he is, how he's doing, and where he works. Just knowing that he's OK gives me some peace."

Others, like Zoe, found children who bore no resemblance to them or to their expectations. "I kept trying to warm up to her," Zoe says. "To find common ground. I wanted to love her. But the more I extended myself to her, the harder she resisted. I'd invite her to luncheons, and she'd arrive in see-through tops, just to shock me. She'd belch, like a beer guzzler, at the table at dinner parties. She told my mother to 'buzz off' more than once. She'd do anything to offend or alienate everyone. I understood that she was angry, that she'd felt rejected because she was relinquished. But there *had* to be some limits. For years, I'd been desperate to find her. After I found her, I became desperate to escape."

Even when they did not face disappointment or rejection, re-united birthmothers and adoptees were often unprepared for what they found. Women seeking lost babies found adults. Adoptees seeking idealized madonnas found middle-aged, imperfect women. Even in the most successful situations, birthmothers re-united with their relinquished children confronted confusion about their roles. They both *were* and were *not* mothers, since their children already had adoptive mothers. Neither, however, did they consider themselves merely "friends" to the people to whom they had given birth. Their children, moreover, were not children; they'd grown up and had independent identities, relationships, and histories that did not involve their biological relatives. Having found each other, birthmothers and their children were usually left to search further: this time, for places in each others' lives.

Mechanisms of Search

The techniques of search varied. Some birthmothers hired private investigators; others worked independently through networks of search support groups. A number sought information from their states, requesting copies of birth certificates or driver's licenses. Some found that bureaucratic mistakes combined with white lies gave them information to which, legally, they were not entitled.

"I wrote to the state," Sue says, "pretending to be my son. I asked for a copy of my birth certificate, stating my name at birth and my birth date. But, since 'I' was under eighteen, my request was rejected. I tried again. I wrote and said I was the adoptive mother and asked for a birth certificate. I was amazed that I received it, along with a birth number that allowed me to seek further information, including his adoptive family's name and address."

A number of birthmothers like Sue falsely claimed to be the adoptive mothers, weaving explanations for lost birth certificates and altered last names. Divorce, remarriage, and relocation were commonly conjured up as part of elaborate, carefully conceived fabrications. Some read books that detailed methods, resources, and alternatives for search. Others wrote to adoption agencies openly seeking nonidentifying information about their relinquished children and adoptive families, then used that information to try to trace the families' whereabouts. Advertisements, search professionals, and volunteer networks of cooperating adoptees and birthparents were among the tools most frequently employed by searchers.

Some birthmothers did not actively search but instead made themselves available to be *found*, should their children search for them. These women wrote letters or waivers of confidentiality permitting sealed adoption records to be opened should their children initiate searches after they reached legal age.

Guess Who?

Some women whose children searched for them, however, were *not* willing to be found. Some were, in fact, distraught at discovery and unceremoniously turned their children away, relinquishing them a second time.

"I got pregnant because I was raped," Mary declares. "It took me years to recover from that. I gave birth to the baby, but that was the most anyone could ask of me. It wasn't the child's fault that I was raped, but it wasn't mine either, and I don't see why I should be saddled with a child I never wanted, that I never chose to have, and who's birth was the result of a horrible violent attack. I couldn't face her when she called and I never will. When she called, I said she had the wrong number. And, the fact is that, if she was looking for a mother, she *did* have the wrong number."

Search support groups estimate that only about 5 percent of the birthmothers found by their relinquished children actually reject them; another small percentage accept the children only reluctantly. For these women, being found by the children they relinquished years ago was not merely upsetting; it was shattering. One woman rejected her son because she'd kept the biracial affair she'd had prior to her marriage secret. She dreaded the possibility that, someday, her secret might be discovered not because she was ashamed of her past but because she feared the intolerance of others. "My husband knows nothing about the baby I gave up twenty-four years ago. I don't think he could accept the fact that I'd had a child prior to marriage, much less that I'd had it with a black man. If he ever found out, I'm sure he'd leave me. I'd lose my home, my marriage, my kids—I'd lose everything. When the agency contacted me, it was as if my worst nightmares were coming true. I refused to see the young man. But I'm still afraid he'll show up at my house unannounced."

Another birthmother, named Gail, rejected her searching daughter because the child's birth had almost destroyed her marriage; she'd become pregnant by her husband's business associate. "My husband and I survived that affair only because I agreed to relinquish the child and never mention her again. Now, four kids and twenty-five years later, here she is to haunt us. My husband has never forgiven me or his friend for betraying him. I made a bad mistake, but that was long ago, in the past. Behind a closed door. She has two parents, and I'm not one of them. I have my own children, and I don't consider her one of them. That was the agreement we made when she was adopted and I intend to stand by it. I wish she would, too. We want her to let us be."

Although such statements sounded harsh, they reflected the fragility of some birthmothers' lives after relinquishing. Many feared that their spouses either could not or would not accept the truth and kept their relinquishments and prior relationships secret, anticipating that they themselves would be rejected if their pasts were revealed. These women were consumed by insecurities, guilts, and anxieties that dominated their lives and prevented them not only from participating in even minimal contact with their offspring but also from examining their feelings about or motivations for avoiding this contact.

When the Truth Won't Fade

Some women, however, were unable to evade their searching children and, accordingly, were forced to confront both the past and their related feelings. Cindy, who'd been abused by her mother during childhood, was one of these women.

"I thought about my son all the time," she says, "but I never would have searched for him. I *couldn't* search because I'd lied about his conception—I'd told everyone that I'd been raped. If that lie were ever exposed, I thought my whole life would crumble. Everything had been built upon that lie. I'd lied to my husband, my sister, my parents. Still, if I were ever to see my son again, I knew that I couldn't tell him his father was a rapist! No one should be told a lie like that. But telling the truth, I believed, would alienate everyone who'd ever trusted me. Either because I'd been promiscuous or because I was a liar."

Like others who had not shared the facts about their relinquishments with their families, Cindy was paralyzed by the threat of the fearful consequences the truth could bring. Her own imagination prevented her from revealing and dealing with the truth and, therefore, from integrating her experiences and healing. Despite her fears, however, when the adoption agency actually called to ask if she wanted to meet her searching son, Cindy was unable to refuse. She asked for time to think about it but, as she hung up the phone, she began to confront the truth.

"I was overwrought," she says. "It must have scared my other kids, to see me so out of control, crying for no apparent reason. But, finally, I decided that I had to tell my husband the truth. I was cornered. I saw no other way out, but to confess my lie, even though it meant risking my husband's trust and love. So I gathered up all my nerve and told him the truth, without looking at him. To hear myself say it, that I had never been raped all those years ago, that I had slept with lots of boys and didn't know who the father was, that I had lied so that my mother wouldn't beat me to death, it sounded so alien, as if I was talking about somebody else. But he listened calmly. He didn't shudder or wince.

"In fact, he simply took my hand and said, 'No one can blame you for what you did back then. Or for lying about it. You did what you had to in order to survive.' For the first time ever, I felt forgiven! I felt really accepted for who I am. Loved."

The initial relief and elation about their reunions, however, were premature. Like Cindy, many birthmothers found that what they'd expected to be difficult about their reunions was far less traumatic than what actually, unexpectedly occurred.

Expectations and Reality

A number of birthmothers who had believed that they had long since "healed" from the effects of relinquishing fell apart when they were found by their searching children. Long-kept secrets, denied feelings, and suppressed grief exploded, blowing the facades off their outwardly "normal" lives.

"I was a mess," one woman says. "My world fell apart. Even though my family stood by me, after all these years, I had to face what had happened. Memories I'd buried—the past came back to haunt me. I began to remember all the humiliation, shame, fear, and, worst of all, all the pain of relinquishing that I'd buried and hidden away. All the loss came flooding through. I couldn't eat or sleep. I lost fifteen pounds in ten days. I cried all the time, just wept constantly, after the day I finally met my son."

Delayed grief and reawakened emotions were experienced by many birthmothers found by their relinquished children. In the previous chapter, a woman described actually passing out during her reunion, reliving acute symptoms of labor. Other women found that, along with their children, they were reunited with lost pieces of their pasts, memories they had suppressed, emotions they had denied. Many were compelled to resume the grieving they'd abandoned years ago and to confront the toll relinquishing had taken on their lives. Many required professional counseling or the support of other birthmothers to help them through this process.

Cindy's reunion took place at the adoption agency. "I was terrified. If he'd been the slightest bit angry or cold to me, I couldn't have handled it. I was sweaty and shaking so bad I thought I'd pass out. But when I first looked at him, I'll never forget it—I saw my own eyes. I can't tell you the feeling, the recognition that occurred—I knew, when I saw his eyes, that it would be OK, that he wasn't angry with me, that it would be OK.

"And I heard the nun say it would be all right if I wanted to hug him. And I did, I hugged him and, oh, he hugged me back! And in that one embrace, one short moment, years of longing were released. Decades of torment eased. I'd needed that hug for twenty-three years. When it finally came, it seemed like it couldn't be true—it had to be a fantasy. But I knew it was real, because the weight was lighter in my heart and I was finally, instantly free."

After the Hug

Many reunions, like Cindy's, started out intensely, full of curiosity, anticipation, emotion, and relief. Birthmothers frequently felt that they could tell, as soon as they laid eyes on their children, the direction that their relationships would take. Even when that direction initially appeared positive, however, there were miles of ground to be covered and the roads often turned bumpy.

For some, reunions proved to be almost as traumatic as relinquishment. Sometimes, although the reunions themselves were positive, the emotions they evoked were unsettling, at best. Cindy's reunion, for example, went swimmingly well. "We were like magnets," she declares. "We were drawn to each other as if we'd never been apart. We shared pictures and talked for hours. I didn't want to tell him about his father that day, but he asked. When I explained, he simply said that, since I wasn't sure who his father was, he wouldn't bother to search for him. He didn't seem shocked or judgmental, ashamed or disappointed. In fact, he just kept asking more questions and said he wanted to meet his brothers—my other boys. We didn't want to leave at the end of our visit. We hugged and exchanged phone numbers. Afterwards, I cried all the way home."

Even though the reunion itself went well, the latent feelings of loss and rage that it awoke shook the very foundations of the birthmother's life. "Our reunion took place over a year ago," Cindy says. "I still cry all the time, day or night. Out in the open or in private. I cry at TV commercials that show babies, at pregnant women. It's terrible, but I can't help it. I have twenty-three years of loss to go through. I love this boy, and I've missed out on so much. I'm angry at my family for making me give him up. I can't handle the anger sometimes, and I certainly don't want it, but here it is."

Another woman says that her grief after reunion was unbearable. Her sense of irreparable loss and guilt was so powerful that she considered suicide simply to end her anguish. "The grief was terrible, the pain was bad. At first I wanted to have another baby.

I needed a baby, I thought, but I was just beginning to plow through my pain. When I realized that the baby I wanted was gone forever, for three or four months, the pain was so severe that I didn't want to live—I just wanted to die so the pain would go away. My husband stayed home from work to watch me, he was so worried. I hid under the blanket in bed, like in the womb. I wouldn't eat or sleep. I just cried. I wanted to die, but instead I went to a psychiatrist. I'm too strong, I guess, to kill myself. I'm a survivor. And, besides, I'm blessed. I'm free of secrets now, and I have people who love me and stand by me. I've got my husband and children—all my children—to live for."

While most birthmothers did not find their reunions life-threatening, many were thrown by unexpected aspects of meeting their children. The senses of tragedy and loss they had experienced at relinquishment resurfaced. Many lost control and dissolved into tears inspired by anything suggesting babies: diaper displays in the supermarket, TV commercials, pregnant women on the street. Most saw these crying bouts as unloading or releasing years of pent-up emotions and did not strive to repress their expression. Even after their emotions had poured forth, time had passed, and their relationships with their reunited offspring had solidified, however, many were unable to resume the normal pre-reunion lives they'd struggled so hard to build. Reunion put them in touch with the harsh truth of their pasts and the reality of what they had lost; postreunion life would never be the same.

"I'm thrilled at our reunion," Cindy says. "My eldest son fits right in with my other boys. My husband loves him, too. I finally feel that my life is complete. I'm a grandmother—my son has a son, and he brings him over to visit. I love them both to distraction. But even though he drops by all the time, I still cry when he leaves. I feel emptiness as soon as his car turns the corner and he's out of sight. I have a terrible fear of separation. I feel a wave of loss and worry that something will happen, something will go wrong. I think our reunion will last forever. But I feel insecure, anyway. I was only fifteen years old when I gave him up. He's twenty-four, now. A man. I long for him as a three- or four-year-old. Not my husband, not my other sons, not even he as a grown man can ease that longing. Despite our strong bonds, I'll always have feelings of sadness for what we've lost. In some ways, although it was like being half-dead, the days before our reunion, the days of suppression were easier."

Finding Out What's Been Lost

Even in mutually rewarding reunions, most birthmothers experienced profound sensations of loss. Although they regained contact with their children and had the opportunity to establish ongoing relationships for the future, they inevitably confronted their feelings about the years and the relationships they had not shared. Even many who were confident that they had completed their grieving faced unanticipated regrets when faced with their actual rather than conceptual children.

"Meeting my son," Sylvia says, "was like meeting myself. We looked the same. The bones in his feet cracked just like mine. We have the same personality, same wily sense of humor, the same nonconformist behavior, the same contempt for rules. He was always getting in trouble at school for having a 'bad attitude.' We're small-boned, unlike his adoptive family. They're all giants; he's five seven and hates being short. He's a loner like I am, but he grew up in a gregarious Texan slap-on-the-back family. It was good for him to see where he came from. It explained to him who he was, made him feel less different. But for me, finding him wasn't enough. We'd lost all those years. It was like finding your son after World War II after he was raised by Russians. They did the best they could, but he's not your son anymore. Not as you'd have raised him. I feel guilty, that he missed what he was entitled to if he'd have grown up with me, that he missed out on the travel, on seeing the world, on feeling that he belonged. And he grew up frustrated, trying to be like the people who raised him, even though he didn't fit. Even reunions can't make it right."

After reunions, many birthmothers similarly lamented that they had not personally been able to give their children shared memories and securely rooted identities during their formative years. Others mourned but found it more difficult to identify the sources of their sadness. Jean and her twenty-four-year-old daughter had both been searching when they found each other four years ago. Despite her initial joy at reunion, Jean felt confused by overwhelming depression. Finally, she realized that, in finding a daughter, she'd lost one as well

"Every year," she says, "I'd bought a birthday present and card for the little girl I'd named Stephanie. I'd put all these presents in the closet in the spare bedroom and saved them for her, each with a card special for that year. When I met her, I brought her the teddy bear I'd bought for her first birthday. I told her I'd been waiting twenty-four years to give it to her. We both cried.

"But that's the only one of those gifts that I ever gave her. Because as I got to know her, I realized that she was not my 'Stephanie,' she was her adoptive mother's 'Melissa.' She wasn't the child I'd imagined and bought gifts for; she was a very different person than the one I'd created in my mind. And in order to have a real relationship with the real young woman I had found, I had to let go of the fantasy child I'd carried with me all the years. And it surprised me how difficult it was to do that, how deeply depressed I got when I finally had a chance to know my daughter as she *is*. But I had to do that, and I gave all the presents I'd bought Stephanie to charity. Now when I buy presents, I buy them for Melissa. There is no Stephanie."

Now That I've Found You ...

After reunion, many birthmothers felt awkward and uncertain of their roles. Even when adoptive parents supported their children's reunions, birthmothers were unsure of how to define their relationships in ways that would not compete or overlap. Creating these roles meant defining themselves as other than "parents," divesting themselves of their "fantasy" children, and enduring doubts about whether their efforts would be successful. Often, as their relationships evolved, birthmothers remained plagued by fears of rejection and failure.

"Melissa looks just like me," Jean says. "We even have the same handwriting. But she is my friend more than my daughter. I wasn't the one who patched her scraped knees or kissed her tears away, after all. Someone else did that. So we're taking it slowly, trying to discover our own ground. Neither of us wants to lose the other again, so we take it step by step. There's no rush, even though it feels like there is. But, truly, we have the rest of our lives. We talk several times each week and, even after four years, I pinch myself whenever I hear her voice on the phone. And when we hang up, I worry that she'll have enough of me, that she'll disappear from my life. But that is my insecurity and not based on fact. The fact is, she invited me to her wedding last year and introduced me to some of her friends as her mother, even though her adoptive mother was there, too. I was bursting inside, but I didn't want to interfere with whatever my daughter has to work through about her adoption, so I kept quiet about it. All I know is that there *is* room for all of us, and we will find our niche together, even if we can't find a name for it."

Many birthmothers emphasized that reunion was *not* a cure for the regrets, angers, or grief they faced after relinquishing. Reunion, in fact, offered additional risks of rejection, disappointment, and confrontation with the events, issues, and emotions of the past. Many reunions that seemed to be going well terminated temporarily or permanently months or years later; reunion itself offered no guarantees of successful long-term relationships. Despite these limitations and risks, however, whether their children welcomed them or rejected them, whether their reunions unleashed pent-up emotions or left them suppressed, whether they developed stable relationships or floundered with insecurity, most birthmothers who had found their children felt they had benefited. Knowledge itself was sufficient reward.

"I could not have survived much longer without knowing," says one. "I needed to *know*, not to wonder, if my son was OK. I don't know how our relationship will evolve now. He may not want me in his life permanently. He may shut me out altogether, and I worry that I might lose him again. But, no matter what happens, I have the peace of knowing that he's healthy and happy. And of having *told* him, after all these years, that I love him, always have and always will."

Timing and Premature Searches

Many of the birthmothers interviewed postponed their searches until after their children were eighteen. Even if they had conducted their searches earlier, most made no effort to contact the children until after they'd reached maturity. The desire to find out about their children did not, in most cases, seem to justify disruptive intrusions into the children's lives. At times, however, the temptations were great.

"I searched for my son when he was just fifteen," Sue says. "I had planned on searching for him when he was eighteen, but I realized that it might take years, so I started early. Surprisingly, it took only a few months to find him, so I knew where he was—just ten miles from my home. I had no intention of contacting him but, as time went on, it became more and more difficult to stay away. I became obsessed with catching just a glimpse of him. I plotted with my girlfriends different ways to get to see him without letting him know who I was.

"Finally, I went to his high school, pretending that I was considering a move to that neighborhood and that I was investigating the school. I asked to see a yearbook and looked him up. When I saw his picture, it was as if I'd always known what he looked like—he had my face, only male. I saw, in the yearbook, that he was on the baseball team—a jock, like his birthfather. I felt like a spy. My heart was racing the whole time. I walked through the corridors, hoping to bump into him and actually asked a boy if he knew him. I pretended to be an old family friend. He did, but he said he was out sick that day. So I left. But I attended all the school's home games. I watched him play from the stands. Whenever he made a hit, I was on my feet, yelling and cheering—I couldn't help it. I even took my mother to a game! And I went to his graduation. I followed him at a distance, so he wouldn't see me. I watched him kiss his girlfriend and hang around with his friends while his parents took pictures. I needed to *see* his life, even if I couldn't participate in it."

A number of birthmothers confided that they observed their children from a distance, unseen and anonymous, like Sue. Some, especially those who had achieved a degree of self-respect or social status in their roles as professionals, community leaders, wives, or mothers, felt humiliated by their need for camouflage and subterfuge; nevertheless, they accepted it as not only the most gentle but often the *only* way they could keep track of their children without disturbing or damaging their lives.

Finding Worst Fears

Usually, birthmothers who searched early did so partially to confirm that their children were healthy or even alive. Occasionally, however, they discovered that they were not. A few searches uncovered tragedies, such as death or severe illness. Some revealed facts that heightened rather than relieved regrets about relinquishment.

"I searched like a maniac," Alexis says. "I would stop at no lengths until I was satisfied that my kid was OK. I'd had dreams about him, beginning after my second child was born, and the dreams nagged at me so that I couldn't rest. I searched fervently, through state records, the maternity center, and the adoption agency. All my efforts through these channels were thwarted. In fact, the agency told me that the adoptive parents had responded to my queries with a curt letter that said, 'We wish no contact with the birthmother. The boy is doing fine.'

"So I joined support groups and began therapy because I was so frustrated. My psychiatrist specialized in birthparent problems and told me in plain English that I needed to find my son for my own mental health. He gave me permission to find him, in a way. So I hired a private investigator, and, when my son was eleven, I found out his name and address. I contacted other birthparents in the area and hired a search consultant to find out more about him. Two weeks later, I found out that my son is severely mentally and physically handicapped. I would *never* have relinquished him if I'd known."

Like many birthmothers, Alexis found that having information about her relinquished child fueled rather than satisfied her desire to see him. However, given the adoptive parents' attitudes and his disabilities, she proceeded with care.

"I went to see him participate in the Special Olympics," she says. "I *needed* to see him. I made contact with him, incognito, like a fan. I took his picture and talked to him about how well he did. He kept looking at me, quizzically. He resembles me strongly. Maybe he saw that, or felt familiar. But he's mentally six years old, and he's going to stay that way. Ironically, as much as it made me want to keep him with me, finding out that he's handicapped freed me of a lot of guilt, because I know he won't be able to fester about the unknowns of his biological heritage, the subtleties of his identity, or the questions of rejection. I sleep better knowing that his handicap saves him from many of the painful complexities of emotion."

Even after the shock of learning about tragedies involving their children, most birthmothers had no regrets about their searches. *Not* knowing their children's fates was consistently deemed worse than knowing even dire or painful facts.

"Now that I've found him, I'm no longer obsessed," Alexis says. "I know that he's handicapped, but I'm grateful that he's loved and well cared for. Of course, I'd like to have him in my life someday. I just don't know how that can happen or what he'd be able to understand about our relationship."

Searching for Disaster

Most birthmothers who tracked their children before they'd reached maturity disguised their motivations and identities. They were driven to address their own concerns but determined not to disturb their children. There were, however, a few whose cravings to find out about their children so overpowered their objectivity that they failed to consider either the impact or the repercussions of their actions.

Annie literally stalked her son for months before she impulsively rushed up to him one day in the schoolyard. "I'd written to the adoptive family, telling them that I'd like to be in touch with my son. They wrote back, irate, and ordered me to leave my son alone. I did, for three whole years. But then I couldn't stand it anymore. I approached him after school when he was eleven years old. I asked if he were William. He said he was. I asked if he were adopted. He grunted, and I assumed that meant yes. I told him that I was his birthmother, that I'd always thought about him, and I asked if he had anything to ask me. He asked only where he'd been born. I gave him some letters I'd written him over the years and my phone number, and that was it. Of course, his mother called me later, furious and frantic. She said that, in fact, they'd *not* told him that he'd been adopted and that he was extremely upset. Well, how was *I* supposed to know they'd never told him? It was his right to know! Since then, I've sent him presents at Christmas and on his birthday, that is, for nine years, but the packages have always come back unopened and the checks I send him have never been cashed."

Unlike Annie, most birthmothers were aware that successful reunions between birthmothers and children required mutual interest, delicate preparation, and careful timing. Even the most zealous women restrained their impulses to storm into their children's lives, appalled at the thought of confusing their children or precipitating emotional problems during their formative years. Reunions that were sloppily handled, selfishly motivated, or prematurely timed, before both parties were ready, often proved, like Annie's, to be disastrous.

"Even today," Annie says, "my son won't talk to me. He's got a job and an apartment of his own, but he won't talk to me. He's had his phone number changed to get me to stop calling. But I won't go away. I *can't*. I'll wait forever if I have to. I back off for a while and try again. We got off to a bad start, and he just won't let us move past that, even after all these years. Sometimes I think he's just like his birthfather—they both rejected me. They even look alike."

When birthmothers like Annie imposed reunions irresponsibly, without concern for the needs and emotions of all members of the adoption triangle, they often exhibited the same patterns of self-destructive, damaging behavior that dominated their post-relinquishment lives. In doing so, they destroyed the possibilities not only of successfully integrating their own relinquishment experiences, but also of developing any lasting or positive relationships with their traumatized and wary children.

Searching for Atonement

A number of birthmothers expressed regrets that they had searched too early not because their children were too young but because they themselves had not sufficiently resolved their problems with respect to relinquishment. They cautioned that finding their children while they were still vulnerable could be harmful both to themselves and to their children. One woman realized too late that she should have completed therapy prior to searching. "Once I found my son, I became desperately depressed. I couldn't bear how hostile I felt when I was around him. Everything he said or did irritated or enraged me. I'm not completely sure why. Maybe because he was his own person, not the child I'd envisioned. Maybe he was just like his pig-headed birthfather. But, for whatever reasons, the joy I felt at finding him turned into despair real fast. So I've cut off contact with him. I hate myself for it, in a way. I don't mean to hurt him or disappoint him. But I can't handle a relationship with him, at least not now."

Birthmothers rarely searched before they felt certain that they could be consistently accountable for taking a place in their children's lives. Frequently, however, they were unable to imagine, much less prepare for, all the possible repercussions of having their children in their *own* lives. Zoe, for example, had never overcome her guilts about relinquishing and was, therefore, susceptible to punishing manipulation by the angry daughter she found.

"She calls me up in the middle of the night, drunk or stoned," she says. "She threatens to get even with me for breaking up her family and giving her up. She says that I ruined her life, that *I'm* the cause of all her troubles. Elizabeth is not the girl with lace and curls that I imagined when I searched. She's, instead, angry, vindictive, and sadistic. But I didn't realize that at first, so when she told me I'd ruined her life, I believed her. I tried to make it up to her. I blamed myself for her problems and, really, subjected myself to all kinds of psychological and verbal punishment from her. Because I blamed myself, because I'd not worked out all my guilts, I allowed her to blame me, too. It was really sick."

Most birthmothers emphasized that, no matter how desperately they wished to search, the timing of their searches was critical. It was important to assure the maturity of not only the child but the birthmother as well. They were convinced that reunions should *not* be attempted until women had identified and dealt with their own relinquishment-related problems and considered all of the possible ramifications of reunion, including rejection, failure, or bizarre and unexpected twists.

"You've got to be strong when you approach your child," Zoe says. "You've got to be ready to take on the toughest questions and to withstand the fury of their pent-up emotions. Otherwise you may find yourself subject to lifelong apology, punishment, and desires for revenge."

Uncertainties and Etiquette

Even in the best of reunions, birthmothers found it necessary to take their relationships slowly. Many were so accustomed to being excluded from their children's lives that they were uncomfortable being included. As much as they'd craved contact, they were shy about accepting invitations to graduations or weddings, let alone titles of "Mom" to their relinquished children or of "Grandma" to their children's children. Some had difficulty knowing how to participate without appearing to compete with adoptive parents. Pam is married to her son's birthfather.

"My son's adoptive parents have much less money than we do," Pam says. "He's in college and struggling to pay tuition. We'd love to help him. But we don't want to offend him or his parents by appearing to give him something they can't. We're unsure how to act. We don't want to seem to be buying his love, but we don't want him to miss out on a good education either. We'd love to help, but we don't know how."

Birthmothers like Pam generally found that, despite their desires to rush into their children's lives and help solve all their problems, it was wise to take things slowly, allowing their relationships to develop naturally and mutually before intervening. Where their husbands were also the birthfathers, additional issues arose.

"I had come to terms with my grief about relinquishing long ago," Pam says. "It never went away, but I'd acknowledged it. My husband Jeff, though, had dismissed our first son, pushed his birth and relinquishment out of his mind altogether. Now, when he met our son as a young man, he had to face up to what we did when we relinquished, with all that we lost. For my husband, the reunion has been much more difficult than for me. He's a mess, really. He doesn't sleep; he cries. He's taken over by grief. And I have trouble supporting him because of all the years he ignored my grief. So the reunion has brought out issues that had been hiding in our marriage, as well as those that concern our son."

Effects of reunions extended not only into marriages but across generations. Siblings and half-siblings, biological grandparents, aunts, uncles, and cousins were also involved. Sometimes jealousies emerged when birthmothers paid more attention to their newfound relinquished children than to those they'd raised. Other times, though, the siblings developed close ties of their own.

"My kids all run in the same crowd," Liz says. "They're like a pack. The eldest fit right in, like a missing piece of a puzzle."

Although not every family experienced complete harmony among offspring, many birthmothers experienced a sense of completion and peace after their children had all been introduced. "My husband and I renewed our wedding vows on our twenty-fifth anniversary," Jean says. "All my prayers were answered. My children, all my children, were there together. The whole family was one. I invited my daughter's adoptive parents, too. We were a family, united, in the warmest, most accepting, most loving sense of the word. It was a joyous occasion, I think, for all of us."

Physical Bonding

During reunions, many birthmothers experienced the need for physical contact with their children. Some were surprised that, even though their children were adults and virtual strangers, they were driven to touch, hug, and hold them, just as if they were newborn babies.

"When he walked in," Sue says, "my first impression was that he walked just like Bob, his dad. It was like a flashback, like being a teenager again and seeing Bob coming to get me for a date. He's even built just like Bob. We knew each other right away, and we embraced when we met and he kissed my cheek. I backed away. I was afraid to touch him too much. I wanted to hold onto him, but neither of us was ready to allow too much contact. For me, holding him meant addressing twenty-five years of pain and longing for him and, I admit, for his father."

A number of birthmothers, like Sue, described reunions in terms of memories and flashbacks. In meeting their children, these women also confronted their pasts, lost youth, and often unresolved feelings about relationships with birthfathers.

"I had to back away and look at him," Sue continues. "I watched his hands as he talked. I wanted to clutch him, just grab him, but I felt uncomfortable about that. I didn't know how he'd respond. Finally, I couldn't stand it any more and I explained that, when he was a baby, I hadn't been allowed to hold him. I said, 'I'm sorry, but I have to touch you. I have to hug and kiss you.' I leaned over to kiss his cheek, but he kissed my lips. My other sons kiss my cheeks; lips are for their girlfriends. The kiss wasn't sexual, but it was different than how my other boys kiss me. It was odd, nice, undefined."

Mothers and children who met as adults often had difficulty defining the ambiguously physical nature of their relationships. Many birthmothers felt *physically* rather than sexually, attracted to their children, as if they could not stop touching, holding, or hugging them.

"My daughter was already married by the time we met," Bridget says. "But we clung to each other, like an infant and a new mother. We needed *physically* to fill in the lost stages of our relationship before we could begin to be together as adults. I pushed her hair back, the way mothers do to small children. She lay her head on my shoulder as if she were a little girl, and I caressed her forehead and her cheek. We went to the ocean for the weekend, after that first meeting, and we spontaneously went through progressive kinds of touching, as if from infancy through adulthood. For hours, the first day, I held her and rocked her and sang to her. We hardly talked at all. Then, gradually, we became more verbal, asking and answering and holding hands, rather than clutching each other. But it was as if we couldn't really talk until we had connected physically, like mothers and babies do. Our familiarity was—still is—based on a very primitive, physical level. My other kids and I kiss hello and good-bye. She and I cling to each other at each parting. Neither of us can be the first to let go."

When adult children were of the opposite sex, the need for physical bonding sometimes proved more confusing. "At the end of our first meeting," Sue recalls, "I said, 'I don't want to say good-bye again.' He told me not to worry; he reassured me. He is gorgeous, and I was startled that I felt an attraction to him. I had to remind myself that he was my *son*, that I birthed him. We see each other often now. A couple of times a week. People who see us together often think we're a couple because we're always touching, always making physical contact of some sort, like holding hands. Now, with time, we've both become more relaxed about touching. But we've established some limits, even though we've never talked about it. It's unlike any other relationship, because it's like being with the male version of my younger self. And, I admit, it's sexually confusing because he's male. We are both in control of our actions, but sexual misunderstanding is possible. He tends to be protective of me, to treat me like a date rather than a mom. We both feel an attraction, clearly, but nothing we'd ever consider acting out, just a comfortable bond that's more than a little bit more electric than the bonds I feel with the boys I've raised from birth."

Contact and Confusion

After reunions, some birthmothers experienced physical attractions to their adult children that were clearly sexual in nature. Many attributed their feelings to repressed maternal responses. "All mothers experience the instinct to bond physically with their babies," Barbara says. "But when that baby is a full-grown adult, physical bonding becomes confused with sexual bonding. Adults in our culture don't usually connect physically, at least not intensely, without arousing some sexual response. It's difficult to clarify, let alone to satisfy those passionate mother-child urges when the mother's forty-two and the child's twenty-five."

Other birthmothers believed that attractions between mothers and children occurred only because relinquishment had separated them during critical years. "When your child grows up away from you, there's no incest taboo," Sue comments. "When you raise children from birth, barriers just happen. Your roles and limits evolve naturally in the context of family, growth, and development. Healthy parents do not feel sexually interested in children whose diapers they've changed. But when the 'child' you meet is a stunning, full-grown adult—particularly of the opposite sex—at the peak of their sexual charm, well, you're on your own. It's surprising, but you're not automatically immune to attraction. No incest taboo has evolved and you have to define your limits on your own."

Some women give additional reasons for these attractions. "It's your own youth that you want to embrace," Andrea says. "It's your own ego. You miss your past. You want to connect with a time of life, with lost innocence, with all the losses and disappointments of your own life by connecting with your child. It's narcissism, desire for your own self, and to pretend otherwise is foolish."

Even when they shared this theory, some women found their attractions difficult to control. "I'm so attracted to my son that I can't be in the same room with him comfortably," Barbara says. "All I can think about when he's around is going to bed with him. I act like a fool, an idiot, a sixteen-year-old with a crush. For his own protection, I've talked to him about my feelings and asked him if he shares them. This frightens him away. He must interpret my frankness as a come-on, because he avoids me. When he does see me, he tries not to be alone with me. He sits across the room rather than next to me. He doesn't want to talk about it. He'd rather keep away from me and the whole subject, which makes me suspect he feels some alarming or, at least, uncomfortable impulses, too."

Some who experienced similar sexual attractions said that their impulses were powerful, embarrassing, difficult to understand, and hard to manage. No matter how they tried to explain them, however, they found them extremely threatening. "If you actually were to *act* on your attractions," Barbara says, "your relationship could be firecrackers, an atom bomb. It could explode. These attractions can destroy a reunion, but if they aren't controlled and incest occurs, they can surely destroy lives."

Birthmothers, Electra, and Oedipus

Incest was much more frequently a fantasy than an actual outcome of reunion. Attractions were usually limited to unfulfilled impulses. One woman, however, admitted to having consummated a sexual relationship with her adult son.

"It wasn't a question of right or wrong," she says. "It was a question of 'POW!' Neither of us could control ourselves, the attraction was too powerful. We saw each other sexually for about four years, and our relationship was more intense than anything I've ever experienced. I don't regret it, either. At least, I *miss* it more than I regret it."

Some birthmothers attributed the lack of shame or guilt about their incestuous feelings to Freudian psychology. "Boys are attracted to their mothers, girls to their fathers. That's a normal part of growing up," Zoe says. "They call these attractions Electra and Oedipus complexes, and normally kids pass through them without incident, inhibiting these desires in the face of family relationships. But when young adults meet parents without the structure of family relationship, when those parents seem like older, more mature forms of their own beings, well, their Oedipal or Electra-type desires *can* be more than they can handle."

Occasionally, birthmothers reported sexual attractions between their relinquished children and other members of their biological families. Sisters and brothers who met as adults, birthfathers and their children were also subject to physical attractions, that took sexual turns. Zoe's opinions were based not on her own attractions, but on those between her daughter and the birthfather.

"One of the first things I discussed with her when I met her was that she should *not* contact her father," Zoe says. "I had a strong sense of foreboding, a fear that something awful would occur. I even spoke to her about the Oedipal thing, because I saw such a strong resemblance between Elizabeth and her father that it frightened me. They drank the same kind of beer, wore the same tattoos, rode the same cycles. They were like clones. It was chilling how much they resembled each other.

"But, despite my warning, she did contact Jack. Until she rang his doorbell, he'd had no knowledge that she even existed. I'd kept the pregnancy completely secret from him. But, once they found each other, they both blamed me for keeping them apart all these years. Their need for each other was so great that Jack actually moved out of his home—divorced his third wife. He and Elizabeth are now living together somewhere in Indiana, as man and wife. I have trouble accepting their relationship because it's sick. But I understand it, if I think of it as being like falling in love with a new baby—blissful. It's like being drunk with love, the baby takes over your whole being. That must be what it was like for Jack to meet Elizabeth. Except that Elizabeth was twenty-five, not a newborn. And Jack has no guilt—he has no conscience, so he took the 'love' to its fullest extreme. And Elizabeth, well, Elizabeth must be very needy. Jack gives her an identity, a mirror to define herself. To me, their relationship is a nightmare. It makes me truly sorry—no, truly sick—that I ever found her."

When Seekers Can't Find

Search, of course, did not guarantee reunion. Many birthmothers spent years searching without success. Some became exhausted and gave up; others continued their pursuits no matter how much energy and expense were required. For a few, the frustration of search led to preoccupations, distortions, and even obsessions. These women interpreted every unexplained event in their lives in terms of their fruitless searches.

"I've sent letters to the agency," Jill says. "I've hit dead ends at every turn. But I believe my son will contact me, someday. He's twenty-three years old, now. Old enough to be allowed to make his own decisions. But the agency says, 'It's closed; that's it.'

"Still, whenever the phone rings and someone hangs up, I think it's him. Neighbors saw a strange car driving up and down the street real slow a few weeks ago. I thought *that* might be him. One year, I got an unsigned Easter card. I still think it was from him. I heard a song on the radio dedicated anonymously to 'Jill' and it was 'You Don't Know Me' by Ray Charles. I nearly flipped. I was *sure* it was him, trying to tell me he was nearby, that he knew me, that he was someone I knew. I realize that I have nothing to prove that he's around. But I have to believe—I've been searching so long. It's torture. It really is."

So Near and Yet So Far:
Open Adoption and Reunions

Although birthmothers with open adoptions did not need to search for their relinquished children, some struggled with many of the same reunion issues as women with closed. Their roles and relationships with their children were often unclear, their legal rights vague or nonexistent.

Many who relinquished with open terms had no direct contact with their children. By agreement, all communication regarding the children took place through the adoptive parents. Still, most of these women felt that simply knowing where and how their children were spared them significant anguish.

"I hear about her in an annual phone call, and I receive an annual photo," Donna says. "Those were the terms of our initial agreement. But I hope that I'll actually meet her someday, when she's older. At least I know there's that possibility. Things seem to be moving in that direction, anyway. As time goes on we all become more familiar and trusting of each other. This year, I could hear her voice in the background during the phone call. She knew her mother was talking to me, and she was shouting, 'Tell Donna about my skating lessons! Tell her I got new skates!' Hearing her say my name, I was aching for her mother to hand her the phone and let her talk to me directly. But I couldn't ask. I can't wait, though, for a chance to talk to her in person. Maybe next year."

Birthmothers like Donna were often tortured by feelings of being just slightly out of reach of their children. Many ached for actual contact, by phone, by mail, by touch. "All I want, every year," Donna says, "is to talk to my daughter on the phone for a few minutes. But I have to admit that, if I talk to her on the phone, *that* won't be enough. I'll want to see her in person. No matter what our contact arrangements are, I'll always want more. So I have to step back and wait for a day, some day, when she herself will initiate contact. And even then, I'll have to let her set the pace and make the rules."

Some birthmothers were comforted by messages from adoptive parents that gave details about the children's lives, but others found these facts merely frustrating. "We talk every Christmas," one woman says. "They tell me everything of note that happened that year. Like Jimmy learned to read, Jimmy broke his arm in softball, Jimmy went to summer camp in the mountains. I drink up every word. I'm mesmerized. And then, at the end of call, they say, 'Well, have a good holiday. We'll talk to you next year.' I always offer to help out if they need me for anything, and I always ask them to let me know if anything major happens. And then, there I am. Alone with a disconnected phone line, waiting for another year to pass."

Sometimes, birthmothers found their limited contact so frustrating that they backed off, unable to maintain consistently ambiguous roles. "I felt teased," Laurie says. "I was unsure of how to be part of my daughter's life without actually being there. So even though I'd agreed to call her on her birthday and to send her Christmas gifts, I backed off and missed a few years. I was wrong. But I was a teenager with problems. That's why I relinquished. But now, ten years later, I've straightened myself out. I finished school, and I'm a dental hygienist. Now I can be responsible, and I *want* to have a relationship with my child. But her parents won't allow it because they're afraid I'll disappear and let her down again. They've as much as told me that they think I'm incapable of sustaining a relationship and that they want me to stay out of her life. Even though we agreed to an open adoption, I have no legal rights. *I* know I've grown up and changed. *I* know that, today, I'd never relinquish her. But they don't know who I am, and I'm sure they don't care. They just want me to stay away."

In many states, birthmothers with open adoptions complained that adherence to open agreements depended entirely on the voluntary compliance of the adoptive parents. Because their open terms were not guaranteed by law, they were not legally binding. "It's basically a gentleman's agreement," Lynne says. "The adoptive parents can back out if they so choose and cut off communication with me if they want to. I'm not worried, though, because I have a great relationship with both of them. I feel like I'm part of the family, in a way. I've actually babysat for my daughter when her parents have gone on vacations. But I also know women who have been victimized by private open adoptions. I have a friend who signed relinquishment papers ambivalently, only because the prospective adoptive parents agreed to very flexible and open terms. As soon as the relinquishment was final, though, the adoptive family vanished, left the state, and apparently even changed their names. The birthmother had no legal rights to pursue them to enforce her agreement; open adoption was not protected by the laws of her state."

Patsy had a similar experience. She and the adoptive parents had agreed to communicate by letter and phone call. The adoptive parents abided by the agreement only until the adoption was actually finalized. "As soon as the adoption was legal," she says, "I received a certified letter from the lawyer of the adoptive parents telling me that they had decided that there would be no further contact between them and me. I was appalled. I wrote to them directly and told them that I didn't think they were fit to parent my child because of how they'd lied to me. I wrote that I regretted my decision to let them adopt her, that I would disappear until she was eighteen if they insisted, but that I'd be waiting and watching them and would contact her, and, when I did, they'd have to explain to her why they'd prevented her from having contact with me for all the intervening years. When they received my letter, they had the agency mediate between us. Instead of the terms to which they'd originally agreed, they now are bound only to accept and to send one letter a year. But I doubt their honesty. And I am forever insecure about whether—or when—they'll back out of *this* agreement. It's been only two years, so I still don't know."

Open adoptions have allowed many birthmothers a degree of peace. Knowing where their children lived and that they were loved and well cared for allowed them to avoid much of the anxiety experienced by women who surrendered with closed terms. Even the arrangements that allowed visits or direct communication between birthmother and child, however, have left many birthmothers dissatisfied. "Open adoption," says a particularly cynical birthmother, "is nothing more or less than a marketing tool to get women to relinquish their babies. It's like saying, 'You can be a parent and not be a parent all at once. You can have your cake and eat it, too.' It's false. It's a sham, an illusion offered to women who are reluctant to relinquish, who really don't *want* to give up their babies, but who are impressionable because they have problems, like youth or limited finances. If a woman agrees to an open adoption, what's she's *really* saying is, I don't want to give my baby up completely. These women should simply not relinquish. They're being misled, and they need to seek help not in relinquishment but in how to *keep* their children."

Others disagreed. They saw open adoption as a solution that, if designed to meet the needs of the particular individuals involved, worked well, if not perfectly. Lynne maintained that open adoption provided her with the opportunity to remain in the life of her unplanned child without taking on the responsibilities of raising her, which would have meant losing her own freedom, career goals, and education.

"If a woman gets to know the adoptive parents really well *before* she relinquishes," she says, "she should be able to avoid problems later. The more you know, the fewer surprises you'll be in for. I was not ready to raise my child, but I was able to find a loving couple who longed for a child, and all of our needs were met. It's not like they've adopted me, along with my child, but it *is* like I have a place there, within the definition of their family, so that I'm not a concept to my daughter and she's not a fantasy to me. We will be able to nurture a relationship of our own over time, as she grows."

Finding, Winning, and Losing

Even when reunions were mutually desired, they were not always completely satisfying to participants.Birthmothers who found their adult children often faced many unanticipated losses in the process. Some lost fantasies about "perfect" children; others, who had held images of babies in their minds, lost their infants for the second time when they encountered adults. All faced the reality that the years between surrender and reunion had been forever lost. Many confronted the loss of their own youth, realizing that reuniting with their children could not retrieve the past. Some finally came to terms with lost love, lost hope, or lost romantic notions.

With reunions, many birthmothers lost their dreams of what their lives would be *after* reunion. Problems did not disappear; life did not become perfect. Instead, most discovered that, no matter how happy their reunions were, they brought the loss of whatever had been linked, psychologically and emotionally, to their separations from their children.

Beyond these losses, birthmothers who searched took chances not only of failure and rejection but also of finding out that their worst fears were true. Their children might be dead, handicapped, ill, emotionally disturbed, abused, or neglected. Further, the process of search and reunion often awakened fearful emotions and memories, triggered long-suppressed grief, or aroused symptoms of posttraumatic stress. With reunions, risks were taken, secrets were revealed, truths were confronted.

Most of the time, birthmothers' fears of what might happen were worse than what actually occurred. But some found that their reunions took unexpected twists and turns. Children occasionally rejected their birthmothers outright; sometimes they appeared to welcome them and later, without apparent cause, terminated all contact. Most postreunion relationships took years to stabilize and ran hot and cold, subject to ups and downs and variations in form and intensity. Having lived for years without each other, birthmothers and their children struggled to include each other in lives that had been constructed around each other's absence.

Although reunions often emphasized the losses of the past, they also offered opportunities for birthmothers and their relinquished children to salvage their futures. Many were able to patch together mutually rewarding, individually crafted relationships. At best, finding each other permitted them to open their lives, hearts, and families to include each other and complete their family circles. At least, it permitted them to share the truth of their biological ties. Even in the worst situations, where reunion led to disappointment, rejection, or the discovery of tragedy, the truth was in itself freeing; searchers were released from the bondage of craving to know. Very few reunions were bizarre enough to cause regrets that searchers had ever searched.

"I found my daughter," Zoe says. "But my daughter is a nightmare, a horror, the child from hell. All those years, as I fell asleep praying to find her, I wish someone had warned me to be careful what you wish for: you might get it. Some losses, although they haunt you, are better left alone."

The fear of discovering horrors like Zoe's, however, was usually drowned out by the passion to breach the gaps created by relinquishment. The yearnings that motivated most searches could not have been quelled by any warnings or tales of disappointment, no matter how extreme. Even without guarantees of successful subsequent relationships, most women found reunions to be their own, priceless rewards. One birthmother described this outcome in a poem:

> . . . As I hugged you good-bye, the wind came
> And blew a lock of hair in my face.
> With a gesture that said more than words
> ever could, you reached out and tucked it in place.
> Though reluctant to leave, I felt light
> As a cloud; There was peace in my soul
> At long last. I was whole once again,
> A part of me found: The part I had left
> in the past.

Nancy, 1982

9

Balancing
the Triangle

SUE WAS A LITTLE TIPSY FROM ALL THE TOASTS. BUT THE TIPSINESS WAS not entirely from drinking; she felt high just being there. The restaurant was elegant. Her son and his fiancée glowed in the candlelight. Their engagement party was small, just family. She'd been honored and touched at the invitation. Her husband, of course, had refused to attend, but she'd been relieved. She hadn't wanted to share this evening with anyone, much less to let his jealousy ruin it. She stared into the candles, remembering the years she'd spent longing for her eldest child. Those years, that longing now seemed far away.

Laughter drew her back to the present. "Hey, Mom," her son yelled. "Watch this!"

Sue was startled and somewhat embarrassed that Steve was calling to *her*, not to his adoptive mother, seated at the other end of the table. But she smiled at him anyway and turned to see what he wanted. When she saw that he was juggling the dinner rolls, she laughed out loud. His father, Bob, had juggled, albeit poorly, and had forever attempted magic tricks that failed comically. Steve and Bob were incredibly, unknowingly, alike.

"Steve, you'll get us thrown out of here!" She turned to his adoptive father, Daniel. But Daniel simply shrugged.

"He's *your* son," he laughed.

Sue laughed, too, but her heart skipped at the generosity of his acknowledgment. Something like fear welled up inside her, but before she could think about it, Steve fumbled and dinner rolls were flying everywhere, crashing into flower arrangements and knocking over half-emptied glasses of wine.

Sue felt compelled to apologize to the waiter standing behind her. "I don't know where he came from . . . ."

"No, Mom," Steve interrupted, "*I'm* the one who didn't know where I came from!"

Everyone roared. Sue blushed, overcome by their easy affection and acceptance. After a moment, she excused herself. It was all too much. She needed to collect herself, maybe have a brief cry.

The ladies' room was empty. Good. She sat at the mirror. Steve's face, older and feminine, stared back at her, its eyes filled with tears and memories. Everything was happening so fast. If only Bob could be there, too; if only he could see their son . . . .

The door opened for a woman who moved so fast, so vehemently that Sue instinctively ducked. Something—clothing—a coat—*her* coat came flying into her face. The woman was shrieking.

"What do you want?" Sue struggled with the lining of her coat, trying to get it off her head. "Why couldn't you stay out of our lives? Go home! Just leave! You have your *own* family—you're not welcome to mine!"

The ladies' room door slammed shut behind Steve's adoptive mother. The coat dropped onto the floor. Sue never had time to respond.

The Ripple Effect

As reunions and open adoptions have become more common, so have ongoing relationships among triangle members. Many biological and adoptive families have begun to communicate or even interact face to face. And, for better or worse, many birthparents have reestablished mutual contact as part of their searches or reunions.

With or without openness or reunions, however, connections between often unsuspecting parties have been created with every adoption. Further, birthparents, adoptees, and adoptive parents have not been the only ones affected; connections have extended beyond basic adoption triangles to anyone related by blood, love, or legal bonds. On its surface, adoption has bound strangers into families. Underneath, it has permanently and invisibly linked these new families to people whom they may never have met or even seen, by nature of shared biological ties. How birthmothers felt about their biological and adoptive connections to others and how they wanted to see them evolve are the subjects of this chapter.

The Other Birthparent: Connections with Fathers

Often, birthfathers seemed invisible on the adoption triangle, sharing a side with birthmothers yet maintaining little or no contact with them or others on the triangle. Some had never even been told that they had fathered the relinquished children. Although a few birthfathers had remained close or even married birthmothers, most had lost touch during or after the pregnancy. For some birthmothers, these men represented lost or true love; more often, however, they represented threatening, unsettling unfinished business.

Young Love Grown Old

Despite the passage of time and their marriages to others, a number of women still considered themselves in love with birthfathers. For some, reunions with their relinquished children rekindled their long-concealed passions, adding sparks to the fires they had carried for years.

"My son is just like his father," Sue sighs. "They're both jocks. They walk alike, stand alike. When I'm with my son, I have to pinch myself to stay in the present, to remember that I'm *not* sixteen, that he is *not* Bob. And, after each visit, I can't wait to pick up the phone and tell Bob all about it."

Like Sue, many women who searched and found their children wanted to include birthfathers in their reunions. Often, they did so; some even put fathers and children in touch or arranged their meetings. Those who remained emotionally involved with birthfathers, however, often found that renewed contact with their former lovers was as wrenching as the reunions themselves.

"When I found our son," Sue remembers, "I called Bob to tell him. I'd seen him only once in the years since our child had been born. When he came to the phone, I heard a baby crying in the background and it broke my heart. I'd had three more children of my own, by then, but it tore me apart to hear Bob with a baby. It brought out all my broken dreams about what might have been."

Occasionally, renewed contact led to renewed romances. Like Sue, Bridget had secretly carried a torch for the father of her relinquished child. After an unhappy marriage in which she had raised five additional children, Bridget divorced her abusive husband, reunited with her relinquished daughter, and contacted the man she'd dreamed about for over two decades.

"I called," she confides, "to tell him that I'd found our daughter and to ask if he'd like to meet her. But when he found out who was calling, Doug fell all over me. He told me that he'd finally separated from his wife and literally begged to see me. And there I was, approaching sixty, with my heart fluttering like a schoolgirl. I was still in love with him, after all these years. I'd always compared other men to him, and they'd always fallen short. He was brilliant, handsome, and eminent. No one could compare to him. Nothing could rival our romance. So I agreed to meet him again. I began to imagine my life falling into place, picking up where it had left off all those long and miserably empty years ago."

Like Bridget, a number of birthmothers hoped someday to resurrect and restore the loving relationships with birthfathers that had perished under the traumas of relinquishment. Often, however, the emotional aftermath of relinquishment combined with the events of intervening years had changed both birthparents so profoundly that, even when the desires were mutual, the chances that their relationships could succeed were minimal. More often than not, the closeness actually achieved by reunited birthparents compared poorly to that which they had long imagined and cherished, sacredly and secretly, in their hearts.

Reality, Compromise, and Hope

Even when they recognized that they would not achieve a neat, "happily ever after" reunion with long-lost birthfathers, many birthmothers found it difficult to let go completely. Some became friends with birthfathers; others participated in extramarital affairs. A few were involved too deeply to define their relationships and watched helplessly as the "normal" lives they had struggled to construct crumbled in the face of their storming, confusing emotions.

"A few months after I called to tell him that I'd found our son, Bob had a heart attack," Sue says. "When I found out, I raced to the hospital. I didn't even think about what my husband would say or how it would look to anyone else. It wouldn't have mattered. It was one of those undeniable moments in life when you know, you absolutely know the truth. The truth for me was that Bob was the only man I'd ever really loved, that we *should* have been together but, because of our baby, we'd lost each other. But I couldn't let him die; I couldn't be separated from him forever—at least, not without letting him know that I always had and always would be in love with him. In the hospital, I couldn't leave him. During the long hours of waiting, his wife and I talked. She told me that he should have married me, not her, that their marriage had been a mistake from the beginning. Bob had married her on the rebound—he wasn't over me and she'd known it. As he recovered, still in intensive care, Bob and I finally talked about our relationship and the loss of our son. He'd never told *anyone* how profoundly relinquishment had affected him. Only years later, staring at death, were we able to recognize the truth of our feelings. More amazing, we were able to admit it."

Even when love was revealed and hearts were reunited, however, the realities of commitments and responsibilities to families, children, and spouses often stood in the way of fairy-tale endings. Frequently, too, the passions and intense emotions aroused by renewed contact were downright frightening to birthparents who had survived for decades by remaining rigidly "in control" of their lives and relationships. The prospects of taking emotional risks, making dramatic changes, or sacrificing "normalcy" were, for many, far too threatening. Faced with the opportunity to reclaim each other, many birthparents shied away, hanging onto safe family ties while keeping each other within arm's length.

"Now that Bob and I are in contact again," Sue says, "both of our marriages are in disarray. His wife has told Bob that he never really 'belonged' to her because he always loved me. The fact is, *I've* never 'belonged' with my husband either. He was simply the best alternative I could find after Bob. But he *is* the father of three of my kids. I'm grateful to him for the home he's provided us. And I do love him, in a way. Understandably, he feels left out, since Bob's come back into my life. But I can't do anything about that. I'll do my best to save my marriage, for the sake of the kids and out of commitment. But my heart belongs to Bob more than to my husband. Surely, my husband feels that."

Discarding Illusions

Occasionally, the torches birthmothers carried for birthfathers burned them badly. Some who had imagined romances faced rejection or disappointment instead. Although the loss of their fantasies devastated some women, others found that the truth finally set them free.

"Doug courted me by phone," Bridget says. "He was just as charming, witty, and intelligent as I remembered him. He referred to places we'd been, conversations we'd had years ago. It was clear that he'd missed me every bit as much as I'd missed him. He'd forgotten *nothing*.

"After several months, we met for a long weekend. It was perfect. My head was in the clouds. I was literally whirling with happiness. I was infatuated, afraid to believe that we might have a chance together. I couldn't wait for him to meet our daughter, so that all three of us could be together, as a family, at last. So I arranged another getaway and asked her to join us.

"But what happened there is something I may never understand. Doug was a different person. He was belligerent and publicly disruptive. He cursed at me, told her she was a 'bitch' and a 'whore' just like me! Our daughter ran out of the restaurant in tears. I ran after her—I was terrified that he'd messed up *my* relationship with her, since I'd told her how wonderful he was! I took her back to our hotel and was so concerned about *her* and the harm he may have done to her that I didn't even think about my own feelings until later, when she fell asleep.

"More than anything else, I felt baffled. Who was Doug? Did he have a split personality? A brain tumor? Some rare allergic reaction to his dinner? Was he taking drugs that mixed poorly? Was he possessed? It was a puzzle, a painful one. One minute he was a distinguished gentlemen; the next he was shouting expletives at us, for no apparent reason."

Although Bridget's experience was bizarre, it was not unlike those of other birthmothers who were reluctant to let go of their dreams. Some hung on to their hopes and illusions, struggling to ignore the undeniable, unbearable facts that would extinguish their romances forever. Eventually, however, the disparities between dreams and reality became so large that they could not be reconciled. Letting go, some of these women discovered that they were no longer the prisoners of their pasts; they were, finally, able to participate in their present lives—even, perhaps, to enter into romantic relationships with real, rather than ideal, partners.

"I actually gave Doug one more chance," Bridget admits. "I'd spent so many years pining for this man that I couldn't write him off right away. So I saw him again, without our daughter. This time he was, if anything, worse. I was driving him home from the train station when he suddenly changed. Like Dr. Jekyll and Mr.

Hyde. He became so offensive and physically threatening that I made him get out of my car and threw his suitcase after him. I was furious. He stood in the road, in my own community, shouting, gesticulating, and publicly accusing me of unnatural sexual acts! Again, I thought that his behavior, because it had changed so suddenly, must have been drug-induced or chemically influenced. I called his sister and learned that he had, in fact, been taking medications that had side effects, but I don't know and don't *want* to know why. He's an adult. He alone is responsible for his behavior and his effect on others. I can't be with someone who's cruel, no matter what's causing his cruelty.

"So after all these years I've lost him, my dream of him. It's an empty feeling. But, in a way, losing him has released me from him, so that I can begin to live again."

Partnerships and Paternity

Some women did not need to reestablish contact with birthfathers: they had married them. Some birthparent couples communicated openly, shared their feelings about relinquishment, and searched for their children together. Others, however, did not. Occasionally, birthmothers searched independently, compelled to separate their needs to find their children from their husbands' needs to suppress or deny the past. Forced to choose between search and marriage, many took the road that might lead to their children.

"Jeff, my husband, pretended to be indifferent about search, at first," Pam says. "He hoped that if he ignored the subject, it would go away. It didn't. I found our son and, as our reunion approached, Jeff became vehemently against it. He even threatened to divorce me. But I wouldn't abandon my son again, not for anyone. Jeff drew a line. I crossed it. There was no going back. Jeff, not I, would have to change."

Most whose husbands protested their searches said that the birthfathers had neither grieved for their surrendered children nor supported them in their own grief. Many believed that the birthfathers would have preferred to remain in permanent denial rather than risk confrontations with their long-buried emotions. Nonetheless, these women persevered, believing that their families' futures required that their husbands face their pasts.

"I insisted that Jeff meet our son," Pam continues. "He agreed, reluctantly, after postponing and changing the date several times. He was not prepared to deal with it. Meeting our son overwhelmed him. He never expected to care about this young man, but when he *saw* him, how he was so like him, so bright, polite, and well spoken—well, Jeff fell apart. They look just alike. They talk and walk like mirror images. Jeff crumbled. The reality of what we'd lost when we relinquished hit him hard. For months, he was a mess, withdrawn and moody. I must admit that *my* reunion was much simpler, much more happy than his. I'd been grieving for years, ever since relinquishment, while Jeff had wiped out the whole event. So when Jeff finally felt it, if anything, I was glad. Because only now, with his grief, was our loss real to him. Only now, when he can admit to the tragedy that's shaped our lives, can we really be united as a couple, as parents and as a family."

Blocking Out Dad

Some birthmothers feared that renewed contact with birthfathers would in some way endanger them, their relinquished children, or both.

"I married the birthfather," Helen says. "But I divorced him a few years later. He beat me up for getting pregnant too soon and 'humiliating' him by relinquishing. He said I'd ruined his life. I'm sure that he married me to make things look better, but he was violent and tremendously immature. I don't want our son to find him. I don't want him to find out what a louse his father is."

Despite their fears, birthmothers who disliked birthfathers rarely discouraged their children from searching for them. Most merely refrained from encouraging these searches and kept their protective instincts and opinions to themselves. No matter how much they wanted to prevent paternal reunions, they hesitated to interfere with their children's pursuits of biological and historical information.

Occasionally, however, birthmothers deliberately blocked contact between their children and birthfathers. When they did, they were often trying to protect themselves as much as the children. Peg was afraid that a reunion with Peter, the birthfather, would impair her own postreunion relationship, so she made her son swear that he would never search for his father.

"Peter's hurt me every time I've had contact with him, ever since we were teenagers," she says. "When I got pregnant, he dropped me. That's why I had to give the baby up. I never got over losing him or our son the *first* time, and it took me years until I could even date again. But Peter breezed off and got married right away. As soon as he got divorced a few years later, he began calling me again. I'd just begun to get my life back together and was afraid that he just saw me as a plaything that he could come back to whenever he wanted. I told him how I felt and why I was afraid to see him. So he stopped calling. And, when he stopped, I was hurt all over again. All the old pain of rejection barreled right through me. I'd wanted him to insist, to tell me that he wouldn't go away, that he'd missed me the same way I'd missed him. But he didn't. He just disappeared again. Now, I'm afraid he'll mess up what I have with my son. I don't want them to meet. I don't want him to come between us or to make our son choose which of us he prefers. I don't want Peter to waltz off with him and leave me alone again. I want him to stay away. He's messed us up enough."

Bad Guys

Birthmothers who adamantly opposed reunions with birthfathers did not always have their own interests in mind. Cindy had been uncertain about the birthfather's identity until she actually met her son. "When he walked in, I knew, without any doubt, who his father was. He looked like a clone of this guy Craig, one of the gang members I'd slept with. Craig still deals drugs. He's scum, slime, a criminal. He never got over street life. He just got lower and lower, and now he crawls in the gutters. So, as much as I don't want my son to find Craig, I don't want Craig to find out that he even has a son.

"I made my son promise on the Bible that he would never search for his father. I told him that his father is disturbed. I've worried about genetics—I've watched for signs of Craig in my son. But, truly, there aren't any. My son is hard-working and gentle. He's a good husband and father. So, right or wrong, I'll do anything I can to prevent them from having contact, or even from being aware of each other."

Efforts by birthmothers to separate their children from troubled birthfathers, however, were not always successful. Zoe's daughter, Elizabeth, not only sought out her father but fell into an incestuous love relationship with him. Together, they reinforced each other's bitter feelings about relinquishment and found that Zoe, alone and recently separated from her husband, made a convenient scapegoat.

"They blame me for all their problems," Zoe says. "They claim that even their sexual relationship is *my* fault, that because I relinquished, they were so starved for each other that they couldn't control their passions. They blame me for their failures in work, in relationships, in anything. They've called me in the middle of the night, drunk or drugged, threatening to get even with me. They've tried to bully me into giving them money. 'You owe us,' they say.

"For my own sanity, I've cut off communication with them. I've moved, had my number changed and unlisted. I've bought a dog and put double bolts on my doors. I remember how Jack threatened to kill me when I was pregnant, and I know that he's crazy when he's mad. I'm afraid of them. I'm sorry that I ever searched. This nightmare might never have happened if I'd just let go and left the past alone."

Birthfathers and Postrelinquishment Patterns

Birthmothers who renewed contact with birthfathers after finding their children frequently discovered men who were struggling with problems that resembled their own. Many fathers showed symptoms of incomplete grief, avoidance of intimacy, difficulties in parenting, generalized guilt, and low self-esteem.

When she contacted Dave after finding their son, Annie concluded that he was stuck in denial. "Dave put on an act of great, exaggerated indifference," she says. "He coldly denied the importance of his son but refused so intensely even to hear about him, that he must have been more threatened than indifferent. Dave's been divorced twice. I think he's afraid of long-term, close relationships. He left me when I got pregnant, and he still leaves women when things get tough. He claims that he's politically opposed to birthparents searching, that he thinks searches should be initiated only by adoptees. But I know Dave. He'll find a political excuse to justify anything he wants, and he simply wants to avoid the responsibility for entering our son's life. He's afraid of facing emotions and of dealing with the mess he's made of so many lives."

Some women found that birthfathers had reacted to relinquishment not only with denial but also with a familiar array of guilty feelings and anxieties. Patterns emerged that included loveless marriages, compulsions to be "perfect," and children born in quick succession.

Alexis resumed communication with her son's birthfather as soon as she began her search. "He claims to be 'fine,'" she says, "but he replaced our relinquished child right away by marrying the very next girl he met and starting a family immediately. His marriage was not based on love. Like me, he married to have another child. But replacing our son didn't work for him any more than it did for me. When each of his other children were born, he became very depressed, just like I did. He denies having interest in our son, but in the same conversation, he tells me about recurring dreams he has about a mysterious little boy. He *says* it's all in the past, but he still calls me a few times each year. He can't entirely let go of me or our son."

Birthmothers observed that birthfathers alternated between being cold and smothering, involved and distant with their children. Many strove to be "the best dad in the world"; others were overprotective and chronically controlling. "I understand him," says one birthmother, discussing the paradoxes of the birthfather's parenting. "He gets frightened by how involved he is so he distances and numbs himself. I was the same way with my kids. I think that birthparents can't simply be moms and dads, as if they'd never given up a child. We adore our children, but we can't always be completely present in our relationships. Part of us 'goes away' sometimes, because of what we lived through and what we've lost."

By renewing contact and tending to long-festering wounds, some birthparents were able to acknowledge each other's pain and help each other heal. When this occurred, reunions between the birthparents were, in their own way, just as important as those shared with their children.

"The birthfather, Girard, fancied that he was still in love with me," Sylvia declares. "Imagine that! He's married and has three children, but when I called him, he was all agog, inarticulate, and as nervous as an infatuated boy. He all but begged me to see him, whispered into the phone that he'd thought of me constantly for all these years. When we finally met, of course, I was able to dispel his glorified idealization of me and of the past. I've aged, and I'm a lot older than he is. I'm not the pert little thing he'd pictured, anymore. And I told him, point blank, that it wasn't *me* he missed; it was that time of our lives, the excitement of our youth. We talked for hours. But, if we hadn't, if we'd never seen each other again and never talked about our relationship and our son, I believe that Girard would have gone to his grave still worshiping some image of me, still feeling that he had failed me, still loving a woman who didn't exist. Our reunion released him from that fate."

Open Adoption, Birthmothers, and Birthfathers

Sometimes birthmothers saw to it that the terms of their open adoptions did not include birthfathers. Where states required birthfathers' permission for relinquishment, some women claimed not to know who the birthfathers were. Even legislation and regulations, therefore, could not always guarantee that birthfathers' rights would be protected. Often, their rights depended on the goodwill of birthmothers.

"Because he was abusive," Donna says, "I didn't tell Nick that I was pregnant. I was afraid for the baby's safety. But I firmly believe that men have the right to know that they've fathered children. In fact, I see it as the obligation of women to tell them. When I finally told Nick that he had a daughter, he was shocked. He'd had no idea that I'd been pregnant. We cried; we held each other. He felt awful—it was bad enough that he'd beaten me up, but he now realized that I'd been carrying our child at the time. Under the circumstances, he felt that he had no right to pass judgment on my decision to relinquish. But he was shaken up, took it hard. It sobered him. Now, he calls and asks me about her, but he feels that he has no right to communicate with her or her adoptive parents directly, because of how he treated me. He feels that it's his fault that I relinquished. But I hope, with time, he'll establish his own contact and have a relationship with her. But he has to be ready, and so does she."

Birthmothers like Donna believed that, for better or worse, information about their children's paternity was not theirs to withhold. Those who believed in openness in adoption could not appoint themselves the sole keepers of the truth. "I realized," Donna says, "that, no matter what *I* think of him, our daughter has the right to know who her birthfather is, and he has the right to know her. I separated them initially for her safety, but as she grows older, deciding whether or not she wants to stay separated from him should be up to her, not me."

Others with open adoptions kept in close communication with birthfathers about every aspect of their children's welfare.

Beginning with the decision to relinquish, some birthparents worked together to find solutions that would provide acceptable compromises for everyone in the adoption triangle.

"I got pregnant by accident," Lynne says. "It was a mistake and we both knew it. Keeping the baby would have been wrong for *me*; having an abortion would have been the wrong for *both* of us. So we agreed to arrange an open adoption. Now, we each keep in touch independently with the adoptive family. I don't keep tabs on how much contact he has with them, but I know that he's in touch pretty regularly and I'm glad, for our child's sake. She knows that all of us—her adoptive and her biological parents—care about and love her. That's got to be important."

A number of birthmothers with open adoptions said that, despite their encouragement, birthfathers did not keep in touch with adoptive families. The birthfathers, they believed, were uncomfortable with their vague roles, reluctant to commit to relationships or still disturbed by unresolved feelings about relinquishment. When the birthfathers did keep in touch with their children, birthmothers generally approved but few wanted this ongoing contact to extend to them. Whether because they wanted to put their former intimacies behind them or because they could not entirely do so, these women tried to keep their postrelinquishment relationships with birthfathers at a polite distance.

The Balancing Point: Adoptive Parents

Some of the most complicated and contradictory feelings expressed by birthmothers were those they had for the people who had adopted their children.

"When we relinquish," one says, "most of us believe that two adoptive parents are better than one biological parent, that a divorced adoptive mother is better than an unmarried birthmother. That's what we are brainwashed into thinking so that we'll relinquish, even today, even in open adoptions. Later, we can't help but resent those people for having *seemed* so much more competent than we did."

In the years that followed relinquishment, some of the regret, anger, and blame felt by birthmothers inevitably fell on the adoptive parents. Often, the feelings birthmothers had for adoptive parents reflected their ambivalence about relinquishing, ranging from jealousy to gratitude, from bitterness to respect. Prior to search or reunion, many women who had participated in closed adoptions imagined adoptive parents in extreme caricatures of perfection or monstrosity. Even in open adoptions, birthmothers often resented the adoptive parents that they had themselves selected.

By getting to know adoptive parents, some birthmothers were able to let go of their rivalries, angers, and fears and acquire genuine respect for the adoptive family. In fact, most of the birthmothers interviewed believed that, if healing within adoption triangles were to be successful, *all* members would have to participate, in both closed and open adoptions. Frequently the adoptive parents actively supported the healing process by facilitating efforts to maintain biological ties; sometimes, however, they did not.

Up Against Mom or Dad

After finding their relinquished children, a number of birthmothers felt that their efforts to build relationships were obstructed by one or both adoptive parents. One woman said that the adoptive parents greeted her "with suspicion, as if they feared that, a full generation later, I'd returned to reclaim my now fully grown son." Sometimes, the distrust expressed by adoptive parents seemed to target birthmothers personally; just as often, however, it reflected more generalized defenses.

"After our reunion, Fran, my son's adoptive mother, became jealous of me," says Pam. "She asked him to stay away from his birthfather—my husband—and me. I couldn't understand why. She'd had him all these years, why couldn't she let us just get to know him? But when my son told us about her life, I understood. After seven miscarriages, Fran had a stillborn child. When her adopted son was about seven, her husband left her, remarried, and quickly fathered two children with his new wife. To Fran, the prompt remarriage and subsequent births seemed like slaps in the face. My son didn't want to add to his mom's losses by appearing to defect to us. He was reluctant to spend time with us, at first. Now he sees us, but he keeps our visits secret. I hope, though, that the healing we're experiencing through our reunion will extend to Fran. We don't have to be rivals. She raised our son with love. That attaches us to her forever. The love my husband and I get from our son is *not* love taken away from her. There's enough for us all."

At times, adoptive parents obstructed relationships not because of their own problems but because of the birthmothers'.

"They cut me off," complains Audrey, the birthmother of a nineteen-year-old, "because they assumed that I was still drinking. Well, I *was* a drunk as a teenager. I had problems, especially after I gave up my baby. I've had my ups and downs—I admit that. But that's the past, and now I want a chance to have *some* contact with my daughter. They say that they have to 'protect' her from me. But I *am* her birthmother, good, bad, or indifferent. All I want is to be able to talk to her on her birthday."

Birthmothers like Audrey felt that adoptive parents were prejudiced against them, unwilling to consider the possibility that they had matured and overcome the problems that had originally led them to relinquish. Although a few admitted that they had, in fact, not entirely overcome these problems, they still did not agree that relationships with them would be harmful to their grown children. They maintained that their status as biological mothers should guarantee them *some* contact with their grown children, regardless of their personal problems or shortcomings. Thwarted by adoptive parents, these women rarely went away permanently; more often, they retreated and waited to try again another day.

Pull-Me, Push-You

Several birthmothers who found adult children were warmly welcomed by one adoptive parent and flatly rejected by the other. Some were confused by this disparity; others assumed that it reflected deeper, ongoing disagreements within the marriage. In fact, some birthmothers felt used by hostile spouses who saw their children's reunions in terms of the problems in their own relationships. Merely by approaching the boundaries of these troubled family circles, some birthmothers became unsuspecting weapons or targets of one or both warring factions.

"Ron's father was superficially very supportive of our reunion," Abby says. "But I suspect that his enthusiasm was only cosmetic, designed to inflame his ex-wife's violent opposition. In fact, he encouraged me in order to enrage her, while he simultaneously endeared himself to Ron by giving him a sports car—his second car—the very week of our reunion. Now, why would an eighteen-year-old college student suddenly need two cars? Was Daddy buying his loyalty? Was Dad threatened that I was on the scene? Whatever it was, there was the adoptive father, lavishing expensive gifts while the adoptive mother ranted to Ron on the phone about how her husband had betrayed her and married her best friend and now Ron was all she had left, and why did he need to meet some woman who'd given him up at birth, anyway?"

When reunions inflamed ongoing battles, some birthmothers found that their children could not take the stress of yet another faction in the family and backed out of new relationships. Others, however, met children who welcomed them as stable and calming influences.

"Ron was upset by his parents' hysteria," Abby recalls, "but he turned to me to talk out what was going on. He saw through his dad's bribery. And he knew that his mom's rage wasn't about me, but about her fears of being alone. Ron was concerned about me, worried that *I* might be hurt. He wanted me to see that I was not the cause of his family's upheaval. It amazed me, but he was genuinely unwilling to let his parents scare me out of his life."

Stepping Out on Mom

Despite the opposition or fears of adoptive parents, many birthmothers maintained postreunion relationships with their children. Some simply avoided adoptive parents; others continued to communicate with them, hoping to win their gradual acceptance.

"After Steve's graduation," Sue says, "I sent a Christmas card to his parents with a picture of my family. His mother called me, demanding to know what I wanted. She has assumed, right from the first contact, that I wanted to take him away from her, somehow. She's afraid of me, needlessly. She wants me to disappear. But I won't, not as long as I know Steve wants me in his life. When I'm with Steve, there's a protective umbrella over us. The world disappears, and nothing, nobody can interfere."

Several birthmothers attributed the insecurities of adoptive mothers to jealousy about maternal territory, fertility, or both. "Look," one says, "I'm fertile Myrtle. I get pregnant every time I even look at my husband. But Tommy's adoptive mother spent nine long years trying to get pregnant before she decided to adopt. All she ever wanted was to give birth, but she couldn't, and that was, for her, a tragedy. All these years, I'm sure, she's tried to pretend that Tommy is her son and hers alone. And then, here I am, showing up twenty years later, shattering that fantasy. My presence, my existence, has robbed her of what she most wanted, the exclusive title of 'Mother.' Of course she resents me. Of course she's jealous. She wants me to disappear and probably hates my guts."

Another birthmother said that the secrecy of seeing her son made her feel like she was having an affair. "He took me to his apartment and showed me pictures of his adopted family, a sister and his parents. He wouldn't talk about his parents, though, only about his sister. It was like he'd be unfaithful if he even talked about them, like a man telling his mistress about his wife. Because he demands secrecy, I write to him at a post office box rather than at his apartment. It's clear that he's conflicted about our relationship, but I can't tell which of us he's protecting with all the secrecy—his adopted family, himself, or me. I've personally had enough of secrecy, but for now, I've decided to roll with it, to let him decide how it goes. After all, he's the one in the middle."

Biding Time

When adoptive parents forbade, opposed, or blocked contact between birthmothers and grown children, some birthmothers simply withdrew. Although they desired relationships with their children, they refused to pressure them into situations that would make them choose between parents.

"I was finished with secrets and lies," one says. "I simply could not see my daughter if seeing her created more secrets and lies. I couldn't ask her to live that way or to risk her parents' trust for my sake. So I told her that I'm here, that I won't go away. And when they are ready to accept me, or when she's ready to be open about having me in her life, I'll be ready to continue our relationship. In the meanwhile, at least I have the peace of mind of knowing who, how, and where she is."

Birthmothers who had relinquished as young teenagers often saw opposition by adoptive parents as temporary setbacks rather than permanent obstacles to their relationships. As middle-aged women, many envisioned their eventual roles in their children's lives as complementary rather than competitive to those of older adoptive parents.

"I can wait," Francine says. "I've waited all these years, so I can wait some more. I'm forty-five. They are in their seventies. When they go—and it's likely that they will before I do—maybe my son will have room for me. I'll be his second mom. I'll be all the parent he has left. And I'm willing to wait and take that place, if that's what it takes."

Waiting for adoptive parents to die and take their rejections with them, however, meant birthmothers risked additional rejection. The attitudes of the adoptive parents were not without impact on their children. As one birthmother put it, "If your child grew up without you, with parents who had no tolerance for you, it's likely that he or she will be able to live without you as an adult, after they're gone."

Nonetheless, age differences between adoptive and biological parents occasionally had potentially important practical implications. Some birthmothers whose children had special needs stood quietly by, prepared to step in and help if needed. Without causing conflicts in their children's lives, they felt that they shared the responsibility for their well-being.

Alexis's relinquished son was severely retarded. "His adoptive parents are almost twenty years older than I am," she says. "My son will always be a child. I worry about what will happen to him when they're too old to care for him. I'm concerned about the future, just from the standpoint of the energy it must take to look after an adult body with a child's mind. But I'm ready, I'll be here, whenever he needs me. Until then, I'll abide by his parents' wishes and stay on the sidelines. I realize that his best interests need to be distinguished from mine and theirs, but I see myself as an insurance policy for him. Including me in his life would be not only in *his* best interests but in everyone's."

Take Me, Take My Mom

Some adoptive parents encouraged birthparent-child contact, as long as the contact also included them. Sometimes, however, their inclusion broadened to the point that their own relationships with birthmothers competed with or eclipsed those of their children.

"I wanted to find my child," Cindy says. "But by finding him, I also found his adoptive mother. Now she won't leave me alone. She wants me to be her best friend. The truth is that I can't stand her. She's always criticizing my son. She complains to me about how bad a teenager he was, that he wore earrings, stayed out all night, took steroids. 'You should be glad to have him now, instead of *then*,' she tells me. I want to smack her when I hear that. How can she tell me I should be grateful to have lost those years with him! How can she tell me that she didn't treasure them!"

Like Cindy, other birthmothers were infuriated by complaints by adoptive parents. Some cynically suspected that the complaints were not genuine, that they were deliberate attempts to form impressions that would alienate them from their children. Most wanted adoptive parents to allow them to form their own opinions and relationships. One birthmother described how the adoptive father belabored his son's shortcomings. "He complained about how tough it was, raising Sean. Certainly, he must know that I'd have given my right arm to raise him. Can he be too blind to notice that I love him unconditionally, without judgment? Whatever Sean did as a kid makes no difference to me, except that I'm sorry I wasn't there to help him deal with it."

When adoptive parents tried to participate in postreunion relationships, many birthmothers interpreted their interest as either insensitivity or an attempt at control. Accordingly, like Cindy, they were suspicious of adoptive parents' offers of friendship and reluctant to become involved. A few saw them as intrusive impediments to their children; others simply found it overwhelming to deal with the children and their adoptive parents all at the same time.

"In order to understand my son, I guess I'll need to get to know the woman who raised him," Cindy admits. "But it's not easy. She's always asking me, 'Can't we be friends?' and I ask her, 'Why?' What does she want or need from me? Maybe I'm too harsh. Maybe she's trying and I'm not, but the truth is, I'm not ready for her yet. I'm still trying to get to know my *son*."

Steel Apron Strings

Sometimes postreunion relationships were strictly controlled by one or both adoptive parents.

"My son's adoptive mother reigns over our relationship," Candy says, "even now that my son's married and has his own son. She allows me to be called 'Grandmother,' but it's an empty title, because she won't allow me to perform any grandmotherly functions. I can't babysit. I can't even visit unless she's there, too. She gets between my son and me and *never* lets us talk alone. He's passive. He let's her run his life. After all, she raised him that way, to give in to her. She's very condescending to me, very obvious in her tolerance. She treats me like a distasteful charity project. It's almost laughable. But she openly winces if I want to hold the baby, as if I might give him a disease or something. And if I bring homemade cookies or cakes, she puts them aside for 'later,' which I'm certain means that she throws them out after I've gone home. Even my food is unworthy for my son or his son to eat."

Although the controlling influence of adoptive parents aggravated some birthmothers, others found that it salvaged their postreunion relationships. Rejected by their children after finding them, these women depended on the cooperation of adoptive parents for subsequent contact. Sometimes, however, these dependencies led more to resentment than to gratitude.

"My son's adoptive mother permits me to call her once a year," Annie says. "It's not that she sees me as a threat. She's secure that he sees her as his mom. She isn't afraid to lose him. But she feels that she is in the middle. He doesn't want to see me or to have anything to do with me, but she understands my viewpoint. So, even though she doesn't encourage our relationship, she sends me pictures of him every year and keeps me informed about what he's doing. She's my only link to him, so I don't dare push her or anger her in any way. If she sets the limit of once a year, that's what I have to accept. Over the years, I've learned that the more I push, the less I get, where my son's concerned. So I've had to let her call the shots and take the crumbs of information she throws my way."

Despite their dissatisfaction, birthmothers like Annie refused to risk confrontations with adoptive mothers. Rather, most tried to ingratiate themselves, hoping that, with time, the affection or approval they earned from adoptive mothers would spread to the children.

Reaching Out Together

Despite these experiences, the majority of the birthmothers interviewed felt that adoptive parents were generally sympathetic and supportive of them. Some even said that their reunions had been due not to their own search efforts but to those of the adoptive parents. Once in a while, though, these well-intentioned efforts went unappreciated.

Mary was a birthmother who refused a reunion with the adult adoptee who found her. "After I refused to talk with her, I received a phone call from the woman who'd adopted her. This woman was distraught, pleading with me to at least meet with her daughter one time. It seems that *she'd* been the one to put her up to searching for me. It had been her idea, because apparently the girl had grown up with problematic notions about who I was or why I'd rejected her at birth. The mother thought, I guess, that if she found me, all her problems would be solved, and so, without thinking about what it might mean to me, that I might not want to be found, she actually began the search herself.

"I told the mother what I'd told the daughter, that, basically, there was no way I could help her. But she still wouldn't leave me alone. She wrote me a letter, which I'm just glad my husband didn't see, in which she begged me to reconsider. 'You gave her life,' she wrote, 'we gave her love.' That was her reasoning as to why I should see her daughter. But her point only supported my position: I gave her life! *My* part was done. Loving her was up to her adoptive family. We agreed, at adoption, that there would be no further contact, that my identity would be secret. I don't appreciate that, two decades later, they want to break their promise."

Although Mary was not typical of the birthmothers interviewed, her experience indicated that a number of adoptive parents in closed adoptions not only encouraged but actually insisted on search. "My son never felt quite at home with his adoptive family," Sylvia says. "His parents knew that and told him, from childhood, that someday he'd be old enough to look for his roots and find out where he came from. They knew that he felt 'different.' He was smaller and quieter than they were. They wanted him to know his biological relatives so that he'd feel more 'normal.' Most important, though, they let him know early in life that they *expected* him to want to find me, that it was not only OK, but that it was natural and right."

Other adoptive parents similarly anticipated their children's curiosity about their origins and encouraged search as soon as an interest was expressed, even if their children were still quite young. Jean coincidentally received pictures of her daughter from the adoptive parents soon after she'd initiated her own search.

"We're all friendly," she says. "They're good people, loving, honest, generous. They did their best to raise their family. I think it's inevitable, though, that when you meet the people who've raised your child, you see the differences more than the similarities. You see them as cut from different cloth. But, even with our differences, there is no enemy here. Ironically, that's the problem. It's tough to be angry, to hold onto your anger about relinquishing, when there's no one to blame, no one who's evil, selfish, or wrong. We're *all* right; each of us did the best we could for the love of a child. Out of that same love, we've been lucky enough, years later, to reunite and create an expanded, loosely defined family. Love is what led me to relinquish her, and love is what led her parents to adopt her. It's what binds us all and keeps us together when other feelings, like jealousy or competition, get in our way."

Birthmothers and Adoptive Parents

Despite the wide range of rivalries, jealousies, and resentments they expressed, most birthmothers emphasized that they saw adoptive parents neither as their rivals nor as the cause of their postrelinquishment problems. Rather, most said that they were loving, well intentioned, and understandably protective of their children and families. If birthmothers found *any* general fault with adoptive parents, it was that they glossed over the repercussions of relinquishment because they could not bear to acknowledge that their *own* families and happiness had emerged from birthmothers' pain.

Nevertheless, most birthmothers did not see their pain as the rightful concern of adoptive parents. "Look," says one, "they didn't steal our children. We gave them up. They appeared when we disappeared, and they, not we, gave the kids homes and families because we didn't. They didn't do anything to us; we did it to ourselves. No one held a gun to our heads and said, 'Relinquish.' No one can expect adoptive parents, who showed up when our kids needed them, to welcome us later, when we are ready, at our convenience. All we can hope for is that they will not bar the doors. They are not our enemies, but they are only human and can feel threatened, protective, or territorial like anybody else. They're trying to be good parents. But, unlike other parents, they have to deal with *us*, the existence of us, even when we are unseen, and they live with the ever-present possibility of us popping into their lives at some unpredictable point. That has to be tough."

No matter what else they said about adoptive parents, most birthmothers tried to empathize and understand their points of view. One birthmother gave some perspective to the relationships between the roles.

"I'm unusual," Jean says, "in that I have a place on all three sides of the adoption triangle. I'm an adoptee, I relinquished a child, and I adopted my son. On a triangle, all three sides are necessary to achieve balance. Each side has to accept, respect, and rely on the others or there can't be any stability. Once you're part of the triangle, you have to see yourself with respect to the other two sides. As an adoptive parent, you can be preciously close to your child, but you can't wish the biological side away, can't deny their importance and legitimacy. Similarly, as a birthmother, you can find a spot in your child's life, but you've got to let go of the parent role. I relinquished my daughter, Stephanie. When I found her years later, she was Melissa and had parents of her own. I had to let go of wanting my baby back and accept a seat on the vacant side of the triangle. It was not the 'mother's' seat. But it was an important one. Even with doting parents, Melissa felt a need for me, just as I did for her. As an adoptive parent, I see it as my responsibility to help my son find his biological parents. I wish him to feel whole. We all need each other; otherwise the triangle is wobbly and incomplete."

The Extended Family and Beyond: Triangles or Polygons?

Some of the people most closely related to adoption have not been clearly represented by adoption's traditional triangular symbol. Biological siblings or half-siblings, grandparents, aunts, uncles, cousins and close friends, spouses of birthparents, and others have also been deeply affected by relinquishment, adoption, and issues of secrecy or openness. Even if both birthparents agreed to surrender, questions about the rights of these others to know and build relationships with their relinquished relatives have remained. Birthmothers struggling to answer these questions have often faced opposition, judgment, and criticism.

"I've told my other kids about their brother," Callie says, "even though my husband was against it. I've even arranged for them to meet each other. My husband has forbidden this. He doesn't want them *ever* to meet. But I can't let him interfere any more. No one approves of what I do, so I'm just going to do what I think is right.

I won't hide my son anymore. I won't be ruled by shame or secrecy. He and my other kids have the right to know each other. After all, my generation will pass on. Let the younger generation have access to each other, let *them* decide what to make of their relationships."

Many birthmothers saw relinquishment as a family rather than an individual affair. They believed that all family members must be involved in reunions and healing, even if they were not party to the decision to relinquish.

"The whole family needs to heal," Pam says. "The loss of a family member—and that's what relinquishment is—affects everyone in the family. The family can be unified by acknowledging and mourning that loss openly and together. My mother was tremendously upset about the loss of her first grandchild. She wishes we'd been able to keep him in the family with cousins or an aunt, rather than given him up to strangers. We all bear scars from the relinquishment. We've all needed counseling, separately and together. Nothing can make the scars go away, but we can help each other by being open about our feelings."

Family Reunions

"My mother hasn't met him yet," Sue says, "but she wants to. She says she wants to meet her eldest grandchild before she dies. She has felt guilty, all these years, about making me surrender him, and, now that my children are teenagers, I'm beginning to realize what my relinquishment meant to *her*. I'd never thought about how it affected anyone but me, Bob, and our son. But it was a tragedy for my parents as well, and my mom's never gotten over her loss or mine."

Even when family members acknowledged the way relinquishment affected them and expressed their desires to reunite, reunion was often a delicate process. Birthmothers were often protective of the relationships they were establishing with their grown children, reluctant to take risks by introducing elements—or people—that they could not control. Starved for their children's company, many were unwilling to share their reunions with others, at least for a while. Some were afraid that, by including the entire family, they'd overwhelm children who were still trying to accept the existence of their birthmothers.

"Timing is important," Sue says. "Understanding how much he can accept or adjust to at one time is critical. I took him to my house on one of our first meetings. He was worried that the other kids or my husband might come in, as if we should be ashamed of being at home together. I realized, then, that he was as unsure of his place in my family as I was of mine in his. Our roles are so unclear that we need to take our time and expand little by little."

Some birthmothers found that bringing their children into their families decades after relinquishment jeopardized their marriages. Several said that their husbands were jealous of the adult children, almost paranoid.

"He feels left out," one said of her husband. "He imagines that my son and I are together whenever he leaves the house, as if we're having an affair or something. He checks up on me, calls to see what I'm doing. My reunion has brought chaos into my marriage. My husband can't deal with it."

Sometimes, this jealousy was not altogether unwarranted. Occasionally, birthmothers shut their spouses out of their postreunion relationships because they wanted their children all to themselves. Others distanced themselves from their marriages when their reunions rekindled romantic sparks for birthfathers. Sue became caught up in so many unresolved issues of the past that she resented her husband's presence and saw him as an intruder.

"Truthfully, I was unwilling to share *that* part of my life, *that* son, with my husband. The reunion stirred up old emotions that pulled me away from my family. The more I withdrew, the more my husband tried to control me. He kept trying to set limits and define what part of our lives the reunion could influence. He ordered me not to tell our children about their half-brother until *he* was ready."

Like Sue, a number of birthmothers found that, although their husbands had accepted relinquishment as part of their pasts, they had been unprepared for it to surface as an active part of the present. "He thought that I'd given up a baby and that that was the end of it," Alexis says. "He didn't think that the child I'd given up was going to reappear as part of his marital package."

When their husbands felt threatened by or jealous of their postreunion relationships, birthmothers usually had little sympathy. After years of yearning for their children, many could not tolerate anyone, even their husbands, who would ask them to hold back. Some found that they were incapable of further secrecy, cover stories, or shame.

"When my husband finally met my son, he liked him very much," Sue recalls. "He stunned me by inviting my son to bring his girlfriend to our home for dinner. I was thrilled—finally, I'd have my whole family together!

"Afterwards, though, my husband told me that he wanted to introduce my son as a 'friend.' I hit the roof! I was done with secrets and refused to lie. He didn't understand why it was so important to me. But I couldn't lie any more. Not to my sons, especially. I insisted on openness. And when I insisted, my husband backed off and honored my wishes, or tried. I discovered that I had some power—more than I'd imagined. I realized that I was the one to direct us through this phase of our lives. Only if I insisted on it would everyone in the family, including my husband, eventually accept the others—*all* of the others."

Even when they realized that their husbands could learn to accept their relinquished children, some birthmothers were concerned about what roles their spouses would play in their children's lives. "What is he going to be to my son?" Sonia asks. "A 'stepbirthfather'? What is that?"

Definitions and titles plagued birthmothers who were trying to establish relationships that would not overlap or compete with those of adoptive families. Most, however, were determined not to let mere labels hold them back. They believed that relationships had to evolve according to the chemistry of those involved. Trying to conform to preconceived definitions, many felt, would add unnecessary strain to the already stressful process of adjusting and expanding the family unit.

"I am confident that there will be room in our family for everyone," Sue says. "But it's not easy. For my part, I realize that I've been largely at fault for the tensions with my husband. I used so much energy trying to forget about my son that I was drained, blocked, and unable to be fully present in my marriage. I never truly participated. My husband naturally reacted to my distance with suspicion, insecurity, and attempts at control. But now, by including my son in our family, I'm finally trying to open up to my husband and include him in the part of my life I'd hidden. The more I share, the less he feels excluded and jealous. One release leads to another, so that we may finally begin to unite as a couple."

Generations, Secrets, and Ties That Bind

Several of the women interviewed had concealed their relinquishments from even their closest relatives. Revealing the truth years later, often after successful searches, they were astonished by reactions that crossed generations.

"It was amazing," Donna says, "how many of my relatives felt guilt, grief, or shame when they found out about my daughter. It surprised me. I'd never thought about how relinquishment would affect other people. I'd been wrapped up in my own grief."

Even those whose families had known about or participated in their relinquishments were often unaware of what their relatives *felt* about it. The topic of relinquishment had remained, even decades later, strictly taboo; they had never even indirectly addressed it with their parents, siblings, or others who'd been involved.

When Sonia decided to search, her family stopped speaking to her. "The illusion that we were a family was all that I lost, in the end," she says. "The truth is that they weren't there for me *ever*. Not when they sent me away while I was pregnant and then ignored my relinquishment. Not when they encouraged me to marry a 'proper' man even though I didn't love him. Not when I tried to find my child. They are not my family even though they raised me. The irony is that I am my child's family, even though I had to give him up."

Eventually, despite years of silence and family pressure, women like Sonia decided to break the bonds of secrecy. When they did, many were surprised to learn how deeply surrender had affected those close to them. Some relationships did not survive the truth; others were renewed.

"My sisters had *no* idea that I'd had a child," Sylvia grins. "They thought of me as an over-the-hill old spinster. I first told them when I brought my son to meet them. I introduced him by name and then said that he was my son. They were agog. I thought my older sister would drop her teeth. They crowded around and hugged and smothered us, as if we'd just returned from a war! Well, in a way, we had. We'd survived years of separation, like refugees. They were thrilled with him, took him in as if he'd always been part of the family.

"Later, though, they cornered me. They were more than a little shocked and hurt that I hadn't come to them when I was pregnant. They wanted to hear everything—why I'd kept it secret from them, why I'd given him to strangers. They demanded explanations. It was only then, almost thirty years later, that it even occurred to me that it was their business. That he had ties to *them* just as he did to me. So our family reunion, though successful, was mixed. They were glad for me because I had a son. And they loved him right away. But they were angry, too, that I'd kept him from them."

The importance of relationships between adoptees and their extended biological families often surprised birthmothers. Most had never considered their relatives' points of view.

"I told my family about my child because I believed that *she* was entitled to know her biological relatives," Linda says. "Her uncles, cousins, and grandparents were still her blood, even if I couldn't raise her. I told my family to prepare them in case, one day, she contacted them. But when I told them about her, they descended on me like a pack of wild dogs. They pointed out, between growling and snarling, that just as she had a right to know them, *they* had the right to know *her*. They did not take kindly to the fact that I'd given away a family member, particularly a helpless baby.

And they all blamed each other—fought among themselves and with me—for having allowed it to happen."

Responsibilities, Reunions, and Relatives

Birthfamilies who found out about surrendered children after relinquishment reacted with a wide range of emotions. Birthmothers' revelations were met with shock, rage, betrayal, and rejection. After these initial responses, though, some families passed through a series of emotions that echoed birthmothers' postrelinquishment reactions. Relatives felt shame, anger, guilt, powerlessness, and loss. When this happened, birthmothers often found themselves counseling their families through phases of denial and anger, even when the denial threatened their relationships and the anger targeted their hearts.

Donna waited over a year to tell her parents about her pregnancy and relinquishment. "I knew that my family had a right to know, but I couldn't bear to talk about it for a while. When I told them, just as I knew she would, my mother broke down. She couldn't eat or sleep and cried for days. Then, denying the permanence of it, she went to the adoption agency to try to get the baby back! She called a lawyer to see what her legal rights were. She wouldn't speak to me, she was so furious that I'd given *her* grandchild away.

"My father didn't want to talk to me either, but for different reasons: he was ashamed. His primary concern was keeping it secret. We had confrontation after confrontation. My mother was in pieces because I'd robbed her of her grandchild; my father felt that I'd dishonored the family. I was sure that they were going to disown me, but I wouldn't back down. I'd done what I'd thought best. Even if they couldn't understand how *I* felt, how hellish it was, they couldn't take any more from me than I'd already given away."

In the consternation that resulted when their families learned of their relinquishments, birthmothers' feelings were often overlooked. Relatives overwhelmed by their own emotions were unable to consider others. When they eventually got around to thinking of the birthmothers, their attitudes, colored by their own concerns, were sometimes less than sympathetic.

"My father ordered me to keep quiet about the baby, to keep her a secret," Donna recalls. "He had *no* idea how impossible, how unbearable that would have been, after all I'd gone through to ensure openness in my child's adoption. I was afraid of him, but I refused. I told him that, even if he couldn't accept the truth, I was not ashamed of it and would not act as if I were. I told him that it was too late for me to be silent; I'd already become active in a support group that gives interviews to media, lobbies for changes in adoption laws, and tries to get birthparents into the public eye. My father was stony and cold. Angry. We were at a standstill. I half expected him to strike me or throw me out of his house. But he didn't. Finally, he muttered, 'We'll talk about this later' and left the room. I was shaking. I realized that I'd never—never—stood up to him before."

Conflicts about how to cope with relinquishment upset long existing family dynamics and patterns of interaction. Sometimes they forced showdowns that led to the breakdown of relationships. Rhonda's sisters rejected her when they found out about her son. "Not only don't they speak to me anymore," she says, "they won't let their children play with my children. They're afraid my kids might mention my relinquishment, and *that's* not a 'fit' subject for their children's ears!"

As the repercussions of surrender rippled through birthmothers' families, relationships changed and sometimes dissolved. Those that survived, however, were often stronger.

One woman recently told her family about the daughter she'd relinquished seventeen years ago. "I made a decision and forced it on everyone else. For that, I bear the burden. When my parents and brothers found out about my child, they had to redefine their notions about me, about trust, and about family. Bringing the truth out meant hurting people, risking relationships, possibly even being rejected. It was scary. But making room for my child to reunite with us made it worth it any risk. I pruned the family tree. Now, I hope the 'tree' will forgive me."

All the Children

Women who had raised families after relinquishing were particularly concerned about how their children would relate to each other after reunions. They worried that their relinquished children would be jealous of the others, that the others would be resentful of the special attention given the newcomers. Some were afraid that the children they'd raised would be upset to learn that a sibling or half-sibling had been surrendered; others worried that their children would think less of them for having had the baby at all. For most, compatibility among their children was of the utmost importance; without it they felt unfinished or incomplete.

Jean was nervous when her son and relinquished daughter first met. "My son is normally shy," Jean says. "But I knew he was especially uncomfortable about meeting his sister. He didn't know how she'd affect his spot in our family. I'm sure that he was jealous of my gushing love for her. I was afraid he'd withdraw or reject her.

"But when they first met, at my twenty-fifth anniversary party, my son walked over and held out his hand to greet her. I heard him say, 'Hi, I'm your brother.' My heart almost burst. Watching them talk, realizing that they might actually *like* each other, having them *both* in my life—well, having that dream come true was unbelievable. Now, two years later, they talk on the phone, ask each other's advice, tell secrets, have had dinner together, share friends. Somehow, without my help, they became their own family. It's incredible and I thank God that I lived to see it."

Several birthmothers found that their relinquished children fit in with the others like missing pieces in a puzzle. Sometimes, the fit was so perfect that it seemed eerie. "My daughter had grown up in the neighborhood where we lived," Liz says. "So all my kids had known each other without realizing they were related. She was older, of course, but they'd all hung out in the same crowd, the same spots. She used to braid my younger daughter's hair on the school bus. So, now that they know they're related, it's not that much different for them than it was before, except they're closer and more bonded. But they'd *already* been drawn to each other. Good genes, I guess."

Brothers, Sisters, and Love

A few birthmothers were reluctant to introduce siblings after reunions. One woman kept her children apart because she had heard anecdotal accounts of postreunion sexual attractions between close relatives.

"My kids have needy, addictive, impulsive personalities," she says. "I'm concerned about how they'd handle their emotions if they met. Frankly, I'm afraid they'd get too involved."

Some birthmothers attempted to prevent confusion by establishing boundaries and defining relationships *prior* to introducing their children to each other. However, defining other relationships usually proved even more difficult than defining their own.

"Look," Dodie says, "I myself was obsessed with my son after I found him. I wasn't entitled to the 'mother' role, so I didn't know *what* I was—a woman? If I were just a woman, then anything, even sex could be OK, in a loving relationship, right? We were both adults, after all. Well, guess what—when my son met my *daughter*, the same feelings came up for *them*, only *she* was twenty-six years younger than me. After a while, their love became so strong that he left his wife and two kids and ran off with her. The rest of us are still spinning, three years later."

Many reunited family members and siblings were unclear about how to express intimacy. Without the framework of conventional relationships, predefined boundaries, or shared histories, some reunited relatives were at a loss about how to deal with mutual love. Sometimes their love went out of control, became confused by sexual attraction, and resulted in incestuous relationships that left birthmothers and others to deal with the repercussions of yet another major family upheaval.

Open Adoption and Relatives

Even in open adoptions that permitted birthmothers to maintain contact with their children, questions arose about relationships between adoptees and the birthmothers' families. Where such relationships existed, they were often tenuous and delicate.

"I'm always afraid," Donna says, "that the adoptive mother will get angry and cut me off. I have to toe the line and please her, in order to keep in touch with my daughter. My mother is dying to write to my daughter. But I don't dare allow that. I'm afraid even to ask about it because it took so long for them to get comfortable about receiving letters from me, even though we'd agreed to them before the adoption."

Sometimes birthmothers found, after explicitly arranging open adoptions, that their own families offered little support in their efforts to maintain contact.

"At first, my father was scandalized by my 'shamelessness,'" Donna says. "He opposed the open aspects of the adoption—my annual letters and phone calls to the adoptive family. He told me, 'You've got to stop doing this to them. Let them raise her in peace!' He saw the adoptive family as having more 'claim' to my daughter than I had, saw their feelings as more important than mine. We almost came to blows. But I wouldn't let up. I insisted that he come to some support group meetings, and, with time, he heard and saw enough not only to accept my position but to become an advocate himself of both birthparents' and birth-grandparents' rights. My dad now even lobbies for open records and legislative changes! He wants to meet his granddaughter someday. She's an unseen but important part of his life."

Because the terms of their open adoptions were not usually protected by law, birthmothers like Donna hesitated to push adoptive parents about allowing relationships with the extended biological families. Not all birthmothers, however, shared the sense that adoptive parents would avoid such contact. Some felt that biological relationships would be encouraged, when the timing was right.

"My child's adoptive family," Lynne says, "feels like it's *my* family, too. They haven't met my parents yet, but I'm sure they will one day. And I know that, as my daughter grows up, they'll encourage her to get to know them. They see adoptees as having

more than other kids, more heritage, more tradition, more relationships than others. I hope that my marriage and family life will
be as good as theirs. I hope I can accept people—and love them—
as openly."

The idea that open adoption redefined and expanded families
was echoed by other birthmothers. One woman suggested that
blending between adoptive and birthfamilies might be the way of
the future. "Today," she says, "most women with unplanned pregnancies either have abortions or keep their babies. They can go on
welfare if they have to. Today, the stigma of relinquishing is far
worse than that of being a single mother. So, when women *do*
relinquish, they can pretty much set their own terms. And, because they are often young enough to be adopted themselves, they
might seek to be included, somehow, in the security of the adoptive family. If they are included, though, their families will have to
be, too, sooner or later. Adoptions may become bridges between
two families, rather than one-way streets."

Room at the Table: New Families, New Bonds

Most birthmothers agreed that relationships in adoption triangles
were evolving, expanding to include more contact with biological
relatives. Although they believed that the level and nature of
contact should be unique to each family, the majority felt that
biological families who wanted it should be guaranteed some
contact with adoptees, even if that contact was strictly regulated
by law. Some felt that progress toward openness was blocked
because of the legal power held by adoptive parents. Others were
even more frustrated by obstacles presented within their own
families. Most hoped that, no matter how change would be accomplished, they would be the final generation of birthmothers to
suffer so much powerlessness and invisibility within the adoption
triangle.

"I hear that adoptees often ask why their birthmothers don't
search for them," Pam says. "Usually, it's because she feels she has
no right to. But we do have the right, and I even think we have the
obligation. My relinquished son was so depressed that he tried

suicide. In therapy, it came out that his depression was linked to feelings of rejection from having been relinquished. After our reunion, our son found not a rejecting but a loving birthmother married to his loving biological dad. Now he's one of us. His family is unlike most. He's got adoptive parents and birthparents, a stepmother, stepsisters, biological brothers and sisters, an adoptive sister, and grandparents on all sides. We all know each other and, for his sake, we're groundbreaking, making the rules up as we go about how to relate to each other. But we are convinced that we're on the right track. Adoptees, adoptive parents, and birthparents need to know that they are not alone, that they are part of a larger family whose shape is still emerging, and that it's OK to open the doors and let each other in."

$\boxed{10}$

The Birthmother
Syndrome

S HE COULD STILL LEAVE. SHE COULD PICK UP HER PURSE AND SLIP OUT the side entrance, before the man stopped talking. Nobody would stop her. She looked out the doorway to the elevator across the hall. There was still time—if she made a run for it, she wouldn't have to say anything. She could think about it some more.

The man was talking about his childhood, something about being a stranger to himself, but Bridget was too nervous to focus on his words. She felt overdressed and self-conscious, conspicuous in her suit and high heels. It was hot, and she worried that she'd get sweat marks under her arms. Silk showed everything. The man next to her was becoming quite animated. It would be rude to leave in the middle of his talk. Waiting for him to pause so she could dash, she looked around the circle and tried to take her mind off her flipping stomach.

Two attractive women sat across from her. One was tanned, in white shorts and sneakers. She looked like she'd come from playing tennis. The other wore a T-shirt promoting the national meeting. They seemed to be friends. Both had large diamond rings and well-manicured nails. They made eye contact often, leaned toward each other as they listened to the man. Yes, they must be friends, the one with short hair just whispered something to the tennis lady, who whispered something back. But they watched the man as they conferred, keeping in touch with whatever he was saying.

The speaker paused for a moment and Bridget panicked. Was it her turn already? Should she run now? Maybe she could simply pass again—claim a sore throat. But then he continued. Her heart raced and she felt a wave of near nausea pass through her.

Breathing deeply to regain her composure, Bridget continued to scan the room. A skinny older woman, with pencils in her hair and a lapful of legislation handouts. A middle-aged man, hair thinning, shirt open to reveal a large gold cross. A perspiring young man, maybe thirty, whose leg kept bouncing in a nervous twitch. A married couple with round bodies, fortyish, huddled together. The wife was crying. A heavyset, pretty woman with a clipboard who looked softly official. A freckled young lady with an auburn perm who seemed to be about twenty, the same age as her daughter.

Beads of sweat swelled on Bridget's forehead, just under her hairline. She remembered the fresh handkerchief in her pocketbook and reached over to get it. As she bent over to pick up her purse, though, the man next to her stopped talking and sat down. There were no follow-up comments or questions. Just silence. It was her turn.

Bridget sat up, pocketbook in hand, ready to bolt. Looking around for the closest route to the stairway, she confronted twenty pairs of eyes in the pattern of a circle, staring at her, patiently waiting.

Her stomach flipped into her throat. In the space of an instant, she argued with herself that she had already postponed this moment for three months, not to mention twenty years, then argued back that it wouldn't hurt to wait another month or two, and besides she didn't think her voice would work with her stomach jammed onto her voice box. Her argument might have continued, but a pair of eyes across the circle grabbed hers and she realized that the gaze felt soothing, that it was not unkind. She hesitated, pocketbook in hand, feeling trapped. She looked slowly from one set of eyes to another, seeing the same softness, the same patience, the same gentle acceptance. They would wait. There was no rush. The eyes were steady and still, and Bridget felt herself settling down, able to find her voice and regain some of her resolve.

She stood, slowly, clutching her purse to hide the trembling. She took a deep breath and deliberately forced her eyes to meet those of the others, straightened her back, held her head up, chest out, and began, shakily, words she had never spoken out loud but had delivered mentally, over and over again, for decades.

"My name is Bridget Dennison Smith. Twenty years ago last April, I relinquished my baby girl. . . ."

Finding a Voice

A growing number of birthmothers are stepping out of the shadows and identifying themselves. Some are angrily outspoken, protesting their feelings of having been manipulated or exploited by society when they were most vulnerable, of having been used as "baby machines" for prospective adoptive couples. Even many who lack a sense of exploitation, however, are beginning to speak up, shed secrecy, and defy stigma, expressing indignation at the prejudiced attitudes and stringent legal limitations they have faced.

"I'm sure," Sonia declares, "that the general public thinks that the only women who'd give up their babies are mentally ill, addicts, convicted felons, or prostitutes. This just isn't so. Some probably are—just as some who don't give up their babies are. The women I've met through support groups, though, are mostly mainstream. They're often professionals. One is the personal aide to a U.S. senator. Many are in helping professions—nurses, therapists, adoption counselors, emergency medical technicians, social workers. The problems we had that led us to relinquish may have become embedded in our personalities and still be there. But I believe that, overall, we are no different than other women. Most of us merely had the misfortune to get pregnant before we were ready to raise children. We've had bad luck and bad timing, but we're not bad people. And I am convinced that the problems we have are more the results of our relinquishments than they were the causes."

Symptoms and Syndromes

Although some admit that they had been predisposed to emotional problems prior to relinquishing, most of the women interviewed were certain, as Sonia was, that the bulk of their problems began afterward. Those problems, discussed in earlier chapters, recurred so often and with such commonality that they appeared to compose the profile of a syndrome specific to birthmothers.

Typically, in the years following relinquishment, this syndrome manifests itself through at least some of the following traits:

1. Signs of unresolved grief, such as lingering denial, anger, or depression
2. Symptoms of posttraumatic stress disorder, such as flashbacks, nightmares, anxiety, avoidance, or phobic reactions
3. Diminished self-esteem, passivity, abandonment of previous goals, or feelings of powerlessness, worthlessness, and victimization
4. Dual identities, divided into outer pretenses of "perfection" or "normalcy" and secret inner feelings of shame, self-condemnation, and isolation
5. Arrested emotional development, typified by the sense of being "stuck" where they were when they relinquished
6. Self-punishment, often inflicted through participation in abusive relationships, abuse of drugs or alcohol, eating disorders, or other self-destructive behaviors
7. Unexplained secondary infertility
8. Living at, or vacillating between, various extremes

The extremes manifested by birthmothers covered a wide range, appearing thematically throughout their lives. Their romances and intimacies, family relationships, child-rearing practices, careers, goals, and self-images often reflected extremes with absolute either/or motifs. Either birthmothers had no additional children or they had many in quick succession. Either they tended to behave promiscuously or they abstained from sexual relationships. Either they strove for perfection or they failed at every opportunity. They were either controlling or passive; they overate or dieted too stringently; they discussed relinquishing openly and often or kept it completely secret.

Vacillating between or clinging to extremes, birthmothers afflicted by the syndrome have seesawed between close intimate relationships and defensive distancing, between parenting overprotectively and numbing themselves from vulnerability to their children. Some have feared discovery, avoided attention, felt unworthy of happiness. Others have overcompensated, seeking out public recognition for excellence and achievement, insatiably seeking acceptability, approval, admiration, and reward.

Whatever extremes or other signs of the syndrome have emerged in their individual life patterns, many of those interviewed have been driven by an underlying theme of hopelessness and loss that has colored the entire fabric of their lives. Indications of the syndrome appeared among birthmothers of all ages, in all parts of the country, and within open and closed adoptions. And though many with closed adoptions blamed their problems on secrecy rather than relinquishment, those with open adoptions experienced many of the same difficulties. Clearly, secrecy alone did not cause the syndrome.

Undoubtedly, there are many who have successfully managed their feelings, received support, eventually integrated their losses, and achieved a degree of healing following relinquishment. Unfortunately, there are many others who have not. For these women, the birthmother syndrome has become the dominant theme of their lives.

Prevention and Treatment

Unwanted pregnancies are simply a fact of life. Millions occur every year in our country alone. For many women facing unplanned pregnancies, adoption has offered an option; for some, undoubtedly, it has seemed to be the *only* option.

Relinquishing children for adoption, however, has often led not to a solution for unwanted pregnancies but to a new set of problems in the form of the birthmother syndrome. Literally millions of women have struggled with this syndrome in secrecy; millions more have yet to confront it. It is, therefore, of critical importance that the effects of relinquishing on birthmothers be examined and understood, so that everyone involved with adoption can be better prepared to deal with the syndrome's impact and to prevent or, at least, minimize its harm. It is important not only to assist those already suffering from the birthmother syndrome but also to eliminate as many of its causes as possible, so that those women who relinquish in the future will be less drastically affected. Accomplishing these goals will require the combined efforts of birthmothers in both open and closed adoptions, other triad members, and society at large.

Social Evolution

At present, changes in social attitudes have already eased some of the harsher aspects of unwanted pregnancies. Because of increased social tolerance, women facing such pregnancies today have options ranging from abortion to relinquishment to single parenting. And, although society does not *reward* unplanned pregnancies, the stigma attached to them has diminished.

As social attitudes have changed, so have procedures associated with relinquishing. "Homes" for pregnant women are just about obsolete. Instead of being sent away in secrecy, most who plan to relinquish are able to remain in school or at work, continuing their own lives in their own homes for the duration of their pregnancies. Many are visited in the hospital by birthfathers, relatives, and friends. Many participate in open adoptions and get to know the prospective adoptive parents prior to delivery, so that both biological and adoptive parents participate cooperatively in pregnancies and births. Further, because of the gradual empowerment of women in society, birthmothers today have increased knowledge of their legal rights, face less shame and stigma, and feel better prepared to continue their lives with dignity.

Even with more public tolerance and flexible terms in adoptions, however, birthmothers must inevitably experience loss and grief. Otherwise, regardless of the terms of their children's adoptions, they will inevitably encounter at least some aspects of the birthmother syndrome.

Self-Help

When it comes to dealing with the syndrome, birthmothers themselves have clear recommendations.

"The first and most difficult thing we birthmothers have to do is to forgive ourselves," says Donna, who now leads an adoption support group. "We have anger, and we often aim it at others. We blame society for making us relinquish, or we blame our parents or the birthfather. But the fact is that, except for a few extreme cases, none of us were *forced* to relinquish. We did it. We need to acknowledge that and accept it and forgive ourselves before we can begin to deal with the rest of our lives. And, having forgiven ourselves, we can become assertive and work openly for changes in adoption-related legislation."

Implicit in Donna's prescription for birthmothers is the rejection of secrecy. Many shared her conviction that the first step for birthmothers in overcoming stigma and shame must be that they themselves refuse to submit to them. By openly acknowledging their relinquishments and coming out with their secrets, some have begun to confront their fears of rejection and judgment and to deem themselves worthy of respect.

"I have become convinced," Bridget says, "that fear of being judged is worse than judgment itself. Secrecy encourages the perpetuation of stigma. As long as we submit to secrecy and act ashamed, we will encourage others to condemn us and continue to live with shame. We must begin to take risks and face up to our mistakes, because that is our only hope of attaining any genuine healing or peace of mind."

Soft Shoulders and Hand Holders

Although most believed that their healing must begin within themselves, many of those interviewed doubted that much progress could be achieved without the help of others. They recommended counseling and other sources of support.

"Without my psychiatrist," Alexis says, "I'd still be unable to relate to anyone, including God, including myself. But I was fortunate, in that I was able to find a professional who had dealt with lots of birthparents and knew what he was doing. He helped me work through the stages of denial, anger, depression, and acceptance. He helped me see and define my needs separately from those of the others in my family, even from those of my relinquished child. He helped me reclaim my self and my life."

If some birthmothers have been helped by psychological counseling, others have had to rely on less professional resources. "The therapists I went to ignored the impact of relinquishment," Annie says. "They actually added to my problems by encouraging me to deny them. It was years before I finally found help and support in dealing with my issues."

Like Annie, many birthmothers found that simply getting counseling was of little benefit. They recommended caution in selecting therapists, suggesting that birthmothers accept counseling only from objective therapists experienced specifically in treating birthparents.

Some birthmothers had other advice regarding therapy. "Include your spouse in your process of working things out," Sue says. "Honesty and openness are critical. Tell your family. Tell your other children. Involve your parents and siblings and extended family in the process. Realize that relinquishment has affected your entire family, not just you. The baby has biological relatives and maybe even siblings. In order for you to heal, you *all* have to work things out together. A member of the family has been lost. That loss has to be acknowledged, felt, and mourned."

As much as they advised including others in the healing process, however, birthmothers cautioned against depending on them. "Whatever you do," Cindy says, "*don't* look to a therapist to cure you or to marriage or a career to protect you from your sorrows—or from stigma. Look to yourself, even while you're accepting help from others; remember that you've got to go through your grief and pain all by yourself. There will, I'm sure, be a longing that never goes away. Don't fight it. We have to learn to manage that longing, to accept it. Because we will long to reconnect, no matter what we do, no matter who we marry or how many other kids we have. Healing isn't a matter of overcoming that longing; it's a matter of learning to live with it."

Coming Out

For many birthmothers, self-help has required not only introspection but also assertiveness and action. Some took action in the form of search; others in political or social involvement. For many, such actions were necessary steps on the road to self-respect, entitlement, and self-expression.

"I didn't have to search," Donna says. "Because of open adoption, I know where my daughter is. But many of the birthmothers I've met have needed to search, not only to try to find their relinquished children but to make the statement that they exist, that they are *not* invisible, that they have *not* conveniently disappeared. In a way, it's ourselves that we seek through search as much as it is our children. And whether or not we succeed in finding those children, we still need to express ourselves. We need to talk about it. We need to communicate, to vent, to let it out. Our feelings have been trapped inside some of us and festered for so long that when we start to let them out, it's often hard to get us to stop or to keep us under control."

The need to express their feelings about relinquishment was so profound that even many who were not successful in search found it necessary to "communicate" with their relinquished children. They wrote letters, journals, poetry, and stories. They painted, sculpted, acted, sang, and played their feelings on musical instruments. Regardless of the form it took, self-expression played a critical role in birthmothers' healing processes.

For support in such expression, birthmothers turned to family, psychiatrists, psychologists, counselors, friends, and religious or spiritual advisors. Among the most effective of all, however, was the support they gave each other.

"No matter what they study in school," Zoe says, "nobody can know the pain of relinquishing except another birthmother. Nobody can give us the understanding or affirmation that we can give each other. We have to be there for each other, to encourage each other, to acknowledge what has happened to us and how we've been scarred. And to share what we know about coping."

"I will never forget the first time I spoke at a support group meeting," Bridget says. "It was the first time I'd told *anyone* other than my husband that I'd relinquished. Physically, the process drained me. Tears streamed down my face, and my head throbbed. But afterwards, when nobody stoned or shunned me, when I was hugged and respected and treated just like a normal person, it sunk in that I'd been partly responsible, all those years, for my own suffering. By remaining silent, I'd allowed myself to be intimidated. I'd anticipated judgment and rejection, and in so doing, *I* had been the harshest judge, the most rejecting person of all."

For self-help, birthmothers recommended counseling geared at assisting the grieving process, self-forgiveness, and rejection of secrecy. They advised honesty and communication, and they encouraged assertiveness and action through search and reunion or through involvement with other birthparents, adoption support groups, or organizations that help triad members or that lobby for change in adoption laws.

"There is no such thing as a happy birthmother," Donna asserts. "Nobody is happy about giving up her baby. But, even so, the trauma can be lessened some if attitudes and policies change. And those changes can be achieved only if the public realizes that birthmothers are not sleazy, scuzzy lowlifes; rather, we are their next-door neighbors, their nurses, their accountants, and the presidents of their PTAs. Only if we birthmothers step out of the shadows and declare ourselves without shame, only if we are open and accept ourselves can we hope to attain the gradual acceptance of others. And I believe we should be open, not only for ourselves but also so that women who relinquish in the future won't have to endure the stigma, secrecy, and shame that we did."

Forewarned, Fore-armed

Many of the women interviewed were concerned about birthmothers of the future. Some warned others not to relinquish under *any* circumstances, and urged them to consider relinquishment as the most "unnatural" act a woman could perform, akin to murder. Others were less adamant, but, universally, they recommended that any woman considering relinquishing undergo counseling first. Most specified that the counselor must be a professional who has worked extensively and specifically with birthmothers. No matter what professional counseling they received, however, birthmothers recommended that women contact birthparent or adoption organizations and consult with other birthmothers before they relinquish.

"Even in the best of circumstances," Lynne remarks, "adoption is *not* going to be a final or an easy solution. There is no easy solution to an unwanted pregnancy. And relinquishment isn't like abortion; it isn't a procedure that ends and is over—it ends with the beginning of a child's life. Relinquishment proceedings may end, but relinquishment is just the beginning of an ongoing, living process: adoption."

Birthmothers like Lynne, involved in open adoptions, often saw relinquishment as permanent but not final. They saw their roles in their children's lives as continuous and lifelong, the place these roles would take in their lives as changeable and fluid, within the context of their combined adoptive and biological families.

Even those who did not participate in open adoptions, however, saw relinquishment as having permanent and widespread repercussions. Many warned women who were considering relinquishment to be prepared for the aftereffects and to be advised of what lies ahead *before* they surrender.

"There are a lot of myths that mislead birthmothers," Alexis says. "It's a myth, for example, that relinquishing is over when papers are signed; it's *not* over, whether the adoption is open or closed. It's a myth that any birthmother will move on and forget about her child. It's a myth that the other children she'll have will make up for the one she's relinquished. It's a myth that, even if she cannot care for her baby now, she will not have second thoughts and regrets later. To any woman considering relinquishment, I want to say: You will mourn, you will grieve, you may regret giving up your child forever. But, even with that knowledge, you may feel surrender is your best option. If you do, take the option *only* if you've examined all your others, only if you have no other choice. And then, be prepared for it to stay with you. There's no use fighting it."

The importance of examining other options was stressed by almost every birthmother interviewed. Pam regrets that she and the birthfather didn't seek help from his parents before they relinquished. "If I could give one piece of advice to women who are thinking about relinquishing, it would be to remember that the baby is a person, too, complete with rights, a unique history, and an individual identity. At birth, that child has not only birthparents but a whole set of biological roots and relatives. If you realize that relinquishing is *not* going to be an easy way out, ask yourself the following: Is it better to begin with openness in the child's biological family and seek help from them before you sign him away permanently to strangers? Are there others who can help you raise him until you can take over on your own? Are there public or social agencies that can help you, such as day care or welfare? Have you received adequate counseling about your legal, financial, and emotional situation? If you've considered all these questions and still feel that relinquishment is right for you, then go ahead. But leave the door open for flexibility and change. You can do that today, by privately arranging open terms for your adoption. I couldn't, and I've regretted it ever since."

Three-sided Solutions

As important as self-help was to birthmothers, they were convinced that overcoming the patterns that nourished their syndrome would require more than their efforts alone. To minimize the permanent damage of relinquishing, they said that not only birthmothers' attitudes but also those of other triad members must change.

"Adoptive parents can help birthparents avoid a lot of heartache if they accept a concept of adoption which includes the biological parents in the family portrait," Lynne says. "We all have to accept the fact that an adoptive family is *not* the same as a biological family, that adoptive parents can not replace their own, unborn biological children by adopting somebody else's. Adoptive families are rich in their own blend of love and bonding. But if adoptive parents try to pretend, or even want to pretend that they are their children's *only* parents, they are doing a disservice not only to the birthparents but also to their adopted children and the whole adoption triad."

The idea that adoptive parents should be prepared to deal not only with their adopted children but also with the children's birthfamilies was expressed frequently in birthmother interviews. Silence, secrecy, and anonymity were *not* acceptable. Some angrily asserted that the sole function of secrecy and closed records was to *support* adoptive parents in the illusion that they were their children's only parents. Others pointed out that the motives behind closed records were irrelevant; secrecy has simply proved to be so harmful to birthmothers and adopted children alike that it should be eliminated.

"Openness is to everyone's benefit," Pam says. "We—adoptive parents and birthparents—are already connected. The children link us. We birthmothers owe our children at least the facts about their biological histories and the reassurance that we have not abandoned them or rejected them. We owe them the knowledge that we have acted out of love. Adoptive parents owe the children *and* their birthparents the opportunity to find out about each other without obstruction or guilt. They owe their adopted children the right to complete identities. And, in turn, birthparents owe the adoptive parents the opportunity to raise the children without interference, remaining available should they be needed for information or other input."

Although they expressed it in a variety of ways, many birthmothers shared the need to have an acknowledged place in their relinquished children's lives. Some expressed anger, openly or indirectly, when state officials, hospitals, adoptive parents, or adoption agencies obstructed their efforts even to learn about their relinquished children. Many lamented the implicit rivalries between the two sets of parents, blaming regulated secrecy for encouraging suspicion, fear, and paranoia among adoptive parents.

"Adoptive parents must know that no woman would go to all the anguish and effort of relinquishing a child only to try to reclaim her," Jean says. "That fear is ridiculous. As an adoptive parent myself, though, I know that that fear is real—it exists, at least for some of us. But birthmothers wouldn't put their children through that—we would never want to rip children away from their family ties. What most of us do want, though, is to know that our children are healthy, that they do not feel rejected because they were relinquished, and that they are as aware of their biological backgrounds as they want to be. We just want the truth to be known or available to them. We believe that the truth can only help; keeping the facts secret makes them seem shameful or evil, and no child needs to be raised feeling that he had shameful origins."

Whose Children Are They?

A few birthmothers were reluctant to support changes in legislation regarding secrecy. Some feared that those who wanted to remain anonymous would lose that option. Others were concerned that legalized openness might confuse adopted children. They expressed concern that children wouldn't know who their "real" mommies or daddies were or with which family they should feel bonded.

The vast majority of those interviewed, however, were confident that such problems would *not* occur. They reasoned that birthmothers could still choose anonymity if they wanted it and pointed out that birthparents' roles would not overlap or compete with those of adoptive parents, that merely revealing their identities to children was not the same as actively parenting them. Many thought that facts about their biological origins would clarify rather than confuse their children's self-images.

"Adoptees who know they've been adopted without knowing why or who gave birth to them are lacking half their stories," Sylvia says. "I think that the objections that some—and I must say *only* some—adoptive families have to telling children the truth come from some very insecure feelings and, frankly, from the desire to own the children. What we have to realize, all of us, is that children are not possessions. They don't *belong* to any of us. Children are their own beings, adopted or not. At best, we adults can guide them. The birthparents have guided them into the world; the adoptive ones guide them through childhood. But we do not own them. We are not in competition for deeds or titles. We are united in love. If we can remember that, we can be resources to each other, for the children's sakes."

Many birthmothers, even with open adoptions, felt that adoptive parents were threatened by or even resentful of them. Even some who had warm and supportive relationships felt that their bonds were superficial, masking uneasy undercurrents. Nevertheless, the majority saw value in continued contact.

"The fact is that the American family is changing," Sue says. "Nobody has a 'normal' family anymore. Almost half of all marriages end in divorce, so kids have stepmoms, stepdads, half-siblings, and stepsiblings. If a mother can accept a stepmother, why can't an adoptive mother accept a birthmother? Why can't an extended adoptive family be seen as including the birthfamily, in some way, in its loosest sense, even if it only means sending birthday and Christmas cards? Why can't we all just know who the others are and be available to each other? I don't mean we birthparents should show up for Sunday dinner, but I do mean we should be acknowledged, so the children know where they came from, that they didn't just land in their adoptive families from a spaceship, and so we birthmothers don't have to hide in shame but can be recognized and respected as the women who carried the children and gave birth to them."

Evolutions, Revolutions, Obligations, and Definitions

As Sue suggests, the American family is changing, adjusting to the effects of divorce and remarriage. The traditional nuclear family is no longer the norm, and many families find themselves creating, inventing, and redefining their roles and relationships idiosyncratically, according to their own needs, construction, personalities, and developmental phases. In this context, the idea of redefining adoptive families to include birthparents in some broad concept of the extended family does not seem so far-fetched. Certainly, it seems less harsh and more realistic than sentencing women who brought adopted children into the world to secrecy and permanent exile.

Overcoming the birthmother syndrome, obviously, cannot be accomplished by birthmothers alone. It will require the cooperation of all triad members and of other members of society. It seems likely, too, that such cooperative efforts would benefit not only birthmothers but adopted children, birthfathers, adoptive parents, and society as well.

"My child isn't going to idealize me and dream that I'm a fairy princess if he knows who I am," Sonia says. "He's not going to feel lost or confused about who he is or why he was adopted if I'm available to tell him. I don't want to compete with his adoptive parents. I want to support them. They appeared when I couldn't take care of my child. I wouldn't think of traumatizing them—or him—by trying to come between them. But I believe that I have something to offer to their family that would make it more complete. And it's my responsibility to make myself accountable and available, at least on an as-needed basis."

Sonia's sense of responsibility to her child, even decades after relinquishment, was echoed by birthmothers of all ages, professions, and circumstances. Because of that responsibility, many believed that no birthmother should be allowed secrecy, even if she claims to want it.

"I was just a child myself when I had my son," Cindy says. "But I still owed him something. If you bring someone into the world, you have a duty to that person forever, no matter what. As a teenager, I wasn't able to live up to that duty, but now I am. That doesn't mean I should move in and take him back after all these years. But it does mean I should let him know that I love him and that I'll do what I can whenever he needs me."

In general, birthmothers believed that the birthmother syndrome could be eased only if the concept of adoption evolved to include them as identifiable, respected triad members. They saw openness in adoption not as a "cure" for the syndrome but as a means of minimizing its worst effects. They felt that it was the responsibility of all triad members to support each other in overcoming the stigma, secrecy, and shame traditionally associated with relinquishment and that respect from and acceptance by adoptive parents was critical, not only to their own postrelinquishment recovery, but also to their children's overall sense of wholeness and well-being.

Past Judgments

Most birthmothers said that the only effective way to eliminate the syndrome would be prevention. Only the elimination of relinquishment could completely eradicate its scars. To this end, they thought that society should help prevent unnecessary relinquishments by providing viable alternatives for pregnant women, making it more feasible for them to keep their babies. Such alternatives include reliable and affordable child-care programs, financial assistance, counseling geared at finding ways to keep unplanned babies within their biological families, or temporary child placement that, unlike traditional foster care, would be geared toward helping mothers take over the independent care of their children.

Even with programs like these, however, some women with unwanted pregnancies would undoubtedly see relinquishment as their only viable option. For these women, there would remain a need to eliminate punitive social attitudes and practices, particularly enforced secrecy. Adoptees and birthparents would have access to their shared histories. Openness in adoption would have to be protected, guaranteed, and regulated by law. Social attitudes toward relinquishing—indeed, the very concept of adoption itself—would have to change.

Stopping the Syndrome

Relinquishment cannot solve the problems of unwanted pregnancies any more than adoption can solve those of infertility. A symbiosis between those who give birth without wanting to and those who want children but don't have them can succeed only if it doesn't damage its participants beyond repair.

If adoption is to be mutually beneficial, it must be seen not as a final solution to a problem but as an ongoing, cooperative effort to ensure the parenting of children. If adoption is to avoid marring triad members, it must be experienced not as a single, finite event but as a step in a lifelong process that includes biological relatives, even if only by identifying them.

To a large extent, the fate of the birthmother syndrome lies in the hands of birthmothers themselves. No matter what society or other triad members do to welcome them out of hiding, birthmothers must deal with the repercussions of their own relinquishments. By allowing themselves to grieve and mourn, to seek support and help when they need it, to assert themselves as individuals, and to forgive themselves, they can begin their own healing.

Further, prior to relinquishing, each prospective birthmother must be made to understand that she will *never* be able to relinquish entirely her responsibilities to her child. Surrendering for adoption should not erase a birthmother's obligations to provide medical and biological information or to provide other forms of help if needed. By insisting on these responsibilities, birthmothers can begin to reclaim the respect due women with names, identities, histories, faces, and voices. When they reveal themselves and the truth, they can begin to fight their syndrome and to overcome their nightmares, flashbacks, phobias, and depressions. Without the need to be saints or sinners, they can hope to be accepted honestly as permanent, rightful members of their children's adoptive extended families.

There is probably no cure for the birthmother syndrome. It is unlikely that any woman can come through relinquishing unscathed. But it *can* be minimized if society at large, adoption triad members, and birthmothers themselves cooperate in seeking legally protected open acknowledgment, recognition, and dignity for these women who have given life. It is not enough for adoption to provide loving homes for surrendered children; it needs to provide respectable, loving roles for birthmothers as well. The double standard that simultaneously encourages adoption and frowns on women who relinquish children must be abandoned. Only when this is accomplished can everyone in the adoption triangle be released from shadows, stigma, and secrecy and be supported on three sides with acceptance, honesty, and love.

. . . Within ourselves we hold the key
through love in all its forms
to grant ourselves true freedom
and unlock unopened doors.
We're all a part of one another,
we're connected one to all.
Why can't we support each other
so no one has to fall? . . .
Oh, Mothers, how I wish you knew
How deeply I love both of you.

Nancy's relinquished daughter Charlene, 1982
(from "Thoughts Along the Way," © 1992, Hannon and Reilly)

APPENDIX

National Organizations Related
to Birthparents' Concerns*

Adoptee Liberty Movement Association (ALMA)
P.O. Box 727, Radio City Station
New York, NY 10101-0727
(212)721-0197

American Adoption Congress
100 Connecticut Ave. NW, Suite 9
Washington, D.C. 20036
1-800-274-6736

Birthparent Connection
P.O. Box 230643
Encinitas, CA 92023-0643

Concerned United Birthparents
2000 Walker St.
Des Moines, IA 50317
(515)263-9558

Council for Equal Rights in Adoption
401 E. 74th St., Suite 17D
New York, NY 10021
(212)988-0110

International Soundex Reunion Registry
P.O. Box 2312
Carson City, NV 10021
(702)882-7755

---

* Excerpted from the *National Adoption Directory—1992*, National Adoption
Information Clearinghouse, Rockville, MD.

Musser Foundation
1105 Cape Coral Pkwy.
Cape Coral, FL 33904
1-800-477-7335 or (813)542-1342

National Organization for Birthfathers and Adoption Reform
P.O. Box 1993
Baltimore, MD 21203

Post-Adoption Center for Education and Research
2255 Ygnacio Valley Rd.
Walnut Creek, CA 94598
(415)935-6622 or (415)654-3099

INDEX

Printed in the United States
206076BV00001B/284/A